SUMMARY ASSESSMENT OF COSTS

SUMMARY ASSESSMENT OF COSTS

KATHARINE SCOTT

CONSULTANT EDITOR: JEREMY MORGAN QC

OXFORD
UNIVERSITY PRESS

This book has been printed digitally and produced in a standard specification in order to ensure its continuing availability

OXFORD
UNIVERSITY PRESS

Great Clarendon Street, Oxford OX2 6DP

Oxford University Press is a department of the University of Oxford.
It furthers the University's objective of excellence in research, scholarship, and education by publishing worldwide in

Oxford New York

Auckland Cape Town Dar es Salaam Hong Kong Karachi
Kuala Lumpur Madrid Melbourne Mexico City Nairobi
New Delhi Shanghai Taipei Toronto

With offices in

Argentina Austria Brazil Chile Czech Republic France Greece
Guatemala Hungary Italy Japan South Korea Poland Portugal
Singapore Switzerland Thailand Turkey Ukraine Vietnam

Oxford is a registered trade mark of Oxford University Press in the UK and in certain other countries

Published in the United States
by Oxford University Press Inc., New York

Reprinted 2008

ISBN 978-0-19-929821-1

FOREWORD

For many years for most advocates, particularly barristers, costs was a subject about which they knew nothing and wanted to know even less. They would happily spend an entire week in court arguing every point in a claim for damages worth no more than £5,000 but then expect to dispose of the £20,000 costs of the action in under five minutes. The courts went along with this approach and all that anyone really needed to know was summed up in Lord Lloyd of Berwick's well-turned dictum, 'As in all questions to do with costs, the fundamental rule is that there are no rules.'

For such advocates those happy days are gone. Lord Woolf chose costs as one of the primary targets of his reforms and the Civil Procedure Rules (CPR) introduced summary assessment. Of all the costs reforms of the CPR it is the one which has attracted the least criticism and seems to have worked best in practice. But the price which advocates have had to pay is that they can no longer afford to maintain a lofty ignorance about costs. All advocates in all forums from the district courts to the Court of Appeal have to be able to conduct a summary assessment.

This book is written not only for those advocates, but also for the judges who have to determine summary assessments and for the solicitors who have to prepare for them. It is written by a costs expert for those who would claim no such expertise. Katherine Scott wears her learning lightly and writes clearly about this essential subject. At all times she puts herself in the position of the reader and asks herself all the questions she would have asked if she had done few, if any, such assessments.

This is a most useful, and portable, book, It is not designed as a substitute for more detailed works but it will work admirably as a manageable introduction to the subject or as an invaluable source of information for those faced with an alarming Schedule of Costs and an imminent court hearing. Whether you are a newcomer to the field of summary assessment or a more experienced practitioner, I recommend that you find a corner of your briefcase for it. Otherwise your great forensic victory may turn distinctly pyrrhic when you find yourself confronted with an opponent carrying Scott's *Summary Assessment of Costs.*

Jeremy Morgan QC
39 Essex Street, London WC2

SUMMARY CONTENTS

DETAILED CONTENTS

ABBREVIATIONS

ADR	alternative dispute resolution
ATE	after the event insurance
BTE	before the event insurance
CCFA	collective conditional fee agreements
CFA	conditional fee agreements
CPR	Civil Procedure Rules
LSC	Legal Services Commission
SCCO	Supreme Court Costs Office
the Code	Solicitors' Costs Information and Client Care Code
the 1974 Act	Solicitors Act 1974
the 1990 Act	Courts and Legal Services Act 1990

TABLE OF CASES

TABLE OF STATUTES

TABLE OF RULES AND PRACTICE DIRECTIONS

STATUTORY INSTRUMENTS

PRACTICE DIRECTIONS TO CIVIL PROCEDURE RULES

RULES

1

INTRODUCTION

A. The scope of this book

It is now the general rule, as set out in the Civil Procedure Rules 1998 (CPR), that there should be a summary assessment of the costs at the end of any application or trial that has taken less than one day.[1] This means that judges and practitioners who would not, prior to 1998, have had any dealings with costs, are now expected to be able to deal with the many legal arguments that can arise at such a hearing. **1.01**

Summary assessments are often difficult hearings to get right. There may be fairly complex arguments that one or both of the parties will want to address and very little time in which to do so. Practitioners often have to make difficult decisions about the way in which these arguments will be run, balancing up on the one hand the need to put before the judge all the relevant statutory material and supporting case law, while on the other hand avoiding the judge coming to the view that the issues are too difficult to be dealt with in the time allotted and that the whole matter should go off to detailed assessment. **1.02**

One of the effects of the rise in the number of Conditional Fee Agreements (CFAs) is that the costs of the winning party have significantly increased (as a result of being able to recover insurance premiums and uplifts from the losing party). It is not unusual for the costs of a fast track one-day trial to far exceed the damages. While parties have always been acutely aware of the issue of costs, it has become even more important that an advocate does his best for a client once the substantive claim has been won or lost. **1.03**

---

[1] Section 13.2 of the Costs Practice Direction which supplements parts 43–48 of the CPR 1998.

1.04 This book is not intended to provide an in-depth analysis of the issues that may arise on a summary assessment, nor does it provide an exhaustive citation of cases, but it does provide enough information to allow the practitioner to deal with the issues that may arise on a summary assessment in the kind of detail that will be required at the assessment itself.

1.05 This book can be used in a number of ways:

(i) A practitioner unfamiliar with summary assessments will be able to read the book from start to finish, to get a feeling for the range of issues that can arise on a summary assessment.
(ii) A practitioner preparing for a summary assessment will be able to go straight to one of the checklists in Chapter 9 to ensure that he is adequately prepared for the hearing. He will then be able to read in more detail on any of the issues likely to be raised in his particular assessment.
(iii) Finally, a practitioner who is faced with an issue that he was not expecting at a hearing will be able to use the book as a reference tool.

1.06 The book is laid out in nine chapters. The first eight chapters explain the principles of summary assessment—what orders the court can make, what to expect at a summary assessment hearing—and take the practitioner through the issues that may arise. Chapter nine includes three checklists to which practitioners may refer, to ensure that they are properly prepared for a summary assessment hearing. The first checklist will help the practitioner when drawing up the statement of costs; the second is to help the practitioner when preparing for the hearing; and the third is a reference tool for use at the summary assessment itself once the costs order has been made. Finally, the book includes relevant extracts from the Civil Procedure Rules, statutes, statutory instruments, and other useful source materials, to ensure that the practitioner has everything he needs to hand.

1.07 Other useful sources of information for practitioners who want to read further into summary assessment are the following:

(i) The Supreme Court Costs Office have produced a document entitled 'The Guide to Summary Assessment of Costs', which is available on their website at <http://www.hmcourts-service.gov.uk>.
(ii) The costs section of 39 Essex Street's website at <http://www.39essex.co.uk>, reports interesting costs cases from the beginning of 2005.

2

SUMMARY ASSESSMENT —AN OVERVIEW

This chapter provides an overview of what summary assessment is and sets out the circumstances in which it is appropriate. Many of the issues introduced in this chapter are developed in more depth later on in the book. **2.01**

A. What is summary assessment?

The summary assessment of costs is the procedure by which a court, having made an order about which party should pay the costs, assesses immediately the amount of costs to be paid under the order instead of ordering fixed costs or detailed assessment.[1] **2.02**

By comparison, detailed assessment is the procedure by which the amount of costs is decided by a costs officer[2] (at a discrete hearing) in accordance with CPR Rule 47.[3] Fixed costs are costs that are awarded in accordance with CPR Rule 45 or 46.[4] **2.03**

The summary assessment of costs is carried out at the end of a hearing. The party who is awarded its costs (the receiving party) will have their **2.04**

---

[1] CPR Rule 43.3.

[2] A costs officer is a costs judge (a taxing master) in the Supreme Court—CPR Rule 43.2(1)(b), a district judge in the county court—CPR Rule 43.2(1)(c), or an authorized costs officer within the meaning of CPR Rule 43.2(1)(d).

[3] CPR Rule 43.4.

[4] It is not strictly accurate to say that no assessment occurs where fixed costs apply. The fixed costs will be determined by the court in accordance with the CPR (for example, fixed trial costs are assessed pursuant to CPR Rule 46.2). In a claim in which fixed costs are awarded pursuant to CPR 45, the court will still need to assess the disbursements (CPR Rule 45.10) and may in any event carry out a summary assessment of the costs pursuant to CPR Rule 45.12.

statement of costs[5] assessed by the judge. Any argument that can be raised at a fully contested detailed assessment hearing can also be raised at a summary assessment. There are, however, two important differences. The first is that the time allotted by the court for dealing with the issue of costs on a summary basis is short. This means that any arguments a party wishes to raise must be presented in such a way as to allow the court to deal with them quickly. The second difference is that neither party is under an obligation to put the other party on notice as to the points they wish to raise. Both of these factors make it even more important that the practitioner is well prepared.

2.05 A practitioner should not be surprised if a judge takes a rough and ready approach to the assessment of costs.[6] Unlike a detailed assessment, the procedure does not demand reasoned judgments in respect of each item that is challenged.

B. When is summary assessment appropriate?

2.06 Section 13.2 of the Costs Practice Direction sets out the general rule as to when summary assessment is appropriate. That is:

(i) at the conclusion of a fast track trial; or
(ii) at the conclusion of a hearing (whether a trial or an application) which has lasted not more than a day[7] (whether at first instance or in the Court of Appeal).
(iii) Section 14.1 of the practice direction to part 52 provides that costs are likely to be assessed by way of a summary assessment hearing in (a) contested directions hearings; (b) applications for permission to appeal at which the respondent is present; (c) dismissal list hearings in the Court of Appeal at which the respondent is present; (d) appeals from case management decisions; and (e) appeals listed for one day or less.

2.07 Once the court has made an order as to where the costs lie it is obliged by the CPR to carry out a summary assessment unless there is a good reason not to do so. Section 13.2(3) of the Costs Practice Direction gives two examples

[5] Chapter 3 explains how to draw up a statement of costs.
[6] *Bryen & Langley v Boston* [2005] EWCA Civ 973.
[7] *Bryen & Langley v Boston* [2005] EWCA Civ 973, where the Court of Appeal did not accede to an argument that due to the amount claimed in the statement of costs, the issue of costs should be sent off to detailed assessment.

of what are considered to be good reasons for not carrying out a summary assessment: (i) where a party shows substantial grounds for disputing the costs claimed and so the issues cannot be dealt with summarily; and (ii) where there is insufficient time to carry out a summary assessment.

Applications where the receiving party is funded by a CFA

2.08 The general rule is that summary assessment is appropriate following an application. However, where the receiving party has the benefit of a CFA or other funding arrangement which entitles that party to recover an additional liability (an additional liability is most commonly an uplift on base costs pursuant to a success fee under a CFA, or an after the event insurance premium (ATE)), CPR Rule 44.3A(1) provides that the court will not assess any additional liability until the conclusion of the proceedings or any part of the proceedings to which the funding arrangement relates.[8] The court can, however, carry out a summary assessment of the base costs and disbursements, adjourning the assessment of the additional liabilities until the conclusion of the proceedings (or the conclusion of the part of the proceedings to which the funding arrangement relates). If the judge does this, the practitioner should request that the judge specifies separate figures for solicitors' fees and counsels' fees, so that when the additional liabilities are assessed (usually by means of a percentage uplift on base costs), the exercise is straightforward.

C. When is summary assessment inappropriate?

2.09 There may be a good reason why the court does not even want to make an order as to where the costs should lie; for example, because the hearing has not finally determined the issue. Following a preliminary trial on liability where a defendant has made an offer that complies with CPR Rule 36[9] in relation to the whole of the claim, the parties will not be in a position to determine whether or not the claimant is going to do better than that offer. In those circumstances parties should communicate the existence of the offer to the court[10] and invite the court to adjourn the issue of costs on the preliminary issue until the conclusion of the claim.[11]

[8] See also para 14 of the Costs Practice Direction.
[9] For a discussion on CPR Rule 36 offers, see paras 4.29–4.41.
[10] CPR Rule 36.19(3)(c).
[11] *HSS Hire Services Group Plc v BMB Builders Merchants Ltd* [2005] 3 All ER 486.

2.10 Having made an order as to where the costs should lie, the court is not obliged to carry out a summary assessment if there is a good reason not to do so.[12]

2.11 In cases that attract fixed costs, summary assessment is clearly not appropriate because only fixed costs are recoverable. Examples of such cases are:

(i) a claim allocated to the small claims track,[13] save where a party has behaved unreasonably,[14] or the value of the claim exceeds the limit for the small claims track;[15]
(ii) cases in which summary judgment is given in a claim for a specified sum of money under CPR Rule 24;[16]
(iii) following judgment in some possession cases.[17]

Children and patients

2.12 Where the receiving party is a child or a patient pursuant to CPR Rule 21 the general rule is that the costs of the child or patient must be subject to detailed assessment.[18] However, the court may carry out a summary assessment of the costs where the solicitor acting for the child or patient waives his right to claim any costs from the child or patient, above and beyond those that are assessed as being payable by the paying party to the child or patient.[19]

2.13 There is nothing to stop the court summarily assessing the costs to be *paid by* a child or patient.

Publicly funded parties

2.14 Where the *receiving* party is funded by the Legal Services Commission (LSC) the court cannot make a summary assessment of his publicly funded costs.[20] These must be assessed at a detailed assessment hearing.

---

12 See the discussion in para 2.07 above.
13 CPR Rule 27.14.
14 CPR Rule 27.14(2)(d).
15 CPR Rule 27.14(5) or where CPR Rule 27.14(2)(b) or (c) applies.
16 CPR Rule 45.1(2)(iv), although the court can make an order that fixed costs do not apply (CPR Rule 45.1(1)).
17 For examples of the cases to which this rule applies, see CPR Rule 45.1(2)(d), (e) and (f).
18 CPR Rule 48.5(2).
19 Sections 51.1 and 13.11 of the Costs Practice Direction.
20 Section 13.9 of the Costs Practice Direction.

The court can make a summary assessment if the LSC funded party is the *paying* party, as this is not a determination of the LSC funded party's liability to pay those costs.[21] **2.15**

It is open to a receiving party to make an application to the court that its costs should be met either wholly or in part by the LSC funded paying party. If such an application is made, the court, having assessed the whole of the receiving party's costs to be met by the LSC funded paying party, can carry out an assessment of the LSC funded party's liability to pay all or part of those assessed costs. Both parties must have filed and served a statement of resources pursuant to s 22.4 of the Costs Practice Direction.[22] The figure the LSC funded client is liable to pay must not exceed that which is reasonable for him to pay taking into account all the matters set out at s 21.3 of the Costs Practice Direction (ie the financial resources of all the parties and their conduct in connection with the dispute). If the parties have not served statements of resources in time for the summary assessment hearing, then this exercise can be carried out by a costs judge at a later hearing. **2.16**

If a party seeks to enforce an order for costs made against an LSC funded client, against the LSC (as opposed to or in addition to the LSC funded client) then he must follow the procedure set out in the Community Legal Services (Costs) Regulations 2000[23] and the Court of Appeal decision in *R v Secretary of State for the Home Department ex parte Gunn* [2001] 3All ER 481 and at [2001] 1WLR 1634. This procedure involves providing written notice to the LSC within three months of a costs order being made against an LSC funded party. Clearly the hearing of this application cannot take place at the summary assessment. Detailed guidance on such applications is outside the scope of this book. **2.17**

[21] Section 13.10 of the Costs Practice Direction.

[22] The statement must comply with s 21.12 of the Costs Practice Direction.

[23] Set out in ss 21–23 of the Costs Practice Direction.

3

PREPARATION FOR SUMMARY ASSESSMENT

The way that costs are claimed at the summary assessment hearing is by the production of a statement of costs which is then assessed by the court. This chapter gives practical guidance on how to draw up the statement of costs and when to serve it. It includes a worked example of a statement of costs. **3.01**

A. The N260

The most important part of preparing for a summary assessment is to draw up a statement of costs. This is the document which shows what costs are being claimed. The CPR encourages parties to use the form N260, or something that closely resembles it. This can be obtained from the court service website at <http://www.hmcourts-service.gov.uk/courtfinder/forms/n260.pdf>. Section 13.5 of the Costs Practice Direction includes general guidance on how to fill it in. The practitioner is obliged to show: **3.02**

(i) the number of hours to be claimed;
(ii) the hourly rate to be claimed;
(iii) the grade of fee earner;
(iv) the amount and nature of any disbursement to be claimed;
(v) the amount of solicitor's costs to be claimed for attending or appearing at the hearing;
(vi) the fees of counsel to be claimed in respect of the hearing;
(vii) any VAT to be claimed on those amounts.

Drawing up the statement

3.03 An accurate description of the fee earners that have worked on the case must be included. There are four grades of fee earners:

(A) solicitors[1] with over eight years' post-qualification experience, including at least eight years' litigation experience;
(B) solicitors and legal executives[2] with over four years' post-qualification experience, including at least four years' litigation experience;
(C) other solicitors and legal executives and fee earners of equivalent experience;[3]
(D) trainee solicitors, para legals and other fee earners.

This information appears at the bottom of the second page of the form N260.

3.04 The hourly rate for each fee earner must be provided. Guideline hourly rates by area appear at Appendix F of this book.[4]

3.05 The statement of costs requires the fee earner to add up the amount of time spent in connection with the case under various headings. As fee earners record time spent in six-minute units, in reality the amount claimed is more likely to reflect the number of units spent on a case as opposed to the actual time spent on a case.

3.06 When a solicitor uses an agent, the agency fees should form part of the solicitors' charges.[5]

3.07 Where a party is claiming an additional liability (a success fee or an insurance premium) the amount does not need to be revealed on the N260.[6] The reason for this is so that a claimant who has entered into a CFA need not disclose to the defendant his solicitor's views of the prospects of success of the claim (as reflected in the success fee) until such time as the court makes an order that the defendant must pay the claimant's costs.

3.08 Section 13.5(3) of the Costs Practice Direction requires the solicitor to sign the statement of costs. The solicitor's signature is effectively a certificate

---

[1] Defined in s 1.4 of the Costs Practice Direction.
[2] This means a fellow of the Institute of Legal Executives (s 4.5(2) of the Costs Practice Direction).
[3] Defined in s 4.5(2) of the Costs Practice Direction.
[4] There is also a discussion at para 5.29 as to which hourly rate the court will apply.
[5] Section 4.16(6) of the Costs Practice Direction.
[6] Section 13.5(5) of the Costs Practice Direction.

from him, as an officer of the court, that he is not seeking to recover more costs than his client is liable to pay him pursuant to the terms of the retainer.[7] This is an assurance to the court that the indemnity principle has not been breached. The indemnity principle is the principle that the paying party is only liable to pay to the receiving party the costs the receiving party has actually incurred.

Without a signature, a court will not make a payment out of the costs assessed.[8] **3.09**

The N260 does not show the dates on which costs were actually incurred. **3.10** Where there is a risk that a partial costs order may be made as a result of a CPR part 36 offer[9] (which usually involves the court making an order that a party is only able to recover its costs over a specified period of time pursuant to CPR Rule 36.20 and 36.21), it is sensible to take the precaution of drawing up a second statement of costs that can be used should such an order be made. This will ensure that the court will be able to complete the summary assessment and will not have to put the matter of costs over to a detailed assessment. This second statement need not be served on the other side unless a partial costs order is made, and should certainly not be served on the court until such an order is made.

Service of the statement of costs

The statement of costs should be filed at court and served on the other **3.11** parties not less than 24 hours before the date of the hearing.[10] Although this provision is not mandatory, failure to comply with it without reasonable excuse will be taken into account by the court when determining what order to make.[11]

The court's reaction to this particular breach of the Costs Practice Direc- **3.12** tion must be proportionate. Thus only if the failure to serve the statement of costs on time has caused prejudice to the paying party should any sanction be imposed on the receiving party. It was suggested in the case of *MacDonald*[12] that where the paying party has been prejudiced by the

[7] *Bailey v IBC Vehicles* [1998] 3 All ER 570.
[8] For a more detailed discussion, see Chapter 7.
[9] For a detailed discussion of partial costs orders and the circumstances in which the court may make such an order, see Chapter 4.
[10] Section 13.5(4) of the Costs Practice Direction.
[11] Section 13.6 of the Costs Practice Direction.
[12] *MacDonald v Taree Holdings Ltd* (*The Times*, 28 December 2000).

late service of the statement of costs there are three possibilities open to the court:

(i) Give the paying party a short adjournment in order to give them time to consider the schedule before proceeding to assessment. During the assessment the court should have in mind the lack of preparation time the paying party has had, and where there is a doubt should err in favour of a light figure rather than a heavy one.
(ii) Adjourn the matter of costs off to a detailed assessment hearing, perhaps with a direction that the receiving party pay the costs of that assessment.
(iii) Adjourn the matter of costs but on a summary basis (preferably with written submissions being made rather than a further hearing).

Only if there is an aggravating feature in the case (such as a deliberate failure to serve the statement of costs on time) should a party be deprived of some or all of his costs for the failure to serve the statement of costs on time.

B. Example of an N260

3.13 The form N260 (opposite) is fairly self-explanatory. The form does not allow for a detailed breakdown of how the time being claimed was spent. This makes it all the more important that the practitioner who is making oral submissions in defence of the statement of costs is fully aware of what work was done in each category. It is a good idea therefore, when preparing the N260, to keep a record of the following information to give to the advocate conducting the hearing:

(i) a list of the work done under the heading 'Others';
(ii) a list of the site inspections undertaken;
(iii) a record of the various stages at which negotiation was undertaken;
(iv) a list of the work 'Other work' covers;
(v) a list of the work included under 'Documents';
(vi) the number of hearings attended.

3.14 Remember to include the time spent drawing up the statement of costs itself. This probably belongs in 'Other work'.

Statement of Costs (summary assessment)

In the Whitefield County **Court**

Case Reference 4 XC 4000 Y

Judge/Master District Judge

Case Title A Person v A N Other

[Party]'s Statement of Costs for the hearing on *(date)* 26/06/2006 **(interim application/fast track trial)**

Description of fee earners*
(a) *(name) (grade) (hourly rate claimed)* Ms Solicitor. Grade B. 130 per hour, qualified 2000
(b) *(name) (grade) (hourly rate claimed)* Mr Trainee. Grade D 90 per hour

Attendances on *(party)* Claimant

(a) *(number)*	3.50	hours at £	130.00	£	455.00
(b) *(number)*	2.00	hours at £	90.00	£	180.00
Attendances on opponents					
(a) *(number)*	4.40	hours at £	130.00	£	572.00
(b) *(number)*		hours at £		£	0.00
Attendance on others					
(a) *(number)*	0.50	hours at £	130.00	£	65.00
(b) *(number)*	3.80	hours at £	90.00	£	342.00
Site inspections etc					
(a) *(number)*		hours at £		£	0.00
(b) *(number)*		hours at £		£	0.00
Work done on negotiations					
(a) *(number)*	2.40	hours at £	130.00	£	312.00
(b) *(number)*	0.80	hours at £	90.00	£	72.00
Other work, not covered above					
(a) *(number)*	4.00	hours at £	130.00	£	520.00
(b) *(number)*	9.60	hours at £	90.00	£	864.00
Work done on documents					
(a) *(number)*	6.60	hours at £	130.00	£	858.00
(b) *(number)*	5.20	hours at £	90.00	£	468.00
Attendance at hearing					
(a) *(number)*		hours at £		£	0.00
(b) *(number)*		hours at £		£	0.00
(a) *(number)*		hours travel and waiting at £		£	0.00
(b) *(number)*		hours travel and waiting at £		£	0.00
			Sub Total	£	4,708.00

N260 Statement of Costs (summary assessment) (10.01)

Printed on behalf of The Court Service

cont.

		Brought forward £	4,708.00
Counsel's fees *(name) (year of call)*	Ms Counsel (2000)		
Fee for [advice/conference/documents]		£	150.00
Fee for hearing		£	400.00
Other expenses			
[court fees]		£	60.00
Others *(give brief description)*	Insurance premium - 500 Medical report - 1000 Medical report - 800 Medical notes - 50	£	2,350.00
Total		**£**	7,668.00
Amount of VAT claimed			
on solicitors' and counsels' fees		£	920.15
on other expenses		£	
Grand Total		**£**	8,588.15

The costs estimated above do not exceed the costs which the *(party)* Claimant is liable to pay in respect of the work which this estimate covers.

Dated 26/06/2006

Signed *Ms Solicitor*

Name of firm of solicitors [partner] for the *(party)* Claimant

* 4 grades of fee earner are suggested:

(A) Solicitors with over eight years' post-qualification experience including at least eight years' litigation experience.

(B) Solicitors and legal executives with over four years' post-qualification experience including at least four years' litigation experience.

(C) Other solicitors and legal executives and fee earners of equivalent experience.

(D) Trainee solicitors, para legals and other fee earners.

"Legal Executive" means a Fellow of the Institute of Legal Executives. Those who are not Fellows of the Institute are not entitled to call themselves legal executives and in principle are therefore not entitled to the same hourly rate as a legal executive.

In respect of each fee earner communications should be treated as attendances and routine communications should be claimed at one tenth of the hourly rate.

N260 Statement of Costs (summary assessment) (10.01)

Printed on behalf of The Court Service

C. VAT

If a receiving party is not registered for VAT, or the legal services that he has received are not supplied in connection with his business, then VAT at the current rate should be added to the between the parties costs to indemnify the winner for the VAT he will pay on the legal services provided to him in the course of the litigation. **3.15**

If the receiving party is registered for VAT and the legal services that he has received are in the course of his business he will be able to recover from HM Revenue and Customs the VAT paid to his solicitor. In these circumstances the receiving party should not claim VAT on the legal services provided as against the paying party. **3.16**

Where a claim is being brought by an insurance company by way of subrogation, VAT should not be added to the costs claimed if the lay client is liable for VAT, irrespective of what the insurance company's VAT status is. **3.17**

Section 5 of the Costs Practice Direction deals with VAT. This provides that: **3.18**

(i) VAT should not be included in a claim for costs if the receiving party is able to obtain credit from HM Revenue and Customs as input tax.
(ii) The VAT number of every person registered under the Value Added Tax 1994 must be included as a part of the claim for costs.
(iii) VAT is not chargeable on work done by a litigant in person.
(iv) VAT should not be added where costs are being paid to a Government Department in respect of services rendered by its legal staff. The same applies in relation to costs incurred by a party's solicitor employee.

4

THE ORDER FOR COSTS

4.01 The order that the court makes as to where the costs lie is not part of the summary assessment procedure. However, the practitioner who is going to carry out the summary assessment of costs must make submissions in relation to that order. In addition, the decisions that the court makes as to (i) which party should pay the costs; and (ii) on what basis those costs should be paid, will inform the basis on which the summary assessment is carried out, and will certainly impact on the amount of costs either paid or received. It is therefore important for practitioners when preparing for summary assessment hearings to consider what order the court is likely to make.

4.02 While in many cases the court will follow the general rule that costs follow the event, the court has a very broad discretion pursuant to CPR Rule 44.3(2)(b) as to what order to make. The orders that the court can make are set out at CPR Rule 44.3(6). These are orders that a party must pay:

(i) a proportion of another party's costs;
(ii) a stated amount in respect of another party's costs;
(iii) costs from or until a certain date only;
(iv) costs incurred before proceedings have begun;
(v) costs relating to particular steps taken in the proceedings;
(vi) costs relating to distinct parts of the proceedings; and
(vii) interest on costs from or until a certain date, including a date before judgment.

4.03 CPR Rule 44.3(4) sets out the matters that the court must take into account when exercising this discretion. These are:

(i) the conduct of all the parties;
(ii) whether a party has been wholly or partially successful in the claim; and

(iii) whether an admissible offer to settle, or payment in to court, has been made, whether compliant with CPR Rule 36 or not.

4.04 What is meant by the conduct of the parties is set out at CPR Rule 44.3(5):

(i) conduct before, as well as during, the proceedings, and the extent to which the parties followed any relevant pre-action protocol;
(ii) whether it was reasonable for a party to raise or contest a particular allegation or issue;
(iii) the manner in which a party has pursued or defended his case or a particular allegation or issue;
(iv) whether a claimant, who has succeeded in his claim, in whole or in part, exaggerated his claim.

A. Who is the winner?

4.05 The starting point undoubtedly is the general rule that the unsuccessful party will be ordered to pay the costs of the successful party.[1] In determining which party has won, the court must look at the proceedings as a whole. In most cases (particularly applications) it is obvious who has won.

4.06 However, it may be that no party can be said to have won, in which case the appropriate order would be no order for costs.[2] Even where the claimant has recovered a sum in damages that exceeds the offer made by the defendant, if that sum is substantially less than was originally claimed and the claimant has lost on a number of arguments, the court is entitled to come to the view, as it did in the case of *Islam v Ali* [2003] EWCA Civ 612, that the claimant is not the overall winner.[3]

4.07 Where there is a claim and a counterclaim it can be difficult to determine who is the overall winner. The Court of Appeal in *Burchell v Bullard* [2005] BLR 330[4] suggested one method; in commercial litigation (ie a claim in which each side is claiming money from the other) the winner can be determined 'by establishing who writes the cheque at the end of the case'.

---

[1] CPR Rule 44.3(2)(a).
[2] *AEI Rediffusion Music Ltd v Phonographic Performance Ltd* [1999] 2 All ER 299.
[3] Another way of dealing with a situation of this kind is to deprive the claimant of costs for their conduct in exaggerating the claim pursuant to CPR Rule 44.3(5). This is dealt with at paras 4.18–4.19.
[4] At para 33.

Where the court gives judgment on the claim and the counterclaim, the court is entitled to make a separate costs order against each party.[5] Generally, however, courts avoid making orders of this nature. **4.08**

B. Partial costs order

The court has the power to make the orders listed in para 4.02 above. Those that appear at para 4.02 (i)–(vi) are sometimes called partial costs orders. **4.09**

When a partial costs order is appropriate

The court must consider whether or not a party has succeeded on part or all of his case or whether it was reasonable to raise or contest a particular allegation.[6] If, in considering these issues, the court comes to the view that a partial costs order is appropriate, then it can readily depart from the general rule that costs follow the event.[7] **4.10**

The Court of Appeal has indicated its approval of partial costs orders 'which reflect not merely the overall outcome of proceeding but also the loss of particular issues'.[8] The reasons are obvious. A partial costs order can in many circumstances reflect the justice of a case more accurately than an all or nothing costs order. For a practitioner trying to persuade a court to make a partial costs order it may help to refer to the Court of Appeal judgment in *Summit Property Ltd v Pitmans* [2001] EWCA Civ 2020, where it was held that a party does not have to have acted unreasonably or improperly for a court to reflect the fact that he has lost on an issue in the order for costs. **4.11**

CPR Rule 44.3(7) provides that where the court is considering making an issue-based order (an order that one party recovers or pays the costs relating to a certain issue in the proceedings) it must instead, if practicable, make a percentage-based order or an order that a party recovers its costs from or until a certain date. The need to do this is even more acute in a summary assessment of costs. The reasons are self-evident; the schedule of costs will not break the time spent into issues. It will be virtually impossible accurately to attribute the costs on a summary basis to any one particular **4.12**

---

[5] CPR Rule 40.13.

[6] CPR Rule 44.3(5)(b).

[7] *AEI Rediffusion Music Ltd.*

[8] *Budgen v Andrew Gardner Partnership* [2002] EWCA Civ 1125 at para 26 (also reported in *The Times*, 9 September 2002).

issue. The time spent trying to carry out this exercise is not consistent with the overriding objective.[9] Further, the judge on a summary assessment, having heard the application or trial himself, will be in a good position to translate into a percentage the proportion of the court's time spent on any particular issue.

4.13 It is only in an exceptional case that a successful party who has been subject to a deduction from its costs pursuant to an issue-based order for failing on a particular issue, will be ordered to pay the costs of the other party in relation to that issue.[10]

C. Conduct

4.14 Not only can the conduct of a party determine the basis on which the costs are to be paid, but conduct can also be taken into account by the court when determining whether a partial costs order is appropriate.[11] The wording of CPR Rule 44.3(5)(a) makes it clear that the conduct that a court can take into account includes the conduct that gave rise to the proceedings as well as conduct within the proceedings itself.[12]

4.15 The Court of Appeal in the case of *Daniels v Commissioner of Police for the Metropolis* [2005] EWCA Civ 1312 considered whether a successful party should be deprived of its costs pursuant to CPR Rule 44.3 for failing to accept a CPR part 36 offer. It was held that only unreasonable conduct by a party would lead to their being deprived of some or all of their costs. Thus where the refusal to accept the CPR part 36 offer was reasonable, this could not be included as conduct that could be taken into account under CPR Rule 44.3(5).

Misconduct in connection with the summary assessment

4.16 CPR Rule 44.14 gives the court the power to disallow all or part of the costs which are being assessed, or to order a party or his legal representatives to pay costs which he has caused any other party to incur. Such an order can only be made where a party or his legal representative has failed to comply

---

9 *English v Emery Reimbold* [2002] 3 All ER 385 at para 115.

10 *Summit v Pitmans.*

11 Para 4.04 sets out the meaning of conduct in this context.

12 *Groupama Insurance Co Ltd v Overseas Partners & Another* [2004] 1 All ER (Comm) 893.

with a rule, court order or practice direction in connection with the summary assessment, or has behaved unreasonably or improperly before or during the proceedings which gave rise to the assessment proceedings.

This provision is limited to misconduct within the summary assessment hearing itself (or where the misconduct only comes to light at assessment stage).[13] This provision will have limited use on a summary assessment hearing as it is unlikely that misconduct will arise in relation to the summary assessment part of the hearing and not the earlier substantive part of the hearing. **4.17**

Exaggeration

Where a claimant consciously exaggerates his claim, even where he has beaten the CPR part 36 payment made by the defendant, the court is entitled to deprive the claimant of a substantial amount of his costs. In the case of *Painting v University of Oxford* [2005] PIQR 65 the claimant pleaded a claim in excess of £400,000. She only recovered £23,000 at trial. As a mark of their disapproval of her exaggeration of the value of her claim, the court held that she was not entitled to her costs after the date a part 36 payment had been made, despite the fact that she had beaten it at trial. **4.18**

In the case of *Allison v Brighton & Hove CC* [2005] EWCA Civ 548 the claimant failed to beat the part 36 offer made at trial and was only awarded 25% of his costs up to the date of the expiry of the offer due to the fact that he had only recovered a very small proportion of what he was claiming. In *Jackson v The Ministry of Defence* [2006] EWCA Civ 46 the claimant reduced his claim from one million pounds to two hundred and forty thousand pounds. He was awarded one hundred and fifty thousand pounds by the court, beating the defendant's part 36 offer by five thousand pounds. The claimant was awarded his costs but with a reduction of 25% for exaggerating his claim. **4.19**

Mediation

A party's unreasonable refusal to mediate can also be taken into account when determining the appropriate costs order to make, even where the offer **4.20**

---

[13] If paying parties were able to rely on this provision in relation to misconduct in the substantive proceedings they would be able to avoid invoking the more complex wasted costs jurisdiction (paras 4.45–4.50).

to mediate occurs before the start of formal proceedings.[14] The Court of Appeal in *Halsey v The Milton Keynes General NHS Trust* [2004] 1WLR 3002 gave guidance to assist courts in assessing when a refusal to mediate is unreasonable. Factors that were relevant included:

(i) the nature of the dispute;
(ii) the merits of the case;
(iii) the extent to which other settlement methods had been attempted;
(iv) whether the costs of Alternative Dispute Resolution (ADR) would be disproportionately high;
(v) whether any delay in setting up and attending the ADR would have been prejudicial;
(vi) whether the ADR had a reasonable prospect of success. (The stronger the court's encouragement to the parties to partake in ADR, the easier it is to show that a party's refusal was unreasonable.)
(vii) Whether the party's view of the prospects of the case was unreasonable (*Hickman v Blake Lapthorn* [2006] EWHC 12 (QB)).

4.21 The Court of Appeal in the case of *Halsey* held that it was for the unsuccessful party to persuade the court that the successful party unreasonably refused to agree to mediation. To succeed, the unsuccessful party needs to persuade the court that there was a reasonable prospect of the mediation being successful. The test is an objective one. Only if the unsuccessful party succeeds in discharging this burden will they have any prospect of persuading a court to reflect that unreasonable refusal in the costs order.

4.22 The court will usually give effect to an unreasonable refusal to mediate by an unsuccessful party by making an order that they must pay the winning party's costs on an indemnity basis. Where the refusal to mediate was that of the successful party the court will sometimes deprive them of some or all of their costs.[15]

4.23 In the *Burchell* case[16] Lord Justice Ward said (at para 41) that a small building dispute was exactly the kind of dispute which lent itself to ADR. Practitioners will have to assess whether this can be said of their particular claim.

---

[14] *Burchell v Bullard* at para 50.
[15] *Dunnett v Railtrack* [2002] EWCA Civ 303.
[16] Para 4.07.

D. Standard or indemnity costs

4.24 Having determined which party shall pay the costs, the court must then go on to determine on what basis those costs should be paid. The normal rule is that costs are awarded on the standard basis. The difference between the standard and the indemnity basis is set out in CPR Rule 44.4. In short, proportionality is a consideration on the standard basis, and any doubt is resolved in favour of the paying party. When costs are assessed on the indemnity basis, proportionality is not a factor, and any doubt is resolved in favour of the receiving party.

4.25 An order for costs to be paid on the indemnity basis is penal in nature, save where the order is made pursuant to CPR Rule 36.[17] For an order for costs to be made on the indemnity basis there has to be 'something in the conduct of the action or the circumstances of the case which takes that case out of the norm'.[18] The misconduct on the paying party's behalf has to be unreasonable to a high degree (although the conduct can fall short of conduct lacking moral probity or deserving moral condemnation).[19] Conduct that is merely wrong or misguided in hindsight is not enough, thus a refusal to accept an offer of settlement on its own will rarely attract an indemnity costs order.

4.26 Below are two examples of cases in which the Court of Appeal has upheld the first instance judge's award of indemnity costs:

(i) In a case in which the claimant made a speculative claim, the defendant made numerous attempts to settle the matter without recourse to the court, and the claimant turned down a part 36 offer which was not beaten; then it was a legitimate use of the discretion to award costs against the claimant on an indemnity basis.[20]
(ii) A claim was misconceived, in which the pleadings were confused and confusing, and which was inadequately prepared for trial.[21]

[17] *Kiam II v MGN Ltd* [2002] 1 WLR 2810 (also at [2002] 2 All ER 242).
[18] *Excelsior Commercial & Industrial Holdings Ltd v Salisbury Hamer Aspden & Johnson* [2002] EWCA Civ 879 at paras 39–40.
[19] *Kiam II v MGN Ltd*.
[20] *Excelsior Commercial* at paras 39–40.
[21] *Silvera v Lovat Fraser Urquhart and Others* [2004] EWCA Civ 580.

4.27 Where a party is found to have lied to the court it is likely that costs will be awarded against that party on an indemnity basis.

4.28 As a matter of principle, indemnity costs can be awarded to a legally aided party.[22]

E. Offers

4.29 Offers can also affect not only who pays the costs, but also on what basis those costs are paid.

Part 36 offers

4.30 If a defendant has made an offer (or payment into court) and that offer/payment complies with the provisions of CPR Rule 36 and the claimant fails to beat this at trial, then the claimant's unreasonable failure to accept the offer will usually be reflected in the costs order made by the court.[23] The first issue that the practitioner must consider therefore is whether the offer complies with the provisions of CPR Rule 36.

Does the offer comply with CPR Rule 36?

4.31 CPR Rule 36.5 sets out the form and content of a CPR part 36 offer. Where there is a defect in the offer, the court must first consider whether this is only a technical breach of the provisions of CPR Rule 36, or whether it is a breach which genuinely misled the other party. If it is a technical breach then the court should ordinarily exercise its discretion under CPR Rule 36.1(2) to treat the offer as a CPR part 36 offer.[24] In determining whether or not the breach misled the other party, the court will bear in mind whether or not that party had competent legal advice.

4.32 An offer that includes provisions as to costs does not comply with CPR Rule 36.[25] Similarly, an offer to settle an appeal that included an offer to waive the uplifted interest under an indemnity costs order that had been awarded to that party following the trial at first instance, does not fall within CPR Rule 36.[26]

---

[22] *Brawley v Marczynski & Another* [2004] 4 All ER 1067.

[23] See paras 4.35–4.39 for full discussion on the costs consequences.

[24] *Mitchell v James* [2004] 1WLR 258; also at [2003] 2 All ER 1064.

[25] *Mitchell v James* at para 29 and *Rio Properties Inc v Gibson Dunn* [2005] EWCA Civ 534.

[26] *Ali-Reza Delta Transport Co Ltd v United Arab Shipping Co Sag* [2004] 1WLR 168.

Has the offer been beaten?

When determining whether or not a party has beaten the part 36 offer, the court must compare like with like. Thus in the case of *Blackham v Entrepose UK* [2004] EWCA Civ 1109 the court held that the interest that had accrued since the offer was made had to be discounted to determine whether or not the offer had been beaten at trial. **4.33**

Has the defendant made a CPR Rule 36 payment?

CPR Rule 36.3 provides that in a money case, unless an offer to settle by a defendant is accompanied by a payment into court, the cost consequences set out in CPR Rule 36 do not apply. However, the court has a discretion under CPR Rules 36.1(2) and 44.3(4)(c) to treat the offer as having those consequences. Guidance was given in the case of *The Trustees of Stokes Pension Fund v Western Power Distribution* [2005] 3 All ER 775 as to when and how this discretion should be exercised. In that case the Court of Appeal held that an offer should usually be treated as having the same effect as a payment into court where (i) the offer is expressed in clear terms so there is no doubt as to what the offer relates to and if it is expressed not to be inclusive of interest, it gives details relating to interest; (ii) the offer must be open for acceptance for more than 21 days; (iii) the offer must be genuine; and (iv) the defendant must be good for the money at the time that the offer is made. If some of those conditions are not satisfied, the offer should be given less weight than a payment into court. Where none of the conditions are satisfied it is likely that the costs consequences that flow from a payment into court will not be extended to that offer. If, however, all the conditions are met, it is likely that the costs consequences will attach to that offer as if it was a payment into court. **4.34**

Cost consequences at trial in CPR Rule 36

If a claimant wins at trial but fails to beat the CPR Rule 36 offer made by the *defendant* then unless the court considers it unjust, the claimant will have to pay the defendant's costs incurred from the latest date on which the payment or offer could have been accepted.[27] This award is usually made on the standard basis.[28] **4.35**

If on the other hand, the claimant does better than the proposal contained in *his* own offer, then unless the court considers it unjust to do so, the **4.36**

[27] CPR Rule 36.20.

[28] *Kiam II v MGN Ltd* [2002] 1 WLR 2810 (also at [2002] 2 All ER 242).

defendant will be ordered to pay interest on damages and/or costs at a rate of up to 10% exceeding base rate, and/or costs on an indemnity basis from the last day that the defendant could have accepted the offer.[29]

4.37 Practitioners may like to remind the court that orders of this nature are not punitive.[30]

4.38 The court has a wide discretion as to when it would be unjust for the cost consequences of CPR Rule 36.20 and 21 to apply. The point has been argued in a number of cases with varying degrees of success:

(i) In *Huck v Robson* [2002] 3 All ER 263 it was argued that an offer to settle liability with a 5% discount was purely tactical. The court held it to be a genuine offer and so indemnity costs were awarded. The court did say, however, that if an offer might be purely tactical then this is a reason for coming to the view that it would be unjust to make such an award.

(ii) In the case of *Nedlloyd Lines UK Ltd & Another v CEL Group Ltd* [2004] 1 Lloyd's Rep 388 the Court of Appeal rejected an argument that the discount offered in the part 36 offer made in relation to an appeal was so small as not to be a genuine and realistic offer to settle. The discount offered in the part 36 offer was £5,000 in a claim worth over £700,000.

(iii) In the case of *Johnson v Gore Wood & Co* [2004] EWCA Civ 14 (also in *The Times*, 17 February 2004) the court considered it unjust to give the paying party the benefit of the provisions of CPR Rule 36 where it disapproved of their conduct during the litigation. Every issue in the claim had been contested at trial.

(iv) In the case of *Ford v GKR Construction* [2000] 1 WLR 1397 (also at [2000] 1 All ER 802) the court considered it unjust to give the defendant the benefit of the provisions of CPR Rule 36 where the defendant had not given adequate disclosure in the substantive claim to enable the claimant to assess whether or not the part 36 offer should be accepted.

(v) In the case of *Nedlloyd Lines* the Court of Appeal rejected an argument that it would be unjust to order indemnity costs against an unsuccessful applicant on the basis that as the respondent had the benefit of a CFA there had been little risk to it in continuing to fight the appeal.

---

29 CPR Rule 36.21.

30 *McPhilemy v Times Newspapers Ltd* [2002] 1WLR 934.

It is worth noting that the cost consequences of CPR Rule 36.20 and 21 only apply at trial. Thus where, for example, a claimant does better than a part 36 payment following a summary judgment application, the court must exercise its general discretion on costs pursuant to CPR Rule 44.3. In the case of *Petrotrade Inc v Texaco Ltd* [2002] 1 WLR 947 (also at [2001] 4 All ER 853) the Court of Appeal held that they would have awarded a claimant who had bettered his part 36 offer following a summary judgment application an order for indemnity costs and enhanced interest. **4.39**

Other offers

If an admissible offer to settle is made[31] that does not comply with CPR Rule 36 then the court is not bound by the provisions of CPR Rule 36 but must take that offer to settle into account pursuant to CPR Rule 44.4(4)(c) when exercising its discretion as to what order it should make. The court should bear in mind in the exercise of its discretion the public interest in encouraging parties to consider and evaluate offers to settle claims made against them, and where the offers are reasonable, to accept them.[32] **4.40**

That said, in the case of *Rio Properties* the court did not take the defective CPR part 36 offer into account even under CPR Rule 44.4(3). The offer made included an offer on costs which was very difficult to evaluate; accordingly the court at first instance did not criticize the defendant for failing to accept the offer. The Court of Appeal held that it was open to the judge in those circumstances to disregard the offer when making the order for costs. **4.41**

F. More than one defendant

Some thought needs to be given to the appropriate order to make where there is more than one defendant. Where the claimant is successful against all of the defendants then there is rarely any difficulty. The situation becomes more complicated where the claimant has succeeded against one defendant and lost against another. In these circumstances the court will usually make one of three orders: **4.42**

(i) Sanderson order[33]—this is an order that the unsuccessful defendant pay the successful defendant's costs. Significant factors in determining

[31] Parties, of course, cannot draw offers that are 'without prejudice' to the attention of the judge.

[32] *Rio Properties v Dunn & Crutcher* [2005] EWCA Civ 534 at para 23.

[33] *Sanderson v Blyth Theatre Company* [1903] 2 KB 533.

whether to make such an order are (i) whether the defendants blamed each other; and (ii) whether it had been reasonable on the part of the claimant to join a particular defendant.[34]

(ii) A Bullock order[35]—this is where the unsuccessful claimant is ordered to pay the costs of the successful defendant, but is entitled to recover these from the unsuccessful defendant as part of the claimant's costs.

(iii) An order that the claimant pay the costs of the successful defendant—this is generally appropriate where the claims against each of the defendants are not brought in the alternative.

4.43 Where a claimant is insolvent, a successful defendant will want a Sanderson order. That order allows the successful defendant to get his costs back by bypassing the insolvent claimant.

4.44 Where the defendant has joined a new party (pursuant to CPR part 20)[36] the usual principle is that the costs of the (successful) part 20 defendant are paid by the defendant—see *Johnson v Ribbins* [1977] 1 WLR 1458.

G. Wasted costs

4.45 CPR Rule 48.7 deals with applications for wasted costs against legal representatives. Such orders are made pursuant to s 51(7) of the Supreme Court Act 1981.

4.46 If the client considers it is appropriate to apply for a wasted costs order against either the other party's legal representatives, or indeed the client's own legal representatives, the client should usually raise the issue of wasted costs before the judge who has dealt with the substantive hearing.[37] It is, however, permissible in some circumstances for the application to be made after the costs have been assessed.[38]

4.47 The jurisdiction to make a wasted costs order depends on two stages of the court's discretion. The first is at the stage when the initial application is made—and can take place at a summary assessment hearing. At this stage the court is invited to exercise its discretion and make an order giving the

---

34 *Irvine v Commissioner of Police for the Metropolis* [2005] EWCA Civ 129.

35 *Bullock v London General Omnibus Company* [1907] 1 KB 264.

36 A discussion of this is outside the scope of this book.

37 *Melchior v Vettivel* [2002] C P Rep 24.

38 *Gray v Going Places Leisure Travel Ltd* [2005] EWCA Civ 189.

legal representative against whom the application is brought an opportunity (at the second stage) to show why the order should not be made against them.[39] This is often called a 'show cause' order.

In determining whether the matter should progress onto the second stage and whether a show cause order should be made, the court must consider the following matters: **4.48**

(i) whether the proceedings are likely to be complex and require detailed investigations into the facts. If so, it would not be appropriate to allow the application to proceed to the second stage. The issue of wasted costs must be capable of being dealt with on a summary basis.
(ii) whether the cost of the enquiries that will be required are likely to be proportionate to the costs claimed in the wasted costs application;
(iii) whether further proceedings are likely to be justified.

Usually a legal representative will only be in the frame for costs relating to a certain issue or for costs incurred over a certain period. The most sensible approach to take when a party makes an application for wasted costs is to: **4.49**

(i) make the costs orders that can be made, and assess the amount of costs due from one party to another;
(ii) consider whether, in all the circumstances, the application should be allowed to progress to the second stage;
(iii) if the matter should progress, make a show cause order.

The second stage of the wasted costs jurisdiction is outside the scope of this book. **4.50**

H. Costs against non-parties

It is possible to obtain costs orders against non-parties pursuant to CPR 48.2. Such orders are outside the scope of this book. **4.51**

---

[39] CPR Rule 48.7.

5

THE SUMMARY ASSESSMENT HEARING

Once the court has made the costs order, the summary assessment itself can begin. This is the procedure by which the court determines the amount of the costs due from the paying party to the receiving party. **5.01**

This chapter explains the procedure that is adopted at hearings and examines the substantive issues that are most commonly argued at summary assessments. The issues occur in the chapter in the order in which they should be raised at the summary assessment. This chapter does not, however, deal with issues that may arise in relation to the funding of a claim (typically by way of a CFA). As these issues can be complex and as they are not relevant to all summary assessments, they have been addressed separately in Chapter 6. **5.02**

A. Procedure for the hearing

All the parties and the judge should have a copy of all statements of costs before the summary assessment begins. Copies of any other relevant materials prepared in accordance with the preparation checklists in Chapter 9 must also be made available to the opposing party and the judge. **5.03**

In particular, practitioners must be sure that the court summarily assesses all the relevant costs: **5.04**

(i) Where the court is summarily assessing the costs of the claim in its entirety, the parties must be clear about precisely what costs the court is being asked to assess. The parties must be aware of all the previous orders for costs that have been made.

(ii) Where the court is assessing additional liabilities at the conclusion of a claim, practitioners must ensure that where, at an earlier hearing, there has been a summary assessment of the base costs with the assessment of the additional liabilities adjourned, the additional liabilities form part of the summary assessment and those sums are included in the final costs order.

(iii) Where the summary assessment is being carried out following a successful appeal (ie one in which there has been a reversal of the decision of the court below), the parties need to be clear as to whether asking the appeal court to assess summarily the costs of the appeal *and* of the costs below. For example, where the hearing at first instance took more than a day it would not be appropriate to assess summarily those costs following the appeal.[1]

5.05 Ordinarily the judge will want to hear from the paying party first so that the issues between the parties can be identified. The receiving party will of course be given an opportunity to respond to each of the issues raised. It is up to the judge whether he hears the paying party make submissions in relation to all the points in issue at one go, or whether he requires each issue to be responded to before going onto the next.

5.06 A summary assessment hearing is, by its very nature, short. Parties must be ready to deal with the issues they wish to raise succinctly. Arguments need to be marshalled into a sensible order and in such a way as to make the best use of the time available. Thus any submissions that go to the overall recovery of costs (such as submissions relating to the solicitor client retainer, or the enforceability of a CFA,[2] proportionality or costs estimates) should be raised first. Next, arguments over the level of fee earner or the hourly rate claimed should be attacked, and then individual items on the bill. The last matter that should be dealt with by the court is the assessment of any uplift claimed by the receiving party.[3]

5.07 The court must carry out a summary assessment of the costs with reference to the statement of costs before it. The court cannot simply award a party a lump sum that it considers appropriate on the basis of its experience of similar cases.[4] Nor can the court simply compare one side's costs schedule

---

1 See Chapter 2 for a discussion as to when summary assessment is appropriate.
2 These are dealt with in Chapter 6.
3 See Chapter 6.
4 *1–800 Flowers Inc v Phonenames Ltd* [2002] FSR 12.

to the other and come to the view that because they are broadly similar, the costs claimed are reasonable.[5]

If, on a summary assessment of the costs of an application, the court comes to the view that some of the costs claimed in the schedule do not relate to the application, but are costs of the action, it must indicate clearly which costs are costs of the action and have not been part of the summary assessment.[6] **5.08**

B. Pointers for the paying party

As the paying party it is important to remind the court that where costs are to be paid on the standard basis the benefit of any doubt must be accorded to them.[7] This can make a substantial difference where the practitioner on the other side does not have good instructions to explain why a particular item on the statement of costs looks high. **5.09**

It can also be helpful, when persuading a court that a particular item claimed by the receiving party is too high, to compare the receiving party's schedule of costs with that of the paying party.[8] **5.10**

C. Preliminary issues

Any arguments that the paying party wants to raise in relation to the solicitor client retainer should be dealt with first. If the retainer is held to be invalid, no costs will be recovered.[9] For the reasons set out at para 5.02 above, where the case is funded by a CFA practitioners should refer to Chapter 6. **5.11**

The Court of Appeal has held that the client care letter should ordinarily be disclosed to the court where a paying party is concerned about the terms of the solicitor client retainer.[10] If this is disclosed, and if the solicitor has signed the statement of costs with the declaration at the bottom of **5.12**

---

5 *Bryen & Langley v Boston* [2005] EWCA Civ 973.

6 *Sterling Publications Ltd v Burroughs* [2000] 2 Costs LR 155.

7 See para 4.24 for a definition of 'standard basis'.

8 This comparison is a 'helpful cross-check in the course of the assessment': *Bryen & Langley v Boston*, but see para 5.07 above.

9 This is because the indemnity principle has been breached; see para 3.08.

10 *Bailey v IBC Vehicles* [1998] 3 All ER 570. It is unclear whether the Court of Appeal considered that disclosure should be made to the paying party as well as to the court.

the N260,[11] then unless there is some evidence to suggest that there is a problem with the retainer, the court should not enquire any further into the enforceability of the retainer nor into whether the indemnity principle has been breached.

Proportionality

5.13 CPR Rule 44.5 sets out the factors that the court must take into account when deciding the amount of costs. Where the costs are to be assessed on the standard basis the court must consider whether or not they were proportionately and reasonably incurred, or proportionate and reasonable in amount. In carrying out this exercise the court must also have regard to the conduct of the parties, the efforts made to resolve the dispute, the value of the claim, the importance of the matter to all parties, the complexity of the matter, the skill and specialist knowledge involved, the time spent on the case, and the place and circumstances in which the work was done.

5.14 Proportionality is a key factor in the conduct of litigation.[12] Parties are expected to conduct litigation in a proportionate manner. This means that the costs must bear some relation to the amount at stake, and the importance of the matters to the respective parties, the complexity of the issues, and the financial position of each party.[13] The increasing importance placed on accurate costs estimates by the courts at both the allocation and pre-trial stage is testament to this.[14]

5.15 If the court is assessing costs on the standard basis the court must only allow costs that are proportionate to the matters in issue.[15] In the case of *SS for Home Department v Lownds* [2002] 1 WLR 2450 (also at [2002] 4 All ER 775) the Court of Appeal held that the court must assess the costs in two stages. The first stage is to look at the costs on a global basis. The court will then be able to come to a view as to whether the costs as a whole are disproportionate. In carrying out this assessment in relation to a claimant's costs the court must bear in mind the sum that it was reasonable for the claimant

[11] Which includes a statement that 'the costs estimates above do not exceed the costs which the [party] is liable to pay in respect of the work which the estimated covers'.

[12] Section 11.1–11.6 of the Costs Practice Direction.

[13] CPR Rule 1.1(2)(c).

[14] Section 6 of the Costs Practice Direction.

[15] CPR Rule 44.4(2)(a) and ss 11.1 and 11.2 of the Costs Practice Direction.

to believe that he might recover at the time that he made the claim on the one hand, as against the costs that have been incurred. In carrying out this assessment in relation to a defendant's costs, the court must have regard to the sum that it was reasonable for the defendant to believe that the claimant might recover. (This is likely to be the pleaded value of the claim.)

The Court of Appeal[16] has approved the following passage of His Honour Judge Alton in the case of *Jefferson v National Freight Carriers Ltd* [2001] 2 Costs LR 313: **5.16**

> In modern litigation, with the emphasis on proportionality, there is a requirement for parties to make an assessment at the outset of the likely value of the claim and its importance and complexity, and then to plan in advance the necessary work, the appropriate level of person to carry out the work, the overall time which would be necessary and appropriate to spend on the various stages in bringing the action to trial and the likely overall cost. While it is not unusual for costs to exceed the amount in issue, it was, in the context of modern litigation such as the present case, one reason for seeking to curb the amount of work done, and the cost by reference to the need for proportionality.

If the court comes to the view that the costs are not disproportionate at this stage then all that is required when carrying out the summary assessment is to determine whether each item claim has been reasonably incurred and if so, whether the cost of that item is reasonable. **5.17**

If, however, the court comes to the view that the costs as a whole are disproportionate, then the court must satisfy itself that the work in relation to each item was necessary, and if necessary, that the cost of the item is reasonable. In deciding whether an item is necessary, the conduct of the parties is highly relevant. The other party, by co-operating, can reduce costs, and by being unco-operative can increase costs. Thus if a party is unco-operative he can render necessary costs which would otherwise have been unnecessary. **5.18**

When considering the issue of proportionality the court must consider the base costs and the disbursements separately from any additional liabilities (such as a success fee or insurance premium and VAT).[17] **5.19**

---

[16] *Lownds*.

[17] Sections 11.5 and 11.9 of the Costs Practice Direction and *Giambrone v JMC Holidays* [2003] 1 All ER 982.

Estimates[18]

5.20 When the court is assessing whether or not the costs being claimed are proportionate or reasonable, it is entitled to take into account any estimate of costs filed by that party.[19]

5.21 The parties must file costs estimates when filing both the allocation questionnaire and the pre-trial checklist.[20] The court may also order a party to file an estimate at any time during the life of the claim.[21] This estimate must include the anticipated costs (base costs and disbursements) up to and including trial; however, there is no need to include a figure for a success fee.[22] This allows the court to keep a tight control on the claim by taking account of the costs estimate when giving case management directions (for example when giving permission for experts).

5.22 The court may have regard to previous costs estimates when assessing whether the costs claimed at the conclusion of a claim are proportionate or reasonable.[23] Where the schedule of costs exceeds the cost estimates by more than 20%, and the receiving party has not provided a satisfactory explanation for the difference, or the paying party has reasonably relied on the estimate of costs, the court may regard the difference as evidence that the costs are unreasonable or disproportionate.[24]

5.23 The court is also able to take into account the estimates that a solicitor has given his own client pursuant to his obligations under rule 15 of the Solicitors Practice Rules and the Solicitors' Costs Information and Client Care Code 1999 (the Code). Where the court comes to the view that there has been a breach of the Code (in failing to give an estimate, or in giving an inadequate estimate), and this has had a calculable effect on the costs incurred by the receiving party, the costs judge is entitled to take the breach into account when deciding whether the amount of costs of the receiving party were reasonably incurred or reasonable and proportionate in amount

---

18 The Court of Appeal looked at estimates in the case of *Leigh v Michelin Tyre* [2004] 2All ER 175. Section 6 of the Costs Practice Direction has been amended to reflect this judgment.

19 Section 6.6 of the Costs Practice Direction.

20 Section 6.4(1) of the Costs Practice Direction and s 2.1 of Practice Directions supplementing CPR Rule 26.

21 Section 6.3 of the Costs Practice Direction.

22 Section 6.2(2) of the Costs Practice Direction.

23 Section 6.6(1) of the Costs Practice Direction.

24 Section 6.6(2) of the Costs Practice Direction.

for the purposes of CPR Rules 44.4 and 44.5.[25] It is of course very difficult for a paying party to get hold of this information, especially on a summary assessment hearing, as a receiving party will not ordinarily disclose these documents to the paying party. The paying party would have to persuade a court to make an order for their disclosure. It is only in exceptional circumstances that such an order would be made (*Garbutt*).

Previous summary assessments

Paragraph 7 of the Supreme Court Costs Office's (SCCO) Guide to the Summary Assessment of Costs[26] requires the party to draw to the judge's attention all previous summary assessments so that the approach to the assessment will be consistent. **5.24**

D. Attacking and defending the detail of the statement of costs

Once the preliminary issues have been dispensed with the practitioner must turn his mind to the detail of the bill. **5.25**

Level of fee earner

The first issue to address is whether the level of fee earner is appropriate for that case. As a general rule the more senior the fee earner, the quicker he can be expected to deal with the claim. **5.26**

Where the grade claimed by the receiving party is too high for the complexity and value of the case, any reasons given by the receiving party for this (such as the fact that the solicitor instructed by the receiving party is a sole practitioner and hence no lower fee earner was available to do the work) is immaterial; a party is entitled to instruct any solicitor he wishes. This does not mean that the hourly rate charged to the receiving party by the solicitor is recoverable from the paying party. The question for the court is whether the hourly rate claimed is reasonable for that particular case. **5.27**

[25] *Garbutt v Edwards, The Times*, 3 November 2005. For a detailed look at the Solicitors' Practice Rules, see Chapter 6.

[26] Available on the SCCO website.

5.28 It is worth remembering that the judge carrying out the summary assessment will have a good grasp of the complexity of the particular piece of litigation having just heard the substantive hearing.

Hourly rate

Solicitors

5.29 The SCCO produce a table of guideline figures for solicitors' rates. The rates set out there vary according to where the solicitor's office is located.[27] These figures are only guideline figures to be used as a starting point in a summary assessment.[28] Thus it is open to a party to persuade a court that a higher figure is appropriate in any given case.[29]

5.30 In choosing which solicitor to instruct, parties must act reasonably. In determining whether a party has acted reasonably the court should take into account the following matters:

(i) the importance of the matter to the receiving party;
(ii) the legal and factual complexities in so far as the receiving party might understand them;
(iii) the location of the receiving party's home, his place of work, and the location of the court in which the proceedings were commenced;
(iv) the location of the solicitors, their accessibility to the client, and their readiness to attend at the relevant court;
(v) what, if anything, the receiving party might reasonably be expected to know about the fees charged by the solicitors compared with the fees of other solicitors whom he might reasonably be expected to have considered.[30]

5.31 As long as the receiving party can show that it was reasonable to instruct the firm of solicitors that he did, he will recover the full rate charged by that solicitor. The fact that a particular client has a habitual connection with a particular firm of solicitors will only be of limited relevance.

---

[27] The guideline figures are reproduced at Appendix F.
[28] Paragraphs 38 and 39 of the SCCO Guide to the Summary Assessment of Costs.
[29] In the case of *Higgs v Camden & Islington Health Authority* [2003] EWHC 15 (QB) (also at 12 BMLR 95) the guideline figure was doubled by the judge on detailed assessment on the basis that the case was a heavy, difficult case run knowledgeably by an expert in that particular field (para 51).
[30] *Wraith v Sheffield Forgemasters Ltd* [1998] 1 WLR 132 (also at [1998] 1 All ER 82).

Where a fee earner has worked on a case for a considerable time, and during that time the hourly rate has increased, it is legitimate to average out the two rates on the statement of costs. **5.32**

It is not uncommon to see several fee earners of different grades working on the same case. While this may mean that there is some duplication of work, it can also be a way of cutting costs, as it allows for the less complex work to be carried out by a lower grade of fee earner. **5.33**

Litigants in person

CPR Rule 48.6 provides that the costs of a litigant in person are payable by another party. These costs can be calculated in two ways: **5.34**

(i) Where the litigant in person can show that he has suffered financial loss he can recover the amount he can prove he has lost while dealing with the litigation.[31]
(ii) Where the litigant in person cannot show financial loss he can recover the rate of £9.25 per hour.[32]

The total amount recoverable by a litigant in person must not exceed two-thirds of the costs that would have been allowed had the party been represented by solicitors (save for disbursements, which may be recovered in full).

Litigants in person are also able to recover as costs payments made by them for legal services relating to the conduct of the proceedings, such as the cost of obtaining advice on a discrete point. **5.35**

Practitioners should also note CPR Rule 48.6(6)(b) and s 52.5 of the Costs Practice Direction. This provides that a solicitor represented by a firm of which he is the proprietor or a solicitor who is represented by himself in his firm's name is not a litigant in person. The consequence of this rule is that those solicitors are able to recover commercial hourly rates for the work done by them on the litigation. Following the case of *McIlwraith v McIlwraith* [2002] EWHC 9028 (costs) a solicitor who is represented by the firm that employs him does not come within this rule. In that case the court found that the solicitor was a litigant in person in substance if not in form (as his employer's firm was on the record as representing him), and he **5.36**

---

31 CPR Rule 48.6(4)(a).
32 CPR Rule 48.6(4)(b) and s 52.4 of the Costs Practice Direction.

was allowed to recover the rate of £9.25 per hour for the work he had done on the claim.

Amount of costs

5.37 The Guide to the Summary Assessment of Costs 2005 Edition[33] gives some guidance on the amount of time that is reasonable to claim in some hearings before the Court of Appeal. No such guidance is given for first instance hearings. Para 50 provides that, 'There can be no guidance as to whether the time claimed has been reasonably spent, and it is for the Judge in each case to consider the work properly undertaken by Solicitors and Counsel and to arrive at a figure which is in all circumstances reasonable.' The guidance for hearings in the Court of Appeal can be summarized as follows (all the figures are for preparation, attendance, travel and waiting):

(i) *Contested Directions Hearings/Applications for permission to appeal at which the respondent is present and appeals from case management directions*:
Where the hearing is attended by solicitor and counsel, it would be reasonable for a solicitor to spend four hours for a one-hour appointment.
Where counsel does not attend, it would be reasonable for the solicitor to spend five hours for a one-hour hearing, and 10 hours for a half-day hearing.
For a litigant in person, it would be reasonable for them to spend nine hours for a one-hour hearing, and 14 hours for a half-day hearing, with an additional allowance for the expense and time for travelling.

(ii) *Dismissal hearing at which the respondent is present (listed for less than an hour)*:
If the hearing is attended by solicitor and counsel, a solicitor may reasonably spend two hours.
If the solicitor attends without counsel it would be reasonable for him to spend three hours.
It would be reasonable for a litigant in person to spend six hours, with an additional allowance for the expense and time for travelling.

(iii) *Appeals listed for one day or less*:
As these appeals vary enormously it is not possible to give guidance as to the number of hours reasonably spent.

---

[33] Available on the SCCO website.

Non-recoverable items

Generally speaking the paying party should only have to pay for the time incurred by the receiving party's lawyers while they are progressing the claim. Thus where administrative tasks have been carried out, or time has been spent developing the solicitor–client relationship, these are not costs that should be visited on the paying party. The difficulty with summary assessment of course, is that it is often difficult to identify whether non-recoverable items are being included in the statement of costs. **5.38**

It is, however, useful to have an understanding of the items that the receiving party is not entitled to recover from the paying party.[34] These include: **5.39**

(i) time charged for photocopying—this is an administrative function;[35]
(ii) solicitor's travel time to see the client—ordinarily the client would expect to attend at the solicitor's office, unless the client is unable to travel;
(iii) local travelling expenses (within a 10-mile radius of the court dealing with the claim);
(iv) reading incoming letters and emails;
(v) diarising court hearings (again this is an administrative function and not fee-earning work);
(vi) time considering law and procedure—the solicitor is expected to know this.

Where a solicitor has used an agent, those fees should be claimed on the basis that they form part of the solicitor's charges.[36] **5.40**

Whether the costs incurred by a party in arranging the funding of a claim (typically by drawing up, explaining and signing a CFA, or researching insurance premiums) are recoverable from the paying party is not clear. It certainly used to be the case that costs incurred in funding a claim were not recoverable from the paying party.[37] However, with the increase in CFAs which place fairly onerous (and time-consuming) obligations upon solicitors to spend time explaining funding issues to their clients, the **5.41**

[34] Section 4 of the Costs Practice Direction.
[35] For an exception to this see para 5.40.
[36] Section 4.16(6) of the Costs Practice Direction.
[37] *Hunt v RM Douglas Roofing Ltd, The Times*, 23 November 1987, in the Court of Appeal. This case went to the House of Lords on a different issue.

court's attitude to this has rather softened. Different judges take different views.

Disbursements

Brief fees

5.42 In a fast track trial, the brief fees are fixed according to (i) for a claimant's advocate, the amount the claimant recovers in the proceedings; and (ii) for the defendant's advocate, the amount the claimant claimed in the claim form.[38]

5.43 The brief fee should include all the preparation for the trial although it is permissible to charge a separate fee for the drafting of a skeleton argument.[39] There is of course an element of overlap between these two items, and the degree of overlap will depend on how far in advance the skeleton argument was prepared. This issue is unlikely to arise on a fast track trial as the advocate's brief fee is fixed.

5.44 The SCCO has produced some figures for counsel's fees for cases which last from between one hour and half a day; they appear at Appendix F. They are not recommended rates, but figures to which judges can refer for guidance.

5.45 The Guide to the Summary Assessment of Costs 2005[40] provides that in Contested Directions Hearings, Applications for Permission to Appeal at which the respondent is present and Appeals from Case Management Directions where the hearing is attended by counsel, it would be reasonable for counsel of between 5–10 years' experience to receive a fee of £550 (plus VAT) for a one-hour hearing and £880 (plus VAT) for a half-day hearing.

5.46 For a Dismissal hearing at which the respondent is present (listed for less than an hour) it would be reasonable for counsel of between 5–10 years' call to receive a fee of £385 plus VAT.

Experts

5.47 The amount charged by experts varies enormously. The factors that should be taken into account are:

(i) the complexity of the issues;

---

[38] CPR Rule 46.2.

[39] There is a Table of Counsel's Fees which is reproduced at para 48.51 of the White Book 2005 and reproduced at Appendix F.

[40] Available on the SCCO website.

(ii) the seniority and experience of the expert;
(iii) whether that level of expertise was required on the particular case;
(iv) the number of hours spent examining evidence;
(v) the length of the report;
(vi) whether the report addressed the relevant issues.

Often paying parties object to a receiving party using an agency to arrange and correspond with the expert on the solicitor's behalf. The question of whether this is a reasonable course of action depends upon whether the involvement of the referral agency has reduced the work that the solicitor has had to do.[41] This can be difficult to establish on a summary assessment of costs as the information provided in the statement of costs does not reveal how much correspondence the solicitor has had to undertake in relation to that expert. If, however, the paying party can convince a court that the instruction of a referral agency has not reduced the amount of work the solicitor has had to undertake (in finding the expert, obtaining disclosure, instructing the expert, and setting up any meetings), then they may have some success in persuading a court to disallow some of the time charged by the solicitor. **5.48**

The paying party may have some success in persuading a court to reduce the fee charged by an agency if it looks too high on the basis that an element of that charge represents an administrative fee. Following *Claims Direct Test Cases Tranche 2* [2003] EWHC 9005 (costs)[42] it is clear that the administrative element of the fee charged by a medical referral agency is not recoverable from the receiving party as it does not amount to a cost of the action. As most agencies will not disclose how much they actually pay the experts it is not always possible for the court to determine how much of the fee paid to the agency represents their administrative fee. In the *Claims Direct* case Master Hurst stated that in his experience £15 was not an uncommon amount to reflect the administrative element. [43] **5.49**

Photocopying

These costs are only recoverable in exceptional circumstances[44] such as where there is an unusual amount of documents for a case of that nature. **5.50**

41 *Stringer v Copley* (Kingston On Thames CC, 17 May 2002).
42 The transcript of this case is available on the Supreme Court Costs Office website.
43 Paragraph 118 of *Claims Direct* case.
44 See para 5.32(i).

Even where photocopying has been carried out by an external agency as a disbursement, it is only recoverable in exceptional circumstances.

Postage/couriers

5.51 These costs are not usually recoverable unless there are unusual circumstances or where the cost is unusually heavy.

6

FUNDING

This chapter is concerned with the issues that may arise in a summary assessment of costs where a claim is funded by a CFA and/or an after the event insurance (ATE) premium, or an additional amount pursuant to s 30 of the Access to Justice Act 1999.[1] The assessment of additional liabilities will only arise at the conclusion of the proceedings (or the part of the proceedings to which the funding agreement relates) pursuant to CPR Rule 44.3A.[2] **6.01**

The most common issues that arise are: **6.02**

(i) Whether the CFA complies with the relevant statutory scheme—if it does not, the paying party will seek to persuade the court that the CFA is unenforceable as between the solicitor and the client. If there is no liability on the part of the client to pay the solicitor's charges and expenses there is nothing for the paying party to indemnify the receiving party for, hence the paying party's liability to the receiving party for costs is nil. This is referred to as the indemnity principle.[3]

---

[1] Section 30 allows for the recovery of an amount (as costs) for provision made by or on behalf of a body (prescribed by the Act) in connection with the proceedings against the risks of having to pay the costs of other parties to the proceedings. It is rare to see an amount claimed under s 30. This particular type of additional liability is outside the scope of this book.

[2] Practitioners should also note CPR Rule 44.3A(2) which allows the court, when dealing with a claim which is subject to a funding arrangement, to make an order either for the summary assessment of all the costs, including the additional liability, a detailed assessment of the additional liability but a summary assessment of the other costs, or a detailed assessment of all the costs.

[3] The indemnity principle is said to be breached if the receiving party claims costs from the paying party, but in fact has no liability to pay those costs to his own solicitor. The paying party is only obliged to indemnify the receiving party for the costs and expenses he has been put to in running the litigation.

(ii) Whether the receiving party was notified in accordance with CPR Rule 44.15 that the receiving party was funding the claim by way either of a CFA or an ATE premium—if this information was not disclosed at the correct time and in the correct manner no uplift on base costs or premium in respect of the ATE premium is recoverable by the receiving party for the period that the information was not provided.

(iii) Whether it was reasonable to take out an ATE premium and if so, whether the premium is reasonable in amount.

(iv) Whether the uplift claimed on the costs is reasonable.

These arguments will be raised at different points during the summary assessment hearing.

A. Conditional fee agreements

6.03 Contingency fees (taking a share of the damages) and conditional fees (only being paid if the client wins, but with an uplift on the base costs) used to be unlawful. It remains unlawful for a legal professional to enter into a contingency fee agreement.

6.04 Section 58 of the Courts and Legal Services Act 1990 (the 1990 Act) made conditional fee agreements lawful (other than in family and criminal work); however, the success fee was not recoverable from the paying party (following the Conditional Fee Agreements Order 1995 and accompanying regulations which came into force on 1 July 1995). Since 1 April 2000 the success fee and any insurance premium is in principle recoverable from the paying party.[4] Section 58 of the 1990 Act as amended specifies that only a CFA which satisfies all of the conditions applicable to it is enforceable. Thus a CFA must comply with the conditions set out in s 58(3) and (4). It must be in writing, it must not relate to proceedings which cannot be the subject of an enforceable conditional fee agreement, if it has a success fee it must state the percentage by which the amount of fees which would be payable if it were not a conditional fee agreement is to be increased, and the percentage must not exceed the percentage specified by order made by the

---

[4] This is because on 1 April 2000, s 27 of the Access to Justice Act 1999 (AJA 1999) substituted a new s 58 of the Courts and Legal Services Act 1990 (the 1990 Act) and introduced a new s 58A.

Secretary of State. In addition, it must comply with the Conditional Fee Agreements Regulations 2000 (the CFA Regulations 2000).

On 1 November 2005 the CFA Regulations 2000 were revoked by the Conditional Fee Agreements, (Revocation) Regulations 2005. The CFA Regulations 2000 continue to have effect for any CFA entered into before 1 November 2005. Paragraphs 6.20–6.31 below set out how CFAs entered into after 1 November 2005 are to be regulated. **6.05**

A CFA made between 1 April 2000 and 31 October 2005 must comply with the conditions set out in s 58(3) and (4) of the 1990 Act as well as the CFA Regulations 2000. A CFA made after 31 October 2005 does not have to comply with the CFA Regulations 2000 but must still comply with the 1990 Act. **6.06**

The CFA Regulations 2000[5]

The provisions of the CFA Regulations 2000 can be summarized as follows: **6.07**

(i) Regulation 2 requires the CFA to specify which proceedings or which part of the proceedings it relates to. It also requires the CFA to include terms relating to the circumstances in which the legal representative's fees and expenses are payable.

(ii) Regulation 3 is concerned with CFAs that provide for success fees. It provides that the CFA must set out the reasons for setting the percentage increase at the level stated in the agreement (and whether any part of that increase relates to the postponement of fees). It also provides that the CFA must include certain terms relating to the assessment by the court, or agreement between the parties, of the success fee.

(iii) Regulation 3A[6] allows parties to enter into CFAs under which the client is only liable for fees and expenses incurred to the extent that they are recoverable from the other side. Regulations 2, 3, and 4 of the CFA Regulations 2000 do not apply to such agreements. These agreements are sometimes referred to as 'CFA Lite' as the provisions with which the CFA has to comply are less onerous than under a regular CFA.[7]

[5] At Appendix B.

[6] Brought into force by the Conditional Fee Agreements (Miscellaneous Amendments) Regulations 2003 in June 2003.

[7] These agreements have not been taken up by many solicitors as they only apply to cases in which the fees *and* expenses are recovered and so will not apply to a 'hybrid' case whereby fees are recoverable only to the extent that they are recovered from the losing party but disbursements are payable by the client in any event.

(iv) Regulation 4 sets out the information that the solicitor must provide the client with before the CFA is entered into.
(v) Regulation 5 provides that the CFA must be signed by the client and the legal representative.
(vi) Regulation 6 is concerned with amending a CFA.

6.08 The solicitor must make appropriate enquiries to satisfy himself that the claimant does not have appropriate before the event (BTE) insurance (reg 4(2)(c)). The steps that a solicitor has to take are set out in the case of *Sarwar v Alam* (2002) 1 WLR 125.[8] In brief the solicitor should do the following:

(i) He should ask the claimant to bring to the first interview any relevant motor, household or other insurance policy. This should extend to a passenger in a motor claim, who should be asked, where practicable, to bring the motor insurance policy of the driver (ie where the passenger is not intending to sue the driver).
(ii) At the first interview the solicitor should ask the claimant whether his liability for costs will be covered by a third party such as a trade union or an employer.
(iii) If there is BTE insurance available and where the claim is a low value simple claim such as a motor claim and the policy cover is adequate, the claimant should be referred to the BTE insurer.

Challenges to the terms of the CFA

6.09 The mandatory nature of the regulations and s 58A of the 1990 Act led to a number of challenges in which it was argued by the paying party that where there was a breach of the regulations, no matter how technical, this rendered the whole agreement unenforceable. On 22 May 2003 the Court of Appeal handed down judgment in six test cases challenging the enforceability of various CFAs in the case of *Hollins v Russell* [2003] 1 WLR 2487.

6.10 The Court of Appeal held that the words 'satisfies all the conditions applicable to it' in s 58(1) of the 1990 Act should be construed realistically so as to reflect the dual purposes of the legislation which were (i) to increase access to legal services; and (ii) to protect the public interest and the interests of clients. In general the court will find that conditions have

[8] Although this case was not looking at compliance with the CFA Regulations 2000 (as it was a pre-2000 CFA) this guidance has been applied to post-2000 CFAs such as in the case of *Culshaw v Goodliffe* (Liverpool County Court, 24 November 2003).

been met when there has been substantial compliance with, or no material departure from, what is required by the regulations.[9]

Costs judges should ask themselves: 6.11

> Has this particular departure from a regulation pursuant to s 58(3)(c) of the 1990 Act or a requirement in s 58, either on its own or in conjunction with any other such departure in this case, had a materially adverse effect either upon the protection afforded to the client or upon the proper administration of justice?

If the answer is yes, the conditions have not been satisfied. If no, the departure is immaterial and the conditions have been satisfied. Sufficiency and materiality depend on the circumstances of the case. It is unclear at present whether one must consider the issue of materiality at the time the CFA was entered into, or at the time of the challenge. The Court of Appeal is due to hear argument on this in the near future. In determining what will have a 'materially adverse effect' it is helpful to look at the way in which the courts have dealt with alleged breaches of the regulations in *Hollins* and beyond: 6.12

(i) In *Dunn v Ward* (one of the *Hollins* test cases) it was alleged that reg 4(2)(e)(ii) of the CFA Regulations 2000, which requires a solicitor who recommends a particular contract of legal expenses insurance to explain 'whether or not he has an interest in doing so', had been breached. The risk which it was designed to guard against was that the lawyer might induce the client to enter into insurance arrangements in which he had an interest. It was held, however, that if the solicitor in fact had no interest there was no risk, and the CFA was not rendered unenforceable by his failure to say so expressly.

(ii) *Dunn v Ward* [2003] 1 WLR 2487; [2003] 4 All ER 590 was also concerned with reg 4(3) and (5) of the CFA Regulations 2000 which require a solicitor to give both a written and an oral explanation of the CFA to the client before the CFA is entered into. It was argued that the standard Law Society model CFA, part of which was the CFA itself and part of it the written explanation, was defective: a document cannot be at once the CFA and the written explanation. It was held that the regulatory intention was that the client should not be left confused. In this case the documents were in clear English and legible, and

[9] *Hollins*, para 106.

the appeal was dismissed, although the Court of Appeal did agree that a free-standing letter of explanation might have been preferable.

(iii) In *Spencer v Wood* [2004] EWCA Civ 352 (also in *The Times*, 30 March 2004) the Court of Appeal (sitting with Senior Costs Judge Hurst) upheld a decision that the entirety of the claimant's profit costs after the claimant and his solicitor had entered into a CFA were to be disallowed because there was a material breach of reg 3(1)(b) of the CFA Regulations 2000. The CFA did not specify how much of the success fee related to the cost to his solicitors of the postponement of receipt of their charges and disbursements. As that element is not recoverable from the paying party the claimant did not know which part of the success fee he would have to pay himself.

(iv) In *Samonini v London General Transport Services* [2005] PIQR 20 (costs) Senior Costs Judge Hurst held that a CFA was unenforceable for breach of reg 4(2)(c) CFA Regulations 2000. The court held that, 'The premium sought for the ATE policy is on its face disproportionate and demands investigation.' The disproportionate size of the premium gave rise to a duty on the solicitor to carry out a careful investigation as to the availability of before the event insurance cover. The enquiries made were insufficient and inadequate and the claimant was not asked about anything other than his motor policy.[10]

(v) In the case of *Hughes v Newham London Borough Council* (SCCO, 28 July 2005) Master O Hare held that where a solicitor had failed to properly inform his client that legal aid was available in a housing disrepair claim brought against the landlord, the solicitor had breached reg 4(2)(d) of the CFA Regulations 2000 which requires solicitors to inform clients about other methods of financing the litigation. This had a materially adverse effect upon the protection afforded to the client as the client had had to take out loans to fund the proceedings and the interest charged under the loan was irrecoverable as against the defendant. The CFA was rendered unenforceable.

(vi) *Richards v Davis* (SCCO, 25 November 2005), where Senior Costs Judge Hurst found that there had been a clear breach of reg 4(2)(c) as the solicitor had not read through the client's motor insurance policy. He also found breaches of reg 4(2)(d) and (e) in that there was a

[10] For the ambit of the investigation that a solicitor is expected to carry out, practitioners should look at the Court of Appeal case of *Sarwar v Alam* [2001] EWCA Civ 1401 and para 6.8 above.

complete failure to consider any funding other than the insurance premium being offered under the TAG scheme. All of these breaches were held to have adversely affected the protection afforded to the client and to have had a materially adverse effect on the proper administration of justice by inflating the claim. Accordingly the CFA was held to be unenforceable.

The recovery of disbursements where the CFA is unenforceable

Practitioners must be aware of the effect on the recovery of disbursements if the CFA is rendered unenforceable. In *Hollins* the receiving party was still able to recover the disbursements (including the insurance premium) even though the CFA was found to be unenforceable. The Court of Appeal had this to say: **6.13**

(i) The ATE premiums are recoverable as costs in any proceedings irrespective of whether or not there is a CFA given the wording of s 29 of AJA 1999.
(ii) Disbursements are recoverable on the following basis: 'if the client has actually paid a debt to a third party, properly incurred in the conduct of the litigation, there seems no reason why this should not be recoverable from the paying party, insofar as it is reasonable and proportionate'.[11]

Thus in the case of *Spencer v Wood* the claimant recovered profit costs incurred before entering into the CFA, no profit costs incurred under the CFA, but the ATE premium and disbursements. **6.14**

Disclosure of the CFA

If the receiving party wishes to recover costs and expenses under a CFA the CFA needs to be disclosed to the paying party to ensure that it complies with the regulations.[12] This disclosure is as relevant in summary assessments as it is in detailed assessments.[13] If the CFA has commercially sensitive material in it, a redacted copy can be disclosed. **6.15**

If a success fee is being claimed, the risk assessment will need to be disclosed to the other side and to the court.[14] **6.16**

[11] *Hollins*, para 115.
[12] *Hollins*, paras 71 and 72.
[13] *Cleanaway Holdings Ltd v Woollam* (Chester County Court, 26 July 2004), a decision of His Honour Judge Barnett.
[14] Regulation 3(2) of the CFA Regulations 2000.

6.17 The CFA itself, and the risk assessment need not be disclosed to the paying party until the order for costs is made by the judge. As the summary assessment of costs will follow immediately, the paying party will need to be able to marshal any challenge they wish to make quickly.

Notification of the funding arrangement

6.18 If the claimant is funded by way of a CFA, and additional liabilities are claimed (typically an uplift on base costs or an ATE premium), notice of how the claim is to be funded must be given to the other side when the claim form is served pursuant to CPR Rule 44.15 and s 19 of the Costs Practice Direction.[15] CPR Rule 44.3B(1)(c) provides that the receiving party cannot receive any additional liability for any period of the proceedings during which the information was not provided. This is a mandatory provision, and the claimant must make a CPR Rule 23 application supported by evidence for relief from sanctions to avoid the consequences of this provision.[16] Paying parties must be aware that in taking a point about notification the assessment of costs could be adjourned. This may well have cost consequences.

6.19 If an application for relief is made, the courts tend to be lenient if the paying party has had notice of the funding arrangements, albeit not in the form prescribed by the CPR.[17] Where no application for relief is made, the courts are not so lenient (*Connor v Birmingham City Council and Birmingham Country Court* (Unreported, 16 March 2005)).

The new regime

Introduction

6.20 The CFA Regulations 2000 have been revoked. It will be the Law Society's rules and guidance that will now regulate solicitors' use of CFAs.

6.21 That said, the provisions of ss 58 and 58A of the 1990 Act as amended remain the same. Thus a CFA will still need to be in writing, not relate to criminal or family proceedings, and where there is a success fee, must specify the percentage increase. A failure to comply with these requirements will render the CFA unenforceable. If there has been a breach of any of

---

[15] Using a form N251.

[16] CPR Rule 3.9(2).

[17] *Montlake & Others v Lambert Smith Hampton Group Ltd* [2004] EWHC 1503 (Comm).

these statutory provisions, it would be quite proper for a paying party to raise these issues before a court on summary assessment.

The professional rules

Section 31 of the Solicitors Act 1974 (the 1974 Act) enables the Law Society to make rules regulating professional practice and conduct of solicitors. Rule 15 of the Solicitors' Practice Rules 1990 provides that solicitors shall give information about costs and other matters in accordance with the Solicitors' Costs Information and Client Care Code 1999 (the Code) to their clients. The Code has statutory force.[18] The Code sets out the costs information that must be given to the client, the stages at which the client should receive such information, and the manner in which the information should be given. Practitioners should also refer to the Law Society guidance entitled 'Your clients—your business' (January, 2006). **6.22**

The Code (as amended) replicates many of the provisions of the CFA Regulations 2000. It places an obligation on a solicitor to explain to a client represented under a CFA the following matters: **6.23**

(i) the circumstances in which the client may be liable for his own costs and for the other party's costs;
(ii) the client's right to an assessment of costs, whether the solicitor intends to seek payment of any or all of their costs from the client; and
(iii) any interest a solicitor may have in recommending a particular policy of insurance or other funding.

Rule 15 of the Solicitors' Practice Rules sets out the effect of breaching the Code. It provides that: **6.24**

(i) A serious breach of the Code or persistent breaches of a material nature will amount to a breach of the rule and may also be evidence of inadequate professional services pursuant to s 37A of the Solicitors Act.
(ii) Material breaches of the Code which are not serious or persistent will not be a breach of the rule but may be evidence of inadequate professional services.
(iii) Non-material breaches of the Code will not be a breach of the rule nor evidence of inadequate professional services.

Inadequate professional services are defined in Sch 1A of the 1974 Act as services provided by a solicitor in connection with any matter in which he **6.25**

[18] *Swain v Law Society* [1982] 2 All ER 827.

or his firm have been instructed by a client, which have in any respect not been of the quality which it is reasonable to expect of the solicitor. Allegations of inadequate professional services are investigated by the Law Society. If a finding is made by the Law Society then they can disallow all or part of the solicitor's costs, and direct that the solicitor pay up to £15,000 compensation to the client.

Challenges to the CFA

6.26 If there has been a breach of the 1990 Act this can properly be raised before a court on a summary assessment hearing. If the breach is made out the court can declare the CFA unenforceable.

6.27 Where there has been a breach of the notification provisions set out in the CPR Rule 44.15,[19] these too can be dealt with by the courts.

6.28 However, the courts' powers to deal with a breach of the Code are less clear. Where there is a breach (or suspected breach of the Code) this may be referred to the Law Society. Any member of the public or any solicitor can make a complaint to the Law Society in respect of a solicitor whom they suspect of breaching either the Code or the rules.

6.29 This puts the practitioner carrying out a summary assessment of costs, faced with a potential breach of the Code in relation to the CFA in a difficult position. The paying party will not be able to avail itself of any of the mechanisms for reducing the receiving party's statement of costs as a result of a breach of the Code unless it refers the matter to the Law Society before the summary assessment, and even then, it is unclear whether a breach of the Code will render the CFA unenforceable.

6.30 In such circumstances, the paying party has only three options:

(i) Ask for an adjournment of the summary assessment of costs to allow the paying party to refer the matter to the Law Society for an investigation. It is possible (but very unusual) to adjourn a summary assessment, but it must be adjourned to the same judge.[20]

(ii) Ask for the matter of costs to go off to a detailed assessment citing s 13.2(3) of the Costs Practice Direction (ie that there are substantial

19 See paras 6.18–6.19 above.

20 *Mahmood v Penrose* [2002] EWCA Civ 457 and s 13.8 of the Costs Practice Direction.

grounds for disputing the sum claimed for costs and those grounds cannot be dealt with summarily).[21] The reason that the costs cannot be dealt with summarily is, of course, that the court will not be able to look into the solicitor's potential breach of the Code on a summary basis. Instead, the paying party must refer the matter to the Law Society, and seek an order that the detailed assessment be adjourned until such time as the Law Society has carried out its investigation.

(iii) Ask the court to look into the breach of the Code and make its own findings. While the case of *Garbutt v Edwards, The Times*, 3 November 2005 makes it clear that (i) not every breach of the Code will amount to a breach of rule 15; and (ii) a breach of the Code of itself does not render the solicitor client retainer unlawful and unenforceable, it does show that (a) the court is willing to look at whether a receiving party's solicitor has breached the Code in his dealings with his own client where that breach can be said to have affected the amount of costs incurred in the litigation (and so the amount of costs a receiving party becomes liable for); and (b) crucially, if the court comes to the view that there has been a breach of the Code, and this has had a calculable effect on the costs claimed, the costs judge is entitled to take the breach into account when deciding whether the amount of costs of the receiving party were reasonably incurred or reasonable and proportionate in amount for the purposes of CPR Rules 44.4 and 44.5.

It is suggested that trying to persuade a court to either adjourn the summary assessment or let the matter go off for detailed assessment some time in the future may be difficult as it will greatly increase the costs of the assessment, something that the summary assessment procedure is designed to avoid. A party is likely to be more successful in persuading the court to undertake the kind of investigation set out in para 6.30(iii). The receiving party will, however, require some evidence that the Code has not been complied with before the court will even consider looking into the matter.[22] Such evidence is not easy for a paying party to come by, especially on a summary assessment. **6.31**

[21] See para 2.07 above.
[22] *Garbutt*.

B. Collective conditional fee agreements[23]

6.32 Collective conditional fee agreements (CCFA) are agreements entered into between bulk purchasers of legal services (typically trade unions or insurance companies) with providers of legal services. They are umbrella agreements that apply to all cases which come within the class of proceedings to which the agreement relates. The mechanism for assessing the risks (and so the uplift) applicable in each individual claim is by way of a risk assessment.

The CCFA Regulations 2000

6.33 The Collective Conditional Fee Agreement Regulations 2000 (CCFA Regulations 2000) came into force on 30 November 2000. They can be summarized as follows:

(i) Regulation 3 defines what a CCFA is.

(ii) Regulation 4 sets out the requirements of a CCFA. This includes a requirement that the CCFA must specify the circumstances in which the legal representative's fees and expenses are payable.

(iii) Regulation 5 sets out the requirements for a CCFA where a success fee is claimed. This includes a provision that the legal representative must, when accepting instructions in relation to specific proceedings, prepare and retain a statement containing his assessment of the amount of the percentage increase in relation to those proceedings having regard to the risk assessment.

(iv) Regulation 6 sets out the form the CCFA must take, and provides that where a CCFA is amended, regs 4 and 5 apply to the amended agreement as if it were a fresh agreement made at the time of the amendment.

(v) Regulation 7 provides that the CFA Regulations 2000 do not apply to CCFAs.

6.34 There have been surprisingly few successful challenges to the compliance of CCFAs with the regulations. While the case of *Hollins* was only concerned with CFAs, the reasoning in relation to material breaches of the regulations applies equally to CCFAs.[24]

---

23 At Appendix B.

24 See para 6.09 above.

Disclosure

6.35 The same principles apply to the disclosure of CCFAs as they do to CFAs.[25] It may be said perhaps more easily of a CCFA that it will have commercially sensitive information within it that should not be disclosed to the other side. This is of course not a reason to withhold disclosure, but is a reason for redacting those sensitive parts.

Notification

6.36 In the same way that a party funding a claim by way of a CFA or ATE insurance premium must notify the other side of this pursuant to CPR Rule 44.15, so too must a party who has entered into a CCFA.[26]

The new regime

6.37 The CCFA Regulations 2000 have been revoked. Thus any CCFA that comes into force after 1 November 2005 must comply with the Law Society's Rules and guidance [27] and will primarily be regulated through the Law Society in the same way that CFAs will be. Thus where a retainer is entered into after 1 November 2005, and that retainer is pursuant to a CCFA that was signed before 1 November 2005, the CCFA Regulations apply to it.

C. Uplifts

6.38 A challenge to the success fee will be the last substantive issue raised at a summary assessment.

6.39 The reasonableness of the success fee is assessed in light of what a reasonable solicitor knew at the time the CFA was entered into.[28] The court is entitled to disregard the solicitor's own risk assessment and consider the matter from the standpoint of a reasonably careful solicitor assessing the risk on the basis of what was known to him at the time.[29]

6.40 This exercise requires the court to look at what evidence was available to the solicitor at the time the success fee was set and disregard what has happened since. However Crane J in *Smiths Dock v Edwards* [2004] EWHC 1116 QB

[25] See paras 6.15–6.17 above.
[26] For a more detailed discussion please see paras 6.18–6.19.
[27] See paras 6.20–6.25 above.
[28] Section 11.7 of the Costs Practice Direction.
[29] *Atack v Lee* [2005] 1 WLR 2643.

accepted the fact that a defendant shows every sign of fighting a claim may be used to lend support to the more pessimistic assessment of the prospects of success made by the claimant's solicitors.

6.41 The ready reckoner is the tool used to translate the practitioner's views on the prospects of success of a particular claim into a success fee. This appears at Appendix F.

6.42 Some of the factors that are relevant in both setting and attacking success fees include:

(i) whether liability has been admitted;
(ii) whether there is a limitation issue;
(iii) if not, the quality of the evidence;
(iv) the prospects on liability;
(v) whether there are risks on causation;
(vi) quantum risks;
(vii) the terms of the CFA—in particular whether the solicitor is entitled to recover any costs if he advises refusal of a part 36 offer that is not beaten at trial;
(viii) the definition of success in the CFA.

6.43 If liability has been admitted within the pre-action protocol, and the terms of the CFA mean that even if the solicitor advises the claimant not to accept a CPR part 36 payment, and the claimant subsequently fails to beat that payment in at trial, the solicitor still gets paid his base costs after the last date that the payment in could have been accepted, then there is very little justification for a high success fee.

6.44 Practitioners also need to be aware that success fees are fixed in certain kinds of cases:

(i) Road traffic accident claims, where the accident took place after 6 October 2003 are subject to fixed success fees.[30] The general rule is that cases that settle prior to trial will attract an increase of 12.5% for solicitors. If they fight to trial the solicitor will recover 100%. The uplifts are slightly different for counsel.
(ii) Employers' liability claims where the injury was sustained after October 2004 are subject to fixed success fees.[31] The general rule is that cases that settle prior to trial will attract an increase of between

---

[30] CPR Rule 45.15–45.19.
[31] CPR Rule 45.20–45.22.

25–27.5% for solicitors. If they fight to trial the solicitor will recover 100%. The uplifts are slightly different for counsel.

(iii) Employers' liability disease claims where the letter of claim is sent after 1 October 2005.[32]

Examples of recent decisions in relation to success fees include: **6.45**

(i) *Callery v Gray* (2001) 1 WLR 2112 (No 2) in a road traffic accident in which the claimant's solicitor reasonably assumed that the claims had every prospect of early settlement on both liability and that quantum 20% was a reasonable uplift.

(ii) *Halloran v Delaney* [2003] 1 WLR 28; also at [2003] 1 All ER 775 in a claim that settled before the issue of proceedings, under a CFA entered into after 1 August 2001; the uplift allowed was 5% for all the costs including those incurred in the costs only proceedings.

(iii) *Atack v Lee* (2005) 1 WLR 2643—this was a road traffic accident claim that fought to trial. The success fee was claimed at 100% and reduced to 50% on appeal to the Circuit Judge. At the time the success fee was set there was a denial of liability, a police report that suggested the claimant was to blame, an independent witness who supported the defendant, and an assessment by the claimant's solicitor that the defendant was to blame. The Court of Appeal held that up to 67% would have been reasonable, but 50% was within the range open to a judge.

(iv) In the case of *Ellerton v Harris* (2005) 1 WLR 2643 (joined with *Atack)* the claimant claimed a success fee of 60%. This was a claim for personal injury arising from an incident in a car park. The claimant was a pedestrian and the defendant had reversed into her. The CFA was signed before the letter of claim was sent. The defendant admitted liability soon afterwards. There was a risk to the solicitor that he would get no fees if a part 36 offer was not beaten pursuant to the terms of the CFA. Only 20% was allowed.

(v) *Edwards v Smith Dock*—this was a mesothelioma case where negligent exposure was admitted but causation and quantum remained live issues. It was at a time that the law in relation to causation was in a state of flux. The fact that the solicitors would receive no costs if a CPR part 36 payment was not beaten was a significant factor in this case. An 87% uplift was allowed.

---

[32] CPR Rule 45.23.

(vi) *Alfa Begum v Supin Klarit* [2005] EWCA Civ 210—this was a summary assessment of a success fee by the Court of Appeal. The court held that there was a 'stone-cold certainty of success'. Accordingly they reduced the success fee to 15% from 100% for counsel and from 70% for the solicitor. The court expressed strong disapproval at the levels at which the success fees had been set.

(vii) *Metcalfe v Clipson* (SCCO, 16 April 2004)—this was a claim for professional negligence against a dentist. The defendant agreed to pay damages following receipt of the letter of claim (without admitting liability) and the matter settled without the issue of proceedings. The success fee was set at 100% but only 20% was allowed.

(viii) *Dent v Huggett* (SCCO, 5 June 2004)—an asbestos claim in which the only concession on liability (that there had been significant exposure) was made shortly before the settlement. 75% fell within what was reasonable.

(ix) *Bowen v Bridgend County Borough Council* [2004] EWHC 9010 (costs)—this was a housing disrepair claim. By the time the CFA was entered into the solicitors had two housing disrepair questionnaires filled in dealing with the issue of giving notice to the landlord (which was the most risky element of the claim). The success fee was claimed at 100% and assessed at 25%.

(x) *KU v Liverpool County Council* [2005] 1WLR 2657 (also in *The Times*, 27 April 2005)—this was a low value tipping claim. The success fee was set at 100% and reduced to 50% on appeal.

(xi) *Designer Guild v Williams* [2003] EWHC 9024 (costs)—it was held by Chief Costs Judge Hurst that in any claim which reached trial a success fee of 100% is easily justified because both sides presumably believe they have a winnable case.

Staged success fees

6.46 The courts have always been keen for parties to enter into agreements that allow for staged success fees.[33] Section 11.8(2) of the Costs Practice Direction gives the court the power to allow different percentages for different items of costs or for different periods. In the *KU* case the Court of Appeal held that where the agreement between the client and the solicitor does not provide for a staged success fee at the outset (as a term of the CFA) then

[33] *Callery v Gray (No 1)* [2001] EWCA Civ 1117.

it is not open to the court to impose a staged success fee as a retrospective measure. In so far as the Costs Practice Direction at s 11.8(2) provides otherwise, it is wrong. Where the CFA provided for a single staged success fee this applies to the whole of the proceedings including the costs of any detailed assessment.

D. After the event insurance premiums

These are recoverable as a matter of principle from a paying party pursuant to s 29 of the Access to Justice Act 1999 which provides that: **6.47**

> where in any proceedings a costs order is made in favour of any party who has taken out an insurance policy against the risk of incurring a liability in those proceedings, the costs payable to him may, subject in the case of court proceedings to rules of court, include costs in respect of the premium of the policy.

A paying party, however, can attack both the principle that the ATE insurance premium should be recovered from them, and the quantum of the premium. **6.48**

In what circumstances is the premium not payable?

The insurance premium remains payable by the paying party even where the CFA is unenforceable.[34] **6.49**

Where, however, the CFA has been held to be unenforceable for the failure to carry out proper investigations to discover whether the client has an existing insurance policy pursuant to reg 4 of the CFA Regulations 2000, the court must then go on to consider whether it was reasonable and proportionate to incur the cost of an ATE insurance premium in those circumstances. In the case of *Richards v Davis* (SCCO, 25 November 2005) the court held that because the client had a BTE policy in place at the time the ATE policy was taken out, it was unreasonable and disproportionate to have taken out that policy and the premium was disallowed. **6.50**

This case is somewhat similar to *Hughes v Newham London Borough Council*. Where the solicitor had failed to discharge his duty under reg 4 of the CFA Regulations 2000 and the Solicitors' Costs Information and Client Care Code para 4(j) (which requires a solicitor to consider and discuss with **6.51**

---

[34] See paras 6.13–6.14 above.

their client whether the client's liability for their own costs may be covered by insurance), it was deemed unreasonable to seek the cost of the insurance premium against the paying party.[35]

Quantum of the premium

6.52 If there is likely to be an issue as to the quantum of the premium evidence may be required.[36] Ideally, this should be in the form of a witness statement setting out the enquiries the solicitor made at the time the premium was incurred, and comparing the prices quoted with the cover bought. Alternatively a copy of one of the tables in *Litigation Funding* [37] will usually do.

6.53 Parties wishing to challenge the quantum of the premium as being unreasonable also need evidence to show that there were other similar and cheaper premiums available on the market at the time which the receiving party might reasonably have taken out.

6.54 In assessing the reasonableness of the premium, the court will be concerned with the following matters that are set out in s 48.26 of the Costs Practice Direction:

(i) the relationship between the premium and the cost of alternative cover;
(ii) whether the premium buys a suitable level of cover for the particular case;
(iii) what the insurance actually covers;
(iv) whether the policy is an off-the-peg policy, or a bespoke one.

6.55 Some examples of premiums that have been allowed in recent cases are as follows:

(i) *Tyndall v Battersea Dogs Home* [2005] EWHC 90011 (costs)—a staged premium in the sum of £1,890 in a fast track road traffic accident was allowed. Three hundred and sixty-seven pounds, fifty pence was payable up to the issue of proceedings, £787.50 was payable after issue and up to 45 days before trial; thereafter it increased to £1,890.

---

[35] (SCCO, 28 July 2005) and at para 6.12(v) above.
[36] *Callery v Gray (No 2)* [2001] EWCA Civ 1246 at para 69.
[37] The Law Society's bi-monthly journal, available on subscription.

(ii) *Woolridge v Hayes* (SCCO, 10 February 2005)—a premium of £7,469 was held to be reasonable in a personal injury case arising from a road traffic accident in which the claimant suffered substantial injuries and settled the case at a figure in excess of £600,000.

(iii) *Pirie v Ayling* [2003] EWHC 9006 (costs)—three hundred and fifty pounds was allowed for a personal injury claim arising from a road traffic accident that was allocated to the fast track.

(iv) *Sarwar v Alam* [2002] 1WLR 125—a premium in the sum of £62,500 in a claim was recoverable for an appeal to the Court of Appeal in a simple road traffic case on an uncertain point of principle in relation to costs.

(v) *Callery v Gray* [2001] EWCA Civ 1246—three hundred and fifty pounds was allowed in a personal injury action.

Disclosure

CPR Rule 44.15 and s 19 of the Costs Practice Direction sets out the disclosure obligations on the receiving party when seeking to claim an ATE insurance premium from the paying party. The information that must be provided is the name and address of the insurer, the policy number, the date of the policy, and information identifying to which claims it relates. **6.56**

CPR Rule 44.3B(1)(c) (the notification provision) applies to ATE insurance premiums in the same way it does to uplifts on CFAs.[38] Accordingly the receiving party cannot receive the premium for any period of the proceedings during which that information was not provided. **6.57**

The wording of CPR Rule 44.3B(1)(c) is worth examining in this context. Taken at face value it means that if the receiving party pays for the insurance policy during the period that he failed to comply with the notification requirements pursuant to CPR Rule 44.3B(1)(c) then the whole of the premium should be disallowed. However, it is not uncommon for courts to adopt a percentage approach. If the receiving party failed to notify the paying party of the existence of the ATE policy for half of the life of the litigation, then he may only be able to recover half the cost of the premium on an application for relief from sanctions. **6.58**

[38] See paras 6.18–6.19 above.

7

PAYMENT

Having completed the summary assessment of costs, and arrived at a figure that the paying party must pay to the receiving party, the court must determine what provisions it will make as to the payment of that sum from one party to another. 7.01

At the conclusion of the proceedings

There is no reason why the assessed sum should not be paid as soon as reasonably practicable. If no date is specified in the order, the payment should be made within 14 days.[1] 7.02

Where the summary assessment is carried out before the conclusion of proceedings

If the hearing that has led to the summary assessment is an interim application, or a trial of a preliminary issue, different issues arise. In the first place, it may not always be appropriate for the monies to be paid over to the receiving party. The paying party may, for example, want the order not to be enforced until the conclusion of the claim, so that they can set off any monies they have to pay against any monies they may eventually be paid. It is entirely a matter for the discretion of the judge whether he accedes to such an application. 7.03

A further complication arises in claims in which the receiving party is funded by way of a CFA. The court must not make an order for payment out of any assessed costs to the receiving party unless the court is satisfied that the receiving party has a liability to pay those costs to his legal representative 7.04

[1] CPR Rule 44.8.

following an interim application.[2] This will depend on the terms of the CFA. The solicitor's signature on the bottom of the statement of costs (the N260) will usually be sufficient proof of the party's liability to pay those costs at an interim stage.[3]

7.05 Where, however, the court has a doubt as to the receiving party's liability to pay the costs to his solicitor, s 14.4 of the Costs Practice Direction allows the court to postpone the receiving party's right to receive those costs. This may be done by directing that any costs that have been assessed shall be paid into court by the paying party to await the outcome of the case, or directing that the order is not enforced until further notice.

Interest

7.06 Interest on costs will run from the date of the judgment.[4] Where summary assessment has taken place, the date of the judgment and the date of the order for payment of the costs is usually the same. Thus although technically interest runs from the date of the summary assessment until the date that the sum is paid, this is not usually claimed.

7.07 However, interest will be payable if the receiving party does not obtain an order for the prompt payment of the assessed costs, as in the circumstances set out in paras 7.03 and 7.05 above. Interest in those circumstances is charged at 8% pursuant to the Judgment Debts (Rate of Interest) Order 1993.[5]

---

[2] Section 14.3 of the Costs Practice Direction.

[3] Section 14.3 of the Costs Practice Direction and para 3.08 above.

[4] CPR Rule 40.8. There is a power for the court to award interest on costs at a discretionary rate from much earlier (CPR Rule 44.3(6)(g)) but this will rarely be appropriate in summary assessment cases.

[5] SI 1993/564.

8

APPEALS AGAINST SUMMARY ASSESSMENTS

It is unlikely that there is a duty on a judge to give extensive reasons for his decisions in a summary assessment of costs where the principal issues between the parties is quantum. **8.01**

In a summary assessment of costs where more substantial issues have arisen, however, the judge may be under a duty to give reasons to allow the parties to understand the basis on which he has arrived at his decision. The Court of Appeal has held that the duty to give reasons only arises where those reasons are not implicit in the order made. *English v Emery Reimbold* [2002] 3 All ER 385, at paras 91–113, shows quite how far the court will go in deducing reasons for a judge's decision. This was a case in which the defendant had offered to settle at £5,500 and the claimant had offered to settle at in excess of £95,000. The claimant succeeded in recovering over £30,000. The judge made no criticisms of either party's conduct, and made an order that there should be no order for costs. The Court of Appeal held that it could be deduced from the order made that the judge had come to the view that the claimant had won half the case and lost on the rest, thus both parties had come to court and won on part of their case. **8.02**

Even in a case in which the judge has given insufficient reasons, appeals from orders for costs where the court is exercising its discretion as to where the costs should fall, and the amount of costs payable, are notoriously difficult to sustain.[1] It was said by the Court of Appeal in *English v Emery Reimbold*, at para 30, that the 'appellate court will seldom be as well placed as the trial judge to exercise a discretion in relation to costs'. **8.03**

---

[1] *Burchel v Bullard* [2005] BLR 330 at para 25.

8.04 Permission to appeal a summary assessment of costs is always required.[2]

8.05 Practitioners should think long and hard before appealing a summary assessment decision, especially on matters of detail such as the time spent on documents or hourly rates.

8.06 On a successful appeal from a summary assessment decision, the Appeal Court will usually summarily assess the costs at first instance, rather than remitting the matter back to the trial judge, thus avoiding incurring further costs.[3]

---

2 *Hosking v Michaelidis* [2003] EWHC 3029 (Ch).
3 *MacDonald v Taree Holdings Ltd, The Times*, 28 December 2000.

9

PREPARATION CHECKLISTS

This chapter provides checklists that practitioners can refer to at the various different stages of a summary assessment. 9.01

(i) The first checklist is for the practitioner to refer to when drawing up the statement of costs.
(ii) The second checklist is for the practitioner to refer to when preparing for the summary assessment.
(iii) The third checklist is for reference at the actual hearing itself, once the substantive issues in the application/trial have been determined.

Checklist 1
The statement of costs

Drawing up a statement of costs for an application is a fairly straightforward exercise, as long as the correct fee earner can be identified, and the number of hours spent on each of the areas of work calculated. For this reason, the checklist below is primarily concerned with drawing up the statement of costs following a trial. 9.02

The first step, of course, is to determine whether or not summary assessment is appropriate.[1] 9.03

All the references in square brackets in this chapter, denote paragraph numbers elsewhere in the book. 9.04

Checklist 1 comprises four steps: 9.05

(i) gathering documents;
(ii) drawing up the statement of costs;

[1] Refer to paras 2.09–2.17 for guidance.

(iii) checking the statement of costs;
(iv) serving the statement of costs.

Step 1: Gathering documents

Ensure that you have the following documents:

(i) N260 or similar [3.02];
(ii) all previous costs orders [5.04(i)];
(iii) where there has been a previous summary assessment the schedules that gave rise to the assessment [5.24];
(iv) any previous costs estimate you have filed, served or provided to your client [5.20–5.24];
(v) accounts ledger;
(vi) a list of all the disbursements on the file.

Step 2: Drawing up the statement of costs

(i) Identify all the relevant fee earners [3.03].
(ii) Identify the relevant hourly rates [3.05, 5.29–5.33].
(iii) By checking the previous costs orders, identify all the work that should be included on the statement [5.04(i)].
(iv) Draw up the statement (include the time spent working on the statement of costs and any post-hearing matters) [3.14].
(v) Keep a running record of the work included in each section [3.13].

Step 3: Checking the statement of costs

(i) Check that the total shown on the statement of costs does not exceed the amount your client is liable to pay [6.02(i)].
(ii) Add up the total amount of base profit costs and check this against the estimates given to your client, to the other side and to the court [5.20–5.24].
(iii) Is there more than a 20% discrepancy between your costs estimate and your schedule? If so, what is the explanation? Do you want to reduce your statement of costs to reflect the estimate?
(iv) Is there a real risk that the existence of an offer will result in a partial costs order? If so, consider drawing up a separate statement of costs to reflect this [3.10].

(v) If the claim is funded by a CFA and it is an interim application, check the terms of the CFA to ensure that the agreement provides for you to be paid if you win an interim application [7.04–7.05].
(vi) Check the client's VAT position [3.15–3.18].
(vii) Check that VAT is added to the relevant disbursements.
(viii) Sign the statement of costs [3.08–3.09].

Step 4: Serving the statement of costs

(i) Serve the statement of costs on the other parties and file with the court at least 24 hours before the hearing.
(ii) Send a covering letter showing when it was served [3.11–3.12].

Checklist 2
Preparing for the summary assessment

This checklist is a reference point for the practitioner who is preparing to attend a hearing at which the costs will be (or may be) summarily assessed. **9.06**

Checklist 2 comprises seven steps: **9.07**

(i) gathering documents;
(ii) understanding your statement of costs;
(iii) preparation where offers have been made;
(iv) preparation where there are arguments about conduct;
(v) preparation where a claim is funded by a CFA/CCFA;
(vi) planning your attack on your opponent's schedule;
(vii) gathering materials to take to the hearing.

Step 1: Gathering documents

Ensure that you have the following documents:

(i) your statement of costs [3.02];
(ii) proof of service of your statement of costs on the other side and the court [3.11–3.12];
(iii) if service was effected late, an explanation [3.11–3.12];
(iv) the other side's statement of costs;
(v) any previous estimates that either side have filed, served or provided to your client [5.20–5.24];
(vi) any previous costs orders made by the court [5.04(i)];

(vii) any offers made by your client [4.29–4.41];
(viii) any offers made by the other side.

Step 2: Understand your statement of costs

Look at the overall costs claimed. Ensure that you are prepared for:

(i) an argument that the costs claimed are disproportionate [5.13–5.19];
(ii) an argument that the costs claimed are more than 20% higher than previous estimates [5.20–5.24].
(iii) Identify any unexpected occurrences.

Ensure that you can persuade the court of the reasonableness of the following:

(i) the level of fee earner used on the case [5.26–5.28];
(ii) the hourly rate [5.29–5.33];
(iii) the work done under each of the headings;
(iv) the nature and level of the disbursements [5.42–5.46].

Step 3: For claims in which there have been offers made

(i) Identify which offers comply with CPR part 36 [4.31–4.32].
(ii) Prepare any arguments as to whether a particular offer complies with CPR part 36.
(iii) Identify the last date on which each of the offers could have been accepted.
(iv) Where there is a real possibility that an offer made by the other side will not be beaten, identify the reasons why the offer was not accepted.
(v) If your opponent has made a CPR part 36 offer and there is a real risk that you will not beat that offer, identify what if any arguments can be put forward to avoid the CPR part 36 cost consequences [4.38].
(vi) Where there is a real risk of a partial costs order being made, draw up a statement of costs that reflects that order.

Step 4: Identify whether there are likely to be arguments about conduct

(i) Has either party exaggerated the claim? If so, has this affected the costs incurred in the claim [4.18–4.19]? Bring evidence.
(ii) Has either party refused to mediate? If so, was it unreasonable [4.20–4.23]? Bring evidence.
(iii) Has any other conduct of either party served to increase costs [4.18–4.23]?

a) Identify the conduct.
b) Identify the prejudice.
c) Prepare evidence to support your arguments.
d) Identify the order you want the court to make, identify the relevant CPR rule, and draw up an order.

Step 5: Where your claim is funded by a CFA/CCFA/ATE insurance

CFA/CCFA

(i) Has the CFA/CCFA been disclosed to the other side [6.15–6.17]? If not, get instructions to disclose it (redacted if necessary). Take copies.
(ii) Identify whether notice of funding was served on the other side [6.18–6.19].
(iii) Identify whether notice of funding complies with the Costs Practice Direction. If not and you are in default draw up an application for relief from sanctions [6.18].
(iv) Serve the application for relief from sanctions on your opponent and court.
(v) Copy the risk assessment to serve on the court and the other side.
(vi) Check that the terms of the CFA comply with the relevant regulations [6.07–6.12].
(vii) Ensure you can justify the uplift by reference to the information that was known to the solicitor/counsel at the time the CFA was entered into [6.38–6.45]; alternatively, if you are the paying party, consider what would be a reasonable uplift.

Insurance premium

(viii) Have the notification requirements in respect of the insurance premium been complied with [6.52]? If not, prepare an application for relief from sanctions.
(ix) Has the premium been paid? Evidence is required [6.47–6.51].
(x) Does the level of ATE premium look reasonable [6.52–6.54]? Provide evidence to support your argument.

Step 6: Prepare your attack on your opponent's schedule

(i) Does your opponent's statement of costs look high in relation to the issues at stake and the value of the claim?
(ii) Is there more than a 20% discrepancy between their previous estimate and their schedule? Can you show that you have relied on previous estimates [5.20–5.24]?

(iii) Check the hourly rate and level of fee earner. Are there any arguments on this [3.03–3.05/5.29–5.33]?
(iv) Compare the overall hours claimed with your statement [5.07].
(v) Do the disbursements look reasonable?
(vi) Have any offers been made? If so, refer to step 3.
(vii) Are there any issues in relation to conduct? If so, refer to step 4.
(viii) Is their claim funded by way of a CFA/CCFA. If so, refer to step 5.

Step 7: List of materials to take to the hearing

All assessments

- Both parties' statements of costs
- Proof of service of the statement of costs
- Previous costs orders
- Costs estimates
- Copies of the guideline figures for hourly rates

Where offers made

- Copies of offers
- Statement of costs to reflect likely partial costs order

Where more than one defendant

- Where they blamed each other (bring correspondence to justify joining both)

Where conduct an issue

- Any evidence that a party unreasonably refused to mediate
- Evidence of exaggeration

CFA claims

- Copies of the risk assessment
- Copies of the CFA itself
- The ready reckoner
- Evidence of the quantum of the insurance premium
- Evidence that the premium has been paid, and when
- Evidence that the premium is reasonable
- Notice of funding
- The CFA Regulations (if appropriate)

Checklist 3
The hearing

The last checklist is a reference tool for practitioners who have just received judgment in the substantive claim or application and are about to embark on arguments about the appropriate order to make and/or the summary assessment hearing. **9.08**

(i) Identify which party has won [4.05–4.08].
(ii) Should costs follow the event [4.02]? If not, why not?
(iii) Have there been any offers that affect the order to be made [4.29–4.41]?
(iv) Should a partial costs order be made [4.09–4.23]? If so, be clear about the reasons you are going to put forward, and the order that you are asking the court to make.
(v) Are there any issues in relation to conduct (either in the substantive hearing or on the summary assessment hearing) [4.14–4.23]?
(vi) Should costs be awarded on the standard or the indemnity basis [4.24–4.28]?
(vii) Are there any issues in relation to proportionality [5.13–5.19]?
(viii) Has either party relied on previous estimates [5.20–5.24]?
(ix) Is the level of fee earner appropriate [5.26]?
(x) Is the hourly rate claimed appropriate [5.29–5.33]?
(xi) Are the number of hours claimed reasonable?
(xii) Has the statement of costs been signed [3.08–3.09]?
(xiii) Was the statement served on time [3.11–3.12]?
(xiv) If the claim is funded by way of CFA, does that CFA comply with the Regulations [6.08–6.12]?
(xv) Has either party complied with the notification provisions?
(xvi) If there is an uplift, is it reasonable [6.38–6.46]?
(xvii) If there is an ATE insurance premium in place, is it justified and reasonable [6.47–6.58]?
(xviii) Should there be an order for payment out of costs within 14 days [7]? If not, why not?
(xix) Do you need permission to appeal the assessment [8]?

APPENDIX A

Statutes (Extracts)

Supreme Court Act 1981 (as amended)[1]

51. Costs in civil division of Court of Appeal, High Court and county courts

(1) Subject to the provisions of this or any other enactment and to rules of court, the costs of and incidental to all proceedings in—
  (a) the civil division of the Court of Appeal;
  (b) the High Court; and
  (c) any county court,
shall be in the discretion of the court.

(2) Without prejudice to any general power to make rules of court, such rules may make provision for regulating matters relating to the costs of those proceedings including, in particular, prescribing scales of costs to be paid to legal or other representatives or for securing that the amount awarded to a party in respect of the costs to be paid by him to such representatives is not limited to what would have been payable by him to them if he had not been awarded costs.

(3) The court shall have full power to determine by whom and to what extent the costs are to be paid.

(4) In subsections (1) and (2) 'proceedings' includes the administration of estates and trusts.

(5) Nothing in subsection (1) shall alter the practice in any criminal cause, or in bankruptcy.

(6) In any proceedings mentioned in subsection (1), the court may disallow, or (as the case may be) order the legal or other representative concerned to meet, the whole of any wasted costs or such part of them as may be determined in accordance with rules of court.

(7) In subsection (6), 'wasted costs' means any costs incurred by a party—
  (a) as a result of any improper, unreasonable or negligent act or omission on the part of any legal or other representative or any employee of such a representative; or
  (b) which, in the light of any such act or omission occurring after they were incurred, the court considers it is unreasonable to expect that party to pay.

[1] As amended by the Courts and Legal Services Act 1990 and the Access to Justice Act 1999.

(8) Where—
   (a) a person has commenced proceedings in the High Court; but
   (b) those proceedings should, in the opinion of the court, have been commenced in a county court in accordance with any provision made under section 1 of the Courts and Legal Services Act 1990 or by or under any other enactment,

   the person responsible for determining the amount which is to be awarded to that person by way of costs shall have regard to those circumstances.

(9) Where, in complying with subsection (8), the responsible person reduces the amount which would otherwise be awarded to the person in question—
   (a) the amount of that reduction shall not exceed 25 per cent; and
   (b) on any taxation of the costs payable by that person to his legal representative, regard shall be had to the amount of the reduction.

(10) The Lord Chancellor may by order amend subsection (9)(a) by substituting, for the percentage for the time being mentioned there, a different percentage.

(11) Any such order shall be made by statutory instrument and may make such transitional or incidental provision as the Lord Chancellor considers expedient.

(12) No such statutory instrument shall be made unless a draft of the instrument has been approved by both Houses of Parliament.

(13) In this section 'legal or other representative', in relation to a party to proceedings, means any person exercising a right of audience or right to conduct litigation on his behalf.

Courts and Legal Services Act 1990 (as amended)

58. Conditional fee agreements[2]

(1) A conditional fee agreement which satisfies all of the conditions applicable to it by virtue of this section shall not be unenforceable by reason only of its being a conditional fee agreement; but (subject to subsection (5)) any other conditional fee agreement shall be unenforceable.

(2) For the purposes of this section and section 58A—
   (a) a conditional fee agreement is an agreement with a person providing advocacy or litigation services which provides for his fees and expenses, or any part of them, to be payable only in specified circumstances; and
   (b) a conditional fee agreement provides for a success fee if it provides for the amount of any fees to which it applies to be increased, in specified circumstances, above the amount which would be payable if it were not payable only in specified circumstances.

[2] As amended by the Access to Justice Act 1999 and the Secretary of State for Constitutional Affairs Order 2003 (SI 2003/1887).

(3) The following conditions are applicable to every conditional fee agreement—
  (a) it must be in writing;
  (b) it must not relate to proceedings which cannot be the subject of an enforceable conditional fee agreement; and
  (c) it must comply with such requirements (if any) as may be prescribed by the Secretary of State.

(4) The following further conditions are applicable to a conditional fee agreement which provides for a success fee—
  (a) it must relate to proceedings of a description specified by order made by the Secretary of State;
  (b) it must state the percentage by which the amount of the fees which would be payable if it were not a conditional fee agreement is to be increased; and
  (c) that percentage must not exceed the percentage specified in relation to the description of proceedings to which the agreement relates by order made by the Secretary of State.

(5) If a conditional fee agreement is an agreement to which section 57 of the Solicitors Act 1974 (non-contentious business agreements between solicitor and client) applies, subsection (1) shall not make it unenforceable.

58A. Conditional fee agreements: supplementary[3]

(1) The proceedings which cannot be the subject of an enforceable conditional fee agreement are—
  (a) criminal proceedings, apart from proceedings under section 82 of the Environmental Protection Act 1990; and
  (b) family proceedings.

(2) In subsection (1) 'family proceedings' means proceedings under any one or more of the following—
  (a) the Matrimonial Causes Act 1973;
  (b) the Adoption and Children Act 2002;
  (c) the Domestic Proceedings and Magistrates' Courts Act 1978;
  (d) Part III of the Matrimonial and Family Proceedings Act 1984;
  (e) Parts I, II and IV of the Children Act 1989;
  (f) Part IV of the Family Law Act 1996;
  (fa) Chapter 2 of Part 2 of the Civil Partnership Act 2004 (proceedings for dissolution etc of civil partnership);
  (fb) Schedule 5 to the 2004 Act (financial relief in the High Court or a county court etc);
  (fc) Schedule 6 to the 2004 Act (financial relief in magistrates' courts etc);

[3] As amended by the Access to Justice Act 1999, the Adoption and Children Act 2002, the Civil Partnership Act 2004, and the Secretary of State for Constitutional Affairs Order 2003 (SI 2003/1887).

(fd) Schedule 7 to the 2004 Act (financial relief in England and Wales after overseas dissolution etc of a civil partnership); and

(g) the inherent jurisdiction of the High Court in relation to children.

(3) The requirements which the Secretary of State may prescribe under section 58(3)(c)—

(a) include requirements for the person providing advocacy or litigation services to have provided prescribed information before the agreement is made; and

(b) may be different for different descriptions of conditional fee agreements (and, in particular, may be different for those which provide for a success fee and those which do not).

(4) In section 58 and this section (and in the definitions of 'advocacy services' and 'litigation services' as they apply for their purposes) 'proceedings' includes any sort of proceedings for resolving disputes (and not just proceedings in a court), whether commenced or contemplated.

(5) Before making an order under section 58(4), the Secretary of State shall consult—

(a) the designated judges;

(b) the General Council of the Bar;

(c) the Law Society; and

(d) such other bodies as he considers appropriate.

(6) A costs order made in any proceedings may, subject in the case of court proceedings to rules of court, include provision requiring the payment of any fees payable under a conditional fee agreement which provides for a success fee.

(7) Rules of court may make provision with respect to the assessment of any costs which include fees payable under a conditional fee agreement (including one which provides for a success fee).

58B. Litigation funding agreements[4]

(1) A litigation funding agreement which satisfies all of the conditions applicable to it by virtue of this section shall not be unenforceable by reason only of its being a litigation funding agreement.

(2) For the purposes of this section a litigation funding agreement is an agreement under which—

(a) a person ('the funder') agrees to fund (in whole or in part) the provision of advocacy or litigation services (by someone other than the funder) to another person ('the litigant'); and

(b) the litigant agrees to pay a sum to the funder in specified circumstances.

(3) The following conditions are applicable to a litigation funding agreement—

(a) the funder must be a person, or person of a description, prescribed by the Secretary of State;

[4] As amended by the Access to Justice Act 1999 and the Secretary of State for Constitutional Affairs Order 2003 (SI 2003/1887).

(b) the agreement must be in writing;
(c) the agreement must not relate to proceedings which by virtue of section 58A(1) and (2) cannot be the subject of an enforceable conditional fee agreement or to proceedings of any such description as may be prescribed by the Secretary of State;
(d) the agreement must comply with such requirements (if any) as may be so prescribed;
(e) the sum to be paid by the litigant must consist of any costs payable to him in respect of the proceedings to which the agreement relates together with an amount calculated by reference to the funder's anticipated expenditure in funding the provision of the services; and
(f) that amount must not exceed such percentage of that anticipated expenditure as may be prescribed by the Secretary of State in relation to proceedings of the description to which the agreement relates.

(4) Regulations under subsection (3)(a) may require a person to be approved by the Secretary of State or by a prescribed person.

(5) The requirements which the Secretary of State may prescribe under subsection (3)(d)—
(a) include requirements for the funder to have provided prescribed information to the litigant before the agreement is made; and
(b) may be different for different descriptions of litigation funding agreements.

(6) In this section (and in the definitions of 'advocacy services' and 'litigation services' as they apply for its purposes) 'proceedings' includes any sort of proceedings for resolving disputes (and not just proceedings in a court), whether commenced or contemplated.

(7) Before making regulations under this section, the Secretary of State shall consult—
(a) the designated judges;
(b) the General Council of the Bar;
(c) the Law Society; and
(d) such other bodies as he considers appropriate.

(8) A costs order made in any proceedings may, subject in the case of court proceedings to rules of court, include provision requiring the payment of any amount payable under a litigation funding agreement.

(9) Rules of court may make provision with respect to the assessment of any costs which include fees payable under a litigation funding agreement.

Access to Justice Act 1999 (as amended)

29. Recovery of insurance premiums by way of costs

Where in any proceedings a costs order is made in favour of any party who has taken out an insurance policy against the risk of incurring a liability in those proceedings, the costs payable to him may, subject in the case of court proceedings to rules of court, include costs in respect of the premium of the policy.

30. Recovery where body undertakes to meet costs liabilities[5]

(1) This section applies where a body of a prescribed description undertakes to meet (in accordance with arrangements satisfying prescribed conditions) liabilities which members of the body or other persons who are parties to proceedings may incur to pay the costs of other parties to the proceedings.

(2) If in any of the proceedings a costs order is made in favour of any of the members or other persons, the costs payable to him may, subject to subsection (3) and (in the case of court proceedings) to rules of court, include an additional amount in respect of any provision made by or on behalf of the body in connection with the proceedings against the risk of having to meet such liabilities.

(3) But the additional amount shall not exceed a sum determined in a prescribed manner; and there may, in particular, be prescribed as a manner of determination one which takes into account the likely cost to the member or other person of the premium of an insurance policy against the risk of incurring a liability to pay the costs of other parties to the proceedings.

(4) In this section 'prescribed' means prescribed by regulations made by the Secretary of State by statutory instrument; and a statutory instrument containing such regulations shall be subject to annulment in pursuance of a resolution of either House of Parliament.

(5) Regulations under subsection (1) may, in particular, prescribe as a description of body one which is for the time being approved by the Secretary of State or by a prescribed person.

Solicitors Act 1974 (as amended)

31. Rules as to professional practice, conduct and discipline[6]

(1) Without prejudice to any other provision of this Part the Council may, if they think fit, make rules, with the concurrence of the Master of the Rolls, for regulating in respect of any matter the professional practice, conduct and discipline of solicitors and for empowering the Society to take such action as may be appropriate to enable the Society to ascertain whether or not the provisions of rules made, or of any code or guidance issued, by the Council are being complied with.

[5] As amended by the Secretary of State for Constitutional Affairs Order 2003 (SI 2003/1887).

[6] As amended by the Access to Justice Act 1999, the Courts and Legal Services Act 1990, and the Secretary of State for Constitutional Affairs Order 2003 (SI 2003/1887).

(2) If any solicitor fails to comply with rules made under this section, any person may make a complaint in respect of that failure to the Tribunal.
(3) Where, under Schedule 4 to the Courts and Legal Services Act 1990 (approval of certain rules in connection with the grant of rights of audience or rights to conduct litigation), the Secretary of State approves any rule such as is mentioned in subsection (1), the requirement of the concurrence of the Master of the Rolls imposed by that subsection shall not apply.
(4) Subsection (3) shall have effect whether or not the rule required to be approved under Schedule 4 to the Act of 1990.

37A. Redress for inadequate professional services[7]

Schedule 1A shall have effect with respect to the provision by solicitors of services which are not of the quality which it is reasonable to expect of them.

SCHEDULE 1A[8]

1.—(1) The Council may take any of the steps mentioned in paragraph 2 ('the steps') with respect to a solicitor where it appears to them that the professional services provided by him in connection with any matter in which he or his firm have been instructed by a client have, in any respect, not been of the quality which it is reasonable to expect of him as a solicitor.
(2) The Council shall not take any of the steps unless they are satisfied that in all the circumstances of the case it is appropriate to do so.
(3) In determining in any case whether it is appropriate to take any of the steps, the Council may—
(a) have regard to the existence of any remedy which it is reasonable to expect to be available to the client in civil proceedings; and
(b) where proceedings seeking any such remedy have not been begun by him, have regard to whether it is reasonable to expect him to begin them.

Directions which may be given

2.—(1) The steps are—
(a) determining that the costs to which the solicitor is entitled in respect of his services ('the costs') are to be limited to such amount as may be specified in the determination and directing him to comply, or to secure compliance, with such one or more of the permitted requirements as appear to the Council to be necessary in order for effect to be given to their determination;

---

[7] As amended by the Courts and Legal Services Act 1990.

[8] As amended by the Courts and Legal Services Act 1990, the Secretary of State for Constitutional Affairs Order 2003 (SI 2003/1887), the Solicitors (Compensation for Inadequate Professional Services) Order 2000 (SI 2000/644), and the Solicitors (Compensation for Inadequate Professional Services) Order 2005 (SI 2005/2749).

(b) directing him to secure the rectification, at his expense or at that of his firm, of any such error, omission or other deficiency arising in connection with the matter in question as they may specify;

(c) directing him to pay such compensation to the client as the Council sees fit to specify in the direction;

(d) directing him to take, at his expense or at that of his firm, such other action in the interests of the client as they may specify.

(2) The 'permitted requirements' are—

(a) that the whole or part of any amount already paid by or on behalf of the client in respect of the costs be refunded;

(b) that the whole or part of the costs be remitted;

(c) that the right to recover the costs be waived, whether wholly or to any specified extent.

(3) The power of the Council to take any such steps is not confined to cases where the client may have a cause of action against the solicitor for negligence.

Compensation

3.—(1) The amount specified in a direction by virtue of paragraph 2(1)(c) shall not exceed £15,000.

(2) The Secretary of State may by order made by statutory instrument amend sub-paragraph (1) by substituting for the sum of £1,000 such other sum as he considers appropriate.

(3) Before making any such order the Secretary of State shall consult the Law Society.

(4) Any statutory instrument made under this paragraph shall be subject to annulment in pursuance of a resolution of either House of Parliament.

Taxation of costs

4.—(1) Where the Council have given a direction under paragraph 2(1)(a), then—

(a) for the purposes of any taxation of a bill covering the costs, the amount charged by the bill in respect of them shall be deemed to be limited to the amount specified in the determination; and

(b) where a bill covering the costs has not been taxed, the client shall, for the purposes of their recovery (by whatever means and notwithstanding any statutory provision or agreement) be deemed to be liable to pay in respect of them only the amount specified in the determination.

(2) Where a bill covering the costs has been taxed, the direction shall, so far as it relates to the costs, cease to have effect.

Failure to comply with direction

5.—(1) If a solicitor fails to comply with a direction given under this Schedule, any person may make a complaint in respect of that failure to the Tribunal; but no other proceedings whatever shall be brought in respect of it.

(2) On the hearing of such a complaint the Tribunal may, if it thinks fit (and whether or not it makes any order under section 47(2)), direct that the direction be treated, for the purpose of enforcement, as if it were contained in an order made by the High Court.

Fees

6.—(1) The Council may, by regulations made with the concurrence of the Secretary of State and the Master of the Rolls, make provision for the payment, by any client with respect to whom the Council are asked to consider whether to take any of the steps, of such fee as may be prescribed.

(2) The regulations may provide for the exemption of such classes of client as may be prescribed.

(3) Where a client pays the prescribed fee it shall be repaid to him if the Council take any of the steps in the matter with respect to which the fee was paid.

(4) In this paragraph 'prescribed' means prescribed by the regulations.

Costs

7.—Where the Council take any of the steps with respect to a solicitor they may also direct him to pay to the Council—

(a) the amount of the fee payable by the Council to the client under paragraph 6(3); and

(b) an amount which is calculated by the Council as the cost to them of dealing with the complaint, or which in their opinion represents a reasonable contribution towards that cost.

Duty of Tribunal

8.—Where the Tribunal—

(a) is considering, or has considered, an application or complaint with respect to a solicitor; and

(b) is of the opinion that the Council should consider whether to take any of the steps with respect to that solicitor, it shall inform the Council.

9. The Council's powers under this Schedule are exercisable in relation to a person even though his name has been removed from, or struck off, the roll and references to a solicitor in this Schedule, so far as they relate to the exercise of those powers, shall be construed accordingly.

APPENDIX B

Statutory Instruments (Extracts)

The Conditional Fee Agreements Regulations 2000 (SI 2000/692) (as amended)[1]

Citation, commencement and interpretation

1.—(1) These Regulations may be cited as the Conditional Fee Agreements Regulations 2000.

(2) These Regulations come into force on 1st April 2000.

(3) In these Regulations—

'client' includes, except where the context otherwise requires, a person who—

(a) has instructed the legal representative to provide the advocacy or litigation services to which the conditional fee agreement relates, or

(b) is liable to pay the legal representative's fees in respect of those services; and

'legal representative' means the person providing the advocacy or litigation services to which the conditional fee agreement relates.

Requirements for contents of conditional fee agreements: general

2.—(1) A conditional fee agreement must specify—

(a) the particular proceedings or parts of them to which it relates (including whether it relates to any appeal, counterclaim or proceedings to enforce a judgement or order),

(b) the circumstances in which the legal representative's fees and expenses, or part of them, are payable,

(c) what payment, if any, is due—

(i) if those circumstances only partly occur,

(ii) irrespective of whether those circumstances occur, and

(iii) on the termination of the agreement for any reason, and

(d) the amounts which are payable in all the circumstances and cases specified or the method to be used to calculate them and, in particular, whether the amounts are limited by reference to the damages which may be recovered on behalf of the client.

---

[1] As amended by the Collective Conditional Fee Agreements Regulations 2000 (SI 2000/2988), the Conditional Fee Agreements (Miscellaneous Amendments) Regulations 2003 (SI 2003/1240), and the Conditional Fee Agreements (Miscellaneous Amendments) (No 2) Regulations 2003 (SI 2003/3344).

(2) A conditional fee agreement to which regulation 4 applies must contain a statement that the requirements of that regulation which apply in the case of that agreement have been complied with.

Requirements for contents of conditional fee agreements providing for success fees

3.—(1) A conditional fee agreement which provides for a success fee—
- (a) must briefly specify the reasons for setting the percentage increase at the level stated in the agreement, and
- (b) must specify how much of the percentage increase, if any, relates to the cost to the legal representative of the postponement of the payment of his fees and expenses.

(2) If the agreement relates to court proceedings, it must provide that where the percentage increase becomes payable as a result of those proceedings, then—
- (a) if—
  - (i) any fees subject to the increase are assessed, and
  - (ii) the legal representative or the client is required by the court to disclose to the court or any other person the reasons for setting the percentage increase at the level stated in the agreement,

  he may do so,
- (b) if—
  - (i) any such fees are assessed, and
  - (ii) any amount in respect of the percentage increase is disallowed on the assessment on the ground that the level at which the increase was set was unreasonable in view of facts which were or should have been known to the legal representative at the time it was set,

  that amount ceases to be payable under the agreement, unless the court is satisfied that it should continue to be so payable, and
- (c) if—
  - (i) sub-paragraph (b) does not apply, and
  - (ii) the legal representative agrees with any person liable as a result of the proceedings to pay fees subject to the percentage increase that a lower amount than the amount payable in accordance with the conditional fee agreement is to be paid instead,

  the amount payable under the conditional fee agreement in respect of those fees shall be reduced accordingly, unless the court is satisfied that the full amount should continue to be payable under it.

(3) In this regulation 'percentage increase' means the percentage by which the amount of the fees which would be payable if the agreement were not a conditional fee agreement is to be increased under the agreement.

Requirements where the client's liability is limited to sums recovered

3A.—(1) This regulation applies to a conditional fee agreement under which, except in the circumstances set out in paragraph (5) and 5(A), the client is liable to pay his legal representative's fees and expenses only to the extent that sums are recovered in respect of the relevant proceedings, whether by way of costs or otherwise.

(2) In determining for the purposes of paragraph (1) the circumstances in which a client is liable to pay his legal representative's fees and expenses, no account is to be taken of any obligation to pay costs in respect of the premium of a policy taken out to insure against the risk of incurring a liability in the relevant proceedings.

(3) Regulations 2, 3 and 4 do not apply to a conditional fee agreement to which this regulation applies.

(4) A conditional fee agreement to which this regulation applies must—

(a) specify—

(i) the particular proceedings or parts of them to which it relates (including whether it relates to any appeal, counterclaim or proceedings to enforce a judgment or order); and

(ii) the circumstances in which the legal representative's fees and expenses, or part of them, are payable; and

(b) if it provides for a success fee—

(i) briefly specify the reasons for setting the percentage increase at the level stated in the agreement; and

(ii) provide that if, in court proceedings, the percentage increase becomes payable as a result of those proceedings and the legal representative or the client is ordered to disclose to the court or any other person the reasons for setting the percentage increase at the level stated in the agreement, he may do so.

(5) A conditional fee agreement to which this regulation applies may specify that the client will be liable to pay the legal representative's fees and expenses whether or not sums are recovered in respect of the relevant proceedings, if the client—

(a) fails to co-operate with the legal representative;

(b) fails to attend any medical or expert examination or court hearing which the legal representative reasonably requests him to attend;

(c) fails to give necessary instructions to the legal representative;

(d) withdraws instructions from the legal representative;

(e) is an individual who is adjudged bankrupt or enters into an arrangement or a composition with his creditors, or against whom an administration order is made; or

(f) is a company for which a receiver, administrative receiver or liquidator is appointed.

(5A) A conditional fee agreement to which this regulation applies may specify that, in the event of the client dying in the course of the relevant proceedings, his estate will be liable for the legal representative's fees and expenses, whether or not sums are recovered in respect of those proceedings.

(6) Before a conditional fee agreement to which this regulation applies is made, the legal representative must inform the client as to the circumstances in which the client or his estate may be liable to pay the legal representative's fees and expenses, and provide such further explanation, advice or other information as to those circumstances as the client may reasonably require.

Information to be given before conditional fee agreements made

4.—(1) Before a conditional fee agreement is made the legal representative must—

(a) inform the client about the following matters, and

(b) if the client requires any further explanation, advice or other information about any of those matters, provide such further explanation, advice or other information about them as the client may reasonably require.

(2) Those matters are—

(a) the circumstances in which the client may be liable to pay the costs of the legal representative in accordance with the agreement,

(b) the circumstances in which the client may seek assessment of the fees and expenses of the legal representative and the procedure for doing so,

(c) whether the legal representative considers that the client's risk of incurring liability for costs in respect of the proceedings to which agreement relates is insured against under an existing contract of insurance,

(d) whether other methods of financing those costs are available, and, if so, how they apply to the client and the proceedings in question,

(e) whether the legal representative considers that any particular method or methods of financing any or all of those costs is appropriate and, if he considers that a contract of insurance is appropriate or recommends a particular such contract—

(i) his reasons for doing so, and

(ii) whether he has an interest in doing so.

(3) Before a conditional fee agreement is made the legal representative must explain its effect to the client.

(4) In the case of an agreement where—

(a) the legal representative is a body to which section 30 of the Access to Justice Act 1999 (recovery where body undertakes to meet costs liabilities) applies, and

(b) there are no circumstances in which the client may be liable to pay any costs in respect of the proceedings,

paragraph (1) does not apply.

(5) Information required to be given under paragraph (1) about the matters in paragraph (2)(a) to (d) must be given orally (whether or not it is also given in writing), but information required to be so given about the matters in paragraph (2)(e) and the explanation required by paragraph (3) must be given both orally and in writing.

(6) This regulation does not apply in the case of an agreement between a legal representative and an additional legal representative.

Form of agreement

5.—(1) A conditional fee agreement must be signed by the client and the legal representative.

(2) This regulation does not apply in the case of an agreement between a legal representative and an additional legal representative.

Amendment of agreement

6. Where an agreement is amended to cover further proceedings or parts of them—

(a) regulations 2, 3, 3A and 5 apply to the amended agreement as if it were a fresh agreement made at the time of the amendment, and

(b) the obligations under regulation 4 apply in relation to the amendments in so far as they affect the matters mentioned in that regulation.

Revocation of 1995 Regulations

7. The Conditional Fee Agreements Regulations 1995 are revoked.

Exclusion of collective conditional fee agreements

8. These Regulations shall not apply to collective conditional fee agreements within the meaning of regulation 3 of the Collective Conditional Fee Agreements Regulations 2000.

The Collective Conditional Fee Agreements Regulations 2000 (SI 2000/2998) (as amended)[2]

Citation, commencement and interpretation

1.—(1) These regulations may be cited as the Collective Conditional Fee Agreements Regulations 2000, and shall come into force on 30th November 2000.

(2) In these Regulations, except where the context requires otherwise—

'client' means a person who will receive advocacy or litigation services to which the agreement relates;

'collective conditional fee agreement' has the meaning given in regulation 3;

'conditional fee agreement' has the same meaning as in section 58 of the Courts and Legal Services Act 1990;

'funder' means the party to a collective conditional fee agreement who, under that agreement, is liable to pay the legal representative's fees;

[2] As amended by the Conditional Fee Agreements (Miscellaneous Amendments) Regulations 2003 (SI 2003/1240), and the Conditional Fee Agreements (Miscellaneous Amendments) (No 2) Regulations 2003 (SI 2003/3344).

'legal representative' means the person providing the advocacy or litigation services to which the agreement relates.

Transitional provisions

2. These Regulations shall apply to agreements entered into on or after 30th November 2000, and agreements entered into before that date shall be treated as if these Regulations had not come into force.

Definition of 'collective conditional fee agreement'

3.—(1) Subject to paragraph (2) of this regulation, a collective conditional fee agreement is an agreement which—

(a) disregarding section 58(3)(c) of the Courts and Legal Services Act 1990, would be a conditional fee agreement; and

(b) does not refer to specific proceedings, but provides for fees to be payable on a common basis in relation to a class of proceedings, or, if it refers to more than one class of proceedings, on a common basis in relation to each class.

(2) An agreement may be a collective conditional fee agreement whether or not—

(a) the funder is a client; or

(b) any clients are named in the agreement.

Requirements for contents of collective conditional fee agreements: general

4.—(1) A collective conditional fee agreement must specify the circumstances in which the legal representative's fees and expenses, or part of them, are payable.

(1A) The circumstances referred to in paragraph (1) may include the fact that the legal representative's fees and expenses are payable only to the extent that sums are recovered in respect of the proceedings, whether by way of costs or otherwise.

(2) A collective conditional fee agreement must provide that, when accepting instructions in relation to any specific proceedings the legal representative must—

(a) inform the client as to the circumstances in which the client or his estate may be liable to pay the costs of the legal representative; and

(b) if the client requires any further explanation, advice or other information about the matter referred to in sub-paragraph (a), provide such further explanation, advice or other information about it as the client may reasonably require.

(3) Paragraph (2) does not apply in the case of an agreement between a legal representative and an additional legal representative.

(4) A collective conditional fee agreement must provide that, after accepting instructions in relation to any specific proceedings, the legal representative must confirm his acceptance of instructions in writing to the client.

Requirements for contents of collective conditional fee agreements providing for success fees

5.—(1) Where a collective conditional fee agreement provides for a success fee the agreement must provide that, when accepting instructions in relation to any specific proceedings the legal representative must prepare and retain a written statement containing—

(a) his assessment of the probability of the circumstances arising in which the percentage increase will become payable in relation to those proceedings ('the risk assessment');

(b) his assessment of the amount of the percentage increase in relation to those proceedings, having regard to the risk assessment; and

(c) the reasons, by reference to the risk assessment, for setting the percentage increase at that level.

(2) If the agreement relates to court proceedings it must provide that where the success fee becomes payable as a result of those proceedings, then—

(a) if—

(i) any fees subject to the increase are assessed, and

(ii) the legal representative or the client is required by the court to disclose to the court or any other person the reasons for setting the percentage increase at the level assessed by the legal representative,

he may do so,

(b) if—

(i) any such fees are assessed by the court, and

(ii) any amount in respect of the percentage increase is disallowed on the assessment on the ground that the level at which the increase was set was unreasonable in view of facts which were or should have been known to the legal representative at the time it was set

that amount ceases to be payable under the agreement, unless the court is satisfied that it should continue to be so payable, and

(c) if—

(i) sub-paragraph (b) does not apply, and

(ii) the legal representative agrees with any person liable as a result of the proceedings to pay fees subject to the percentage increase that a lower amount than the amount payable in accordance with the conditional fee agreement is to be paid instead,

the amount payable under the collective conditional fee agreement in respect of those fees shall be reduced accordingly, unless the court is satisfied that the full amount should continue to be payable under it.

(3) In this regulation 'percentage increase' means the percentage by which the amount of the fees which would have been payable if the agreement were not a conditional fee agreement is to be increased under the agreement.

(4) Sub-paragraphs (b) and (c) of paragraph (2) do not apply to a collective conditional fee agreement under which, except in the circumstances set out in paragraph (6) and (7), the client is liable to pay his legal representative's fees and expenses only to the extent that sums are recovered in respect of the proceedings, whether by way of costs or otherwise.

(5) In determining for the purposes of paragraph (4) the circumstances in which a client is liable to pay his legal representative's fees and expenses, no account is to be taken of any obligation to pay costs in respect of the premium of a policy taken out to insure against the risk of incurring a liability in the relevant proceedings.

(6) A collective conditional fee agreement to which paragraph (4) applies may specify that the client will be liable to pay his legal representative's fees and expenses whether or not sums are recovered in respect of the relevant proceedings, if the client—

(a) fails to co-operate with the legal representative;
(b) fails to attend any medical or expert examination or court hearing which the legal representative reasonably requests him to attend;
(c) fails to give necessary instructions to the legal representative;
(d) withdraws instructions from the legal representative;
(e) is an individual who is adjudged bankrupt or enters into an arrangement or a composition with his creditors, or against whom an administration order is made; or
(f) is a company for which a receiver, administrative receiver or liquidator is appointed.

(7) A collective conditional fee agreement to which paragraph (4) applies may specify that, in the event of the client dying in the course of the relevant proceedings, his estate will be liable for the legal representative's fees and expenses, whether or not sums are recovered in respect of those proceedings.

Form and amendment of collective conditional fee agreement

6.—(1) Subject to paragraph (2), a collective conditional fee agreement must be signed by the funder, and by the legal representative.

(2) Paragraph (1) does not apply in the case of an agreement between a legal representative and an additional legal representative.

(3) Where a collective conditional fee agreement is amended, regulations 4 and 5 apply to the amended agreement as if it were a fresh agreement made at the time of the amendment.

Amendment to the Conditional Fee Agreements Regulations 2000

7. After regulation 7 of the Conditional Fee Agreements Regulations 2000 there shall be inserted the following new regulation:

Exclusion of collective conditional fee agreements

8. These Regulations shall not apply to collective conditional fee agreements within the meaning of regulation 3 of the Collective Conditional Fee Agreements Regulations 2000.

The Conditional Fee Agreements (Revocation) Regulations 2005 (SI 2005/2305)

Citation and commencement

1. These Regulations may be cited as the Conditional Fee Agreements (Revocation) Regulations 2005 and shall come into force on 1st November 2005.

Revocation

2. Subject to regulation 3, the Conditional Fee Agreements Regulations 2000 (the 'CFA Regulations'), the Collective Conditional Fee Agreements Regulations 2000 (the 'CCFA Regulations'), the Conditional Fee Agreements (Miscellaneous Amendments) Regulations 2003, and the Conditional Fee Agreements (Miscellaneous Amendments) (No. 2) Regulations 2003 are revoked.

Savings and transitional provisions

3.—(1) The CFA Regulations shall continue to have effect for the purposes of a conditional fee agreement entered into before 1st November 2005.

(2) Paragraph (1) shall apply in relation to a collective conditional fee agreement as if there were substituted for a reference to the CFA Regulations a reference to the CCFA Regulations.

The Community Legal Services (Costs) Regulations 2000 (SI 2000/441) (as amended)[3]

Assessment of resources

7.—(1) The first £100,000 of the value of the client's interest in the main or only dwelling in which he resides shall not be taken into account in having regard to the client's resources for the purposes of section 11(1) of the Act.

(2) Where, but only to the extent that, the court considers that the circumstances are exceptional, having regard in particular to the quantity or value of the

[3] As amended by the Community Legal Service (Costs) (Amendment) Regulations 2002 (SI 2001/822), and the Community Legal Service (Costs) (Amendment) Regulations 2003 (SI 2003/649).

items concerned, the court may take into account the value of the client's clothes and household furniture, or the tools and implements of his trade, in having regard to the client's resources for the purposes of section 11(1) of the Act.

(3) Subject to paragraph (4), in having regard to the resources of a party for the purposes of section 11(1) of the Act, the resources of his partner shall be treated as his resources.

(4) The resources of a party's partner shall not be treated as that party's resources if the partner has a contrary interest in the dispute in respect of which the funded services are provided.

(5) Where a party is acting in a representative, fiduciary or official capacity, the court shall not take the personal resources of the party into account for the purposes of section 11(1) of the Act, but shall have regard to the value of any property or estate, or the amount of any fund out of which he is entitled to be indemnified, and may also have regard to the resources of the persons, if any, including that party where appropriate, who are beneficially interested in that property, estate or fund.

Statements of resources

8.—(1) Any person who is a party to proceedings in which another party is a client may make a statement of resources, and file it with the court.

(2) A person making and filing a statement of resources under paragraph (1) shall serve a copy of it on the client.

(3) Where a copy of a statement of resources has been served under paragraph (2) not less than seven days before the date fixed for a hearing at which the amount to be paid under a section 11(1) costs order falls, or may fall, to be decided, the client shall also make a statement of resources, and shall produce it at that hearing.

Procedures for ordering costs against client and Commission

9.—(1) Where the court is considering whether to make a section 11(1) costs order, it shall consider whether, but for cost protection, it would have made a costs order against the client and, if so, whether it would, on making the costs order, have specified the amount to be paid under that order.

(2) If the court considers that it would have made a costs order against the client, but that it would not have specified the amount to be paid under it, the court shall, when making the section 11(1) costs order:

(a) specify the amount (if any) that the client is to pay under that order if, but only if:

(i) it considers that it has sufficient information before it to decide what amount is, in that case, a reasonable amount for the client to pay, in accordance with section 11(1) of the Act; and

(ii) it is satisfied that, if it were to determine the full costs at that time, they would exceed the amount referred to in sub-paragraph (i);

(b) otherwise, it shall not specify the amount the client is to pay under the costs order.

(3) If the court considers that it would have made a costs order against the client, and that it would have specified the amount to be paid under it, the court shall, when making the costs order:

(a) specify the amount (if any) that the client is to pay under that order if, but only if, it considers that it has sufficient information before it to decide what amount is, in that case, a reasonable amount for the client to pay, in accordance with section 11(1) of the Act;

(b) otherwise, it shall not specify the amount the client is to pay under the section 11(1) costs order.

(4) Any order made under paragraph (3) shall state the amount of the full costs.

(5) The amount (if any) to be paid by the client under an order made under paragraph (2)(b) or paragraph (3)(b), and any application for a costs order against the Commission, shall be determined in accordance with regulation 10, and at any such determination following an order made under paragraph (2)(b), the amount of the full costs shall also be assessed.

(6) Where the court makes a section 11(1) costs order that does not specify the amount which the client is to pay under it, it may also make findings of fact, as to the parties' conduct in the proceedings or otherwise, relevant to the determination of that amount, and those findings shall be taken into consideration in that determination.

10.—(1) The following paragraphs of this regulation apply where the amount to be paid under a section 11(1) costs order, or an application for a costs order against the Commission, is to be determined under this regulation, by virtue of regulation 9(5).

(2) The receiving party may, within three months after a section 11(1) costs order is made, request a hearing to determine the costs payable to him.

(3) A request under paragraph (2) shall be accompanied by:

(a) if the section 11(1) costs order does not state the full costs, the receiving party's bill of costs, which shall comply with any requirements of relevant rules of court relating to the form and content of a bill of costs where the court is assessing a party's costs;

(b) unless the conditions set out in paragraph (3A) are satisfied, a statement of resources; and

(c) if the receiving party is seeking, or, subject to the determination of the amount to be paid under the section 11(1) costs order, may seek, a costs order against the Commission, written notice to that effect.

(3A) The conditions referred to in paragraph (3)(b) above are that—

(a) the court is determining an application for a costs order against the Commission;

(b) the costs were not incurred in a court of first instance.

(4) The receiving party shall file the documents referred to in paragraph (3) with the court and at the same time serve copies of them:

(a) on the client, if a determination of costs payable under section 11(1) of the Act is sought; and

(b) on the Regional Director, if notice has been given under paragraph (3)(c).

(5) Where documents are served on the client under paragraph (4)(a), the client shall make a statement of resources.

(6) The client shall file the statement of resources made under paragraph (5) with the court, and serve copies of it on the receiving party and, if notice has been given under paragraph (3)(c), on the Regional Director, not more than 21 days after the client receives a copy of the receiving party's statement of resources.

(7) The client may, at the same time as filing and serving a statement of resources under paragraph (6), file, and serve on the same persons, a statement setting out any points of dispute in relation to the bill of costs referred to in paragraph (3)(a).

(8) If the client, without good reason, fails to file a statement of resources in accordance with paragraph (6), the court shall determine the amount which the client shall be required to pay under the section 11(1) costs order (and, if relevant, the full costs), having regard to the statement made by the receiving party, and the court need not hold an oral hearing for such determination.

(9) If the client files a statement of resources in accordance with paragraph (6), or the period for filing such notice expires, or if the costs payable by the client have already been determined, the court shall set a date for the hearing and, at least 14 days before that date, serve notice of it on:

(a) the receiving party;

(b) the client (unless the costs payable by the client have already been determined); and

(c) if a costs order against the Commission is or may be sought, the Regional Director.

(10) The court's functions under this regulation may be exercised:

(a) in relation to proceedings in the House of Lords, by the Clerk to the Parliaments;

(b) in relation to proceedings in the Court of Appeal, High Court or a county court, a costs judge or a district judge;

(c) in relation to proceedings in a magistrates' court, by a single justice or by the justices' clerk;

(d) in relation to proceedings in the Employment Appeal Tribunal, by the Registrar of that Tribunal.

(11) The amount of costs to be determined under this regulation may include the costs incurred in relation to a request made under this regulation.

10A.—(1) Subject to paragraph (2), where the court makes a section 11(1) costs order but does not specify the amount which the client is to pay under it, the court may order the client to pay an amount on account of the costs which are the subject of the order.

(2) The court may order a client to make a payment on account of costs under this regulation only if it has sufficient information before it to decide the minimum amount which the client is likely to be ordered to pay on a determination under regulation 10.

(3) The amount of the payment on account of costs shall not exceed the minimum amount which the court decides that the client is likely to be ordered to pay on such a determination.

(4) Where the court orders a client to make a payment on account of costs—
   (a) it shall order the client to make the payment into court; and
   (b) the payment shall remain in court unless and until the court—
      (i) makes a determination under regulation 10 of the amount which the client should pay to the receiving party under the section 11(1) costs order, and orders the payment on account or part of it to be paid to the receiving party in satisfaction or part satisfaction of the client's liability under that order; or
      (ii) makes an order under paragraph (5)(b) or (5)(c) of this regulation that the payment on account or part of it be repaid to the client.

(5) Where a client has made a payment on account of costs pursuant to an order under paragraph (1) of this regulation—
   (a) the receiving party shall request a hearing under regulation 10 to determine the amount of costs payable to him;
   (b) if the receiving party fails to request such a hearing within the time permitted by regulation 10(2), the payment on account shall be repaid to the client;
   (c) if upon the hearing under regulation 10 the amount of costs which it is determined that the client should pay is less than the amount of the payment on account, the difference shall be repaid to the client.

APPENDIX C

Solicitors' Costs Materials

Solicitors' Practice Rules 1990*

Rule 15

Solicitors shall:

(a) give information about costs and other matters, and

(b) operate a complaints handling procedure,

in accordance with a Solicitors' Costs Information and Client Care Code made from time to time by the Council of the Law Society with the concurrence of the Master of the Rolls, but subject to the notes.

Solicitors' Costs Information and Client Care Code 1999 (as amended)[1]

Code dated 3rd September 1999 made by the Council of the Law Society with the concurrence of the Master of the Rolls under Rule 15 of the Solicitors' Practice Rules 1990, regulating the English and Welsh practices of solicitors, registered European lawyers, registered foreign lawyers and recognised bodies in giving information to clients and operating complaints procedures.

1. Introduction

(a) This code replaces the written professional standards on costs information for clients (see paragraphs 3–6) and the detail previously contained in Practice Rule 15 (client care) (see paragraph 7).

(b) The main object of the code is to make sure that clients are given the information they need to understand what is happening generally and in particular on:
   (i) the cost of legal services both at the outset and as a matter progresses; and
   (ii) responsibility for clients' matters.

(c) The code also requires firms to operate a complaints handling procedure.

(d) It is good practice to record in writing:

---

* Solicitors' Practice Rules 1990, rule 15, and Solicitors' Costs Information and Client Care Code 1999 (as amended) are reproduced by permission of the Law Society © The Law Society 1990 and 2005.

[1] As amended by the Solicitors' Practice (Client Care) Amendment Rules 2005.

(i) all information required to be given by the code including all decisions relating to costs and the arrangements for updating costs information; and
(ii) the reasons why the information required by the code has not been given in a particular case.

(e) References to costs, where appropriate, include fees, VAT and disbursements.

2. Application

(a) The code is of general application, and it applies to registered foreign lawyers as well as to solicitors of the Supreme Court and registered European lawyers (subject to note (v) to Practice Rule 15). However, as set out in paragraph 2(b), parts of the code may not be appropriate in every case, and solicitors should consider the interests of each client in deciding which parts not to apply in the particular circumstances.

(b) The full information required by the code may be inappropriate, for example:
(i) in every case, for a regular client for whom repetitive work is done, where the client has already been provided with the relevant information, although such a client should be informed of changes; and
(ii) if compliance with the code may at the time be insensitive or impractical. In such a case relevant information should be given as soon as reasonably practicable.

(c) Employed solicitors should have regard to paragraphs 3–6A of the code where appropriate, e.g. when acting for clients other than their employer. Paragraph 7 does not apply to employed solicitors.

(d) Solicitors should comply with paragraphs 3–6 of the code even where a client is legally aided if the client may have a financial interest in the costs because contributions are payable or the statutory charge may apply or they may become liable for the costs of another party.

(da) If appropriate solicitors should also comply with paragraph 6A of the code where a client is legally aided.

(e) The code also applies to contingency fee and conditional fee arrangements and to arrangements with a client for the solicitor to retain commissions received from third parties.

3. Informing the client about costs

(a) Costs information must not be inaccurate or misleading.

(b) Any costs information required to be given by the code must be given clearly, in a way and at a level which is appropriate to the particular client. Any terms with which the client may be unfamiliar, for example 'disbursement', should be explained.

(c) The information required by paragraphs 4 and 5 of the code should be given to a client at the outset of, and at appropriate stages throughout, the matter. All information given orally should be confirmed in writing to the client as soon as possible.

4. Advance costs information—general

The overall costs

(a) The solicitor should give the client the best information possible about the likely overall costs, including a breakdown between fees, VAT and disbursements.
(b) The solicitor should explain clearly to the client the time likely to be spent in dealing with a matter, if time spent is a factor in the calculation of the fees.
(c) Giving 'the best information possible' includes:
  (i) agreeing a fixed fee; or
  (ii) giving a realistic estimate; or
  (iii) giving a forecast within a possible range of costs; or
  (iv) explaining to the client the reasons why it is not possible to fix, or give a realistic estimate or forecast of, the overall costs, and giving instead the best information possible about the cost of the next stage of the matter.
(d) The solicitor should, in an appropriate case, explain to a privately paying client that the client may set an upper limit on the firm's costs for which the client may be liable without further authority. Solicitors should not exceed an agreed limit without first obtaining the client's consent.
(e) The solicitor should make it clear at the outset if an estimate, quotation or other indication of cost is not intended to be fixed.

Basis of firm's charges

(f) The solicitor should also explain to the client how the firm's fees are calculated except where the overall costs are fixed or clear. If the basis of charging is an hourly charging rate, that must be made clear.
(g) The client should be told if charging rates may be increased.

Further information

(h) The solicitor should explain what reasonably foreseeable payments a client may have to make either to the solicitor or to a third party and when those payments are likely to be needed.
(i) The solicitor should explain to the client the arrangements for updating the costs information as set out in paragraph 6.

Client's ability to pay

(j) The solicitor should discuss with the client how and when any costs are to be met, and consider:—
  (i) whether the client may be eligible and should apply for legal aid (including advice and assistance);
  (ii) whether the client's liability for their own costs may be covered by insurance;
  (iii) whether the client's liability for another party's costs may be covered by pre-purchased insurance and, if not, whether it would be advisable for the

client's liability for another party's costs to be covered by after the event insurance (including in every case where a conditional fee or contingency fee arrangement is proposed); and

(iv) whether the client's liability for costs (including the costs of another party) may be paid by another person, e.g. an employer or trade union.

Cost-benefit and risk

(k) The solicitor should discuss with the client whether the likely outcome in a matter will justify the expense or risk involved including, if relevant, the risk of having to bear an opponent's costs.

5. Additional information for particular clients

Legally aided clients

(1) (a) The solicitor should explain to a legally aided client the client's potential liability for the client's own costs and those of any other party, including:

(i) the effect of the statutory charge and its likely amount;

(ii) the client's obligation to pay any contribution assessed and the consequences of failing to do so;

(iii) the fact that the client may still be ordered by the court to contribute to the opponent's costs if the case is lost even though the client's own costs are covered by legal aid; and

(iv) the fact that even if the client wins, the opponent may not be ordered to pay or be capable of paying the full amount of the client's costs.

Privately paying clients in contentious matters (and potentially contentious matters)

(b) The solicitor should explain to the client the client's potential liability for the client's own costs and for those of any other party, including:

(i) the fact that the client will be responsible for paying the firm's bill in full regardless of any order for costs made against an opponent;

(ii) the probability that the client will have to pay the opponent's costs as well as the client's own costs if the case is lost;

(iii) the fact that even if the client wins, the opponent may not be ordered to pay or be capable of paying the full amount of the client's costs; and

(iv) the fact that if the opponent is legally aided the client may not recover costs, even if successful.

Liability for third party costs in non-contentious matters

(c) The solicitor should explain to the client any liability the client may have for the payment of the costs of a third party. When appropriate, solicitors are advised to obtain a firm figure for or agree a cap to a third party's costs.

Clients represented under a conditional fee agreement (including a collective conditional fee agreement)

(d) Where a client is represented under a conditional fee agreement, the solicitor should explain:

(i) the circumstances in which the client may be liable for their own costs and for the other party's costs;
(ii) the client's right to assessment of costs, wherever the solicitor intends to seek payment of any or all of their costs from the client; and
(iii) any interest the solicitor may have in recommending a particular policy or other funding.

(2) This rule will come into force on the date of notification of the Lord Chancellor's approval or the date of repeal of the Conditional Fee Agreements Regulations (2000), whichever is the later.

6. Updating costs information

The solicitor should keep the client properly informed about costs as a matter progresses. In particular, the solicitor should:

(a) tell the client, unless otherwise agreed, how much the costs are at regular intervals (at least every six months) and in appropriate cases deliver interim bills at agreed intervals;
(b) explain to the client (and confirm in writing) any changed circumstances which will, or which are likely to affect the amount of costs, the degree of risk involved, or the cost-benefit to the client of continuing with the matter;
(c) inform the client in writing as soon as it appears that a costs estimate or agreed upper limit may or will be exceeded; and
(d) consider the client's eligibility for legal aid if a material change in the client's means comes to the solicitor's attention.

6A. Disclosure of solicitor's arrangements with third parties

(a) The solicitor should disclose to the client any relationship with a third party (for example a funder, fee sharer or introducer) which affects the steps which the solicitor can take on the client's behalf.
(b) The solicitor should explain any constraints or conditions which affect the client.
(c) All information given orally concerning (a) and (b) above should be confirmed in writing to the client as soon as possible.

7. Client care and complaints handling

Information for clients

(a) Every solicitor in private practice must ensure that the client:
(i) is given a clear explanation of the issues raised in a matter and is kept properly informed about its progress (including the likely timescale);
(ii) is given the name and status of the person dealing with the matter and the name of the principal, or director (in the case of a recognised body which is a company), or member (in the case of a recognised body which is a limited liability partnership) responsible for its overall supervision;
(iii) is told whom to contact about any problem with the service provided; and

(iv) is given details of any changes in the information required to be given by this paragraph.

Complaints handling

(b) Every principal in private practice (or, in the case of a recognised body, the body itself) must:
   (i) ensure the client is told the name of the person in the firm to contact about any problem with the service provided;
   (ii) have a written complaints procedure and ensure that complaints are handled in accordance with it; and
   (iii) ensure that the client is given a copy of the complaints procedure on request.

APPENDIX D

Extracts from the Civil Procedure Rules 1998 (as amended)

Part 1 Overriding Objective

1.1 The overriding objective

(1) These Rules are a new procedural code with the overriding objective of enabling the court to deal with cases justly.

(2) Dealing with a case justly includes, so far as is practicable—
  - (a) ensuring that the parties are on an equal footing;
  - (b) saving expense;
  - (c) dealing with the case in ways which are proportionate—
    - (i) to the amount of money involved;
    - (ii) to the importance of the case;
    - (iii) to the complexity of the issues; and
    - (iv) to the financial position of each party;
  - (d) ensuring that it is dealt with expeditiously and fairly; and
  - (e) allotting to it an appropriate share of the court's resources, while taking into account the need to allot resources to other cases.

1.2 Application by the court of the overriding objective

The court must seek to give effect to the overriding objective when it—
  - (a) exercises any power given to it by the Rules; or
  - (b) interprets any rule subject to rule 76.2.

1.3 Duty of the parties

The parties are required to help the court to further the overriding objective.

Part 3 The Court's Case Management Powers

3.8 Sanctions have effect unless defaulting party obtains relief

(1) Where a party has failed to comply with a rule, practice direction or court order, any sanction for failure to comply imposed by the rule, practice direction or court order has effect unless the party in default applies for and obtains relief from the sanction.

(Rule 3.9 sets out the circumstances which the court may consider on an application to grant relief from a sanction)

(2) Where the sanction is the payment of costs, the party in default may only obtain relief by appealing against the order for costs.

(3) Where a rule, practice direction or court order—
  (a) requires a party to do something within a specified time, and
  (b) specifies the consequence of failure to comply,
  the time for doing the act in question may not be extended by agreement between the parties.

3.9 Relief from sanctions

(1) On an application for relief from any sanction imposed for a failure to comply with any rule, practice direction or court order the court will consider all the circumstances including—
  (a) the interests of the administration of justice;
  (b) whether the application for relief has been made promptly;
  (c) whether the failure to comply was intentional;
  (d) whether there is a good explanation for the failure;
  (e) the extent to which the party in default has complied with other rules, practice directions, court orders and any relevant preaction protocol (GL);
  (f) whether the failure to comply was caused by the party or his legal representative;
  (g) whether the trial date or the likely trial date can still be met if relief is granted;
  (h) the effect which the failure to comply had on each party; and
  (i) the effect which the granting of relief would have on each party.

(2) An application for relief must be supported by evidence.

Part 20 Parties and Group Litigation

20.2 Meaning of 'Part 20 claim'

(1) A Part 20 claim is any claim other than a claim by a claimant against a defendant and includes—
  (a) a counterclaim by a defendant against the claimant or against the claimant and some other person;
  (b) a claim by a defendant against any person (whether or not already a party) for contribution or indemnity or some other remedy; and
  (c) where a Part 20 claim has been made against a person who is not already a party, any claim made by that person against any other person (whether or not already a party).

(2) In this Part 'Part 20 claimant' means a person who makes a Part 20 claim.

21.10 Compromise etc by or on behalf of child or patient

(3) In proceedings to which Section II of Part 45 applies, the court shall not make an order for detailed assessment of the costs payable to the child or patient but shall assess the costs in the manner set out in that Section.

Part 27 The Small Claims Track

27.14 Costs on the small claims track

(1) This rule applies to any case which has been allocated to the small claims track unless paragraph (5) applies. (Rules 44.9 and 44.11 make provision in relation to orders for costs made before a claim has been allocated to the small claims track)

(2) The court may not order a party to pay a sum to another party in respect of that other party's costs except—

  (a) the fixed costs attributable to issuing the claim which—

    (i) are payable under Part 45; or

    (ii) would be payable under Part 45 if that Part applied to the claim;

  (b) in proceedings which included a claim for an injunction (GL) or an order for specific performance a sum not exceeding the amount specified in the relevant practice direction for legal advice and assistance relating to that claim;

  (c) costs assessed by the summary procedure in relation to an appeal; and

  (d) such further costs as the court may assess by the summary procedure and order to be paid by a party who has behaved unreasonably.

(2A) A party's rejection of an offer in settlement will not of itself constitute unreasonable behaviour under paragraph (2)(d) but the court may take it into consideration when it is applying the unreasonableness test.

(Rule 36.2(5) allows the court to order Part 36 costs consequences in a small claim)

Part 36 Offers to Settle and Payments into Court

36.1 Scope of this Part

(1) This Part contains rules about—

  (a) offers to settle and payments into court; and

  (b) the consequences where an offer to settle or payment into court is made in accordance with this Part.

(2) Nothing in this Part prevents a party making an offer to settle in whatever way he chooses, but if that offer is not made in accordance with this Part, it will only have the consequences specified in this Part if the court so orders.

(Part 36 applies to Part 20 claims by virtue of rule 20.3)

36.2 Part 36 offers and Part 36 payments—general provisions

(1) An offer made in accordance with the requirements of this Part is called—
  (a) if made by way of a payment into court, 'a Part 36 payment';
  (b) otherwise 'a Part 36 offer'.

(Rule 36.3 sets out when an offer has to be made by way of a payment into court)

(2) The party who makes an offer is the 'offeror'.
(3) The party to whom an offer is made is the 'offeree'.
(4) A Part 36 offer or a Part 36 payment—
  (a) may be made at any time after proceedings have started; and
  (b) may be made in appeal proceedings.
(5) A Part 36 offer or a Part 36 payment shall not have the consequences set out in this Part while the claim is being dealt with on the small claims track unless the court orders otherwise.

(Part 26 deals with allocation to the small claims track)
(Rule 27.2 provides that Part 36 does not apply to small claims)

36.3 A defendant's offer to settle a money claim requires a Part 36 payment

(1) Subject to rules 36.2A(2), 36.5(5) and 36.23, an offer by a defendant to settle a money claim will not have the consequences set out in this Part unless it is made by way of a Part 36 payment.
(2) A Part 36 payment may only be made after proceedings have started.

(Rule 36.5(5) permits a Part 36 offer to be made by reference to an interim payment)
(Rule 36.10 makes provision for an offer to settle a money claim before the commencement of proceedings)
(Rule 36.23 makes provision for where benefit is recoverable under the Social Security (Recovery of Benefit) Act 1971)

36.4 Defendant's offer to settle the whole of a claim which includes both a money claim and a non-money claim

(1) This rule applies where a defendant to a claim which includes both a money claim and a non-money claim wishes—
  (a) to make an offer to settle the whole claim which will have the consequences set out in this Part; and
  (b) to make a money offer in respect of the money claim and a non-money offer in respect of the non-money claim.
(2) The defendant must—
  (a) make a Part 36 payment or Part 36 offer made under rule 36.2A in relation to the money claim; and
  (b) make a Part 36 offer in relation to the non-money claim.
(3) The Part 36 payment notice or Part 36 offer made under rule 36.2A must—
  (a) identify the document which sets out the terms of the Part 36 offer made under this rule; and

(b) state that if the claimant gives notice of acceptance of the Part 36 payment or Part 36 offer made under rule 36.2A he will be treated as also accepting the Part 36 offer made under this rule.

(Rule 36.6 makes provision for a Part 36 payment notice)

(4) If the claimant gives notice of acceptance of the Part 36 payment or Part 36 offer made under rule 36.2A, he shall also be taken as giving notice of acceptance of the Part 36 offer in relation to the non-money claim.

36.5 Form and content of a Part 36 offer

(1) A Part 36 offer must be in writing.

(2) A Part 36 offer may relate to the whole claim or to part of it or to any issue that arises in it.

(3) A Part 36 offer must—

(a) state whether it relates to the whole of the claim or to part of it or to an issue that arises in it and if so to which part or issue;

(b) state whether it takes into account any counterclaim; and

(c) if it is expressed not to be inclusive of interest, give the details relating to interest set out in rule 36.22(2).

(4) A defendant may make a Part 36 offer limited to accepting liability up to a specified proportion.

(5) A Part 36 offer may be made by reference to an interim payment.

(Part 25 contains provisions relating to interim payments)

(6) A Part 36 offer made not less than 21 days before the start of the trial must—

(a) be expressed to remain open for acceptance for 21 days from the date it is made; and

(b) provide that after 21 days the offeree may only accept it if—

(i) the parties agree the liability for costs; or

(ii) the court gives permission.

(7) A Part 36 offer made less than 21 days before the start of the trial must state that the offeree may only accept it if—

(a) the parties agree the liability for costs; or

(b) the court gives permission.

(Rule 36.8 makes provision for when a Part 36 offer is treated as being made)

(8) If a Part 36 offer is withdrawn it will not have the consequences set out in this Part.

36.6 Notice of a Part 36 payment

(1) A Part 36 payment may relate to the whole claim or part of it or to an issue that arises in it.

(2) A defendant who makes a Part 36 payment must file with the court a notice ('Part 36 payment notice') which—

(a) states the amount of the payment;

(b) states whether the payment relates to the whole claim or to part of it or to any issue that arises in it and if so to which part or issue;

(c) states whether it takes into account any counterclaim;

(d) if an interim payment has been made, states that the defendant has taken into account the interim payment; and
(e) if it is expressed not to be inclusive of interest, gives the details relating to interest set out in rule 36.22(2).

(Rule 25.6 makes provision for an interim payment)

(Rule 36.4 provides for further information to be included where a defendant wishes to settle the whole of a claim which includes a money claim and a non-money claim)

(Rule 36.23 makes provision for extra information to be included in the payment notice in a case where benefit is recoverable under the Social Security (Recovery of Benefit) Act 1997)

(3) The offeror must—
(a) serve the Part 36 payment notice on the offeree; and
(b) file a certificate of service of the notice.

(4) . . .

(5) A Part 36 payment may be withdrawn or reduced only with the permission of the court.

36.8 Time when a Part 36 offer or a Part 36 payment is made and accepted

(1) A Part 36 offer is made when received by the offeree.
(2) A Part 36 payment is made when written notice of the payment into court is served on the offeree.
(3) An improvement to a Part 36 offer will be effective when its details are received by the offeree.
(4) An increase in a Part 36 payment will be effective when notice of the increase is served on the offeree.
(5) A Part 36 offer or Part 36 payment is accepted when notice of its acceptance is received by the offeror.

36.9 Clarification of a Part 36 offer or a Part 36 payment notice

(1) The offeree may, within 7 days of a Part 36 offer or payment being made, request the offeror to clarify the offer or payment notice.
(2) If the offeror does not give the clarification requested under paragraph (1) within 7 days of receiving the request, the offeree may, unless the trial has started, apply for an order that he does so.
(3) If the court makes an order under paragraph (2), it must specify the date when the Part 36 offer or Part 36 payment is to be treated as having been made.

36.10 Court to take into account offer to settle made before commencement of Proceedings

(1) If a person makes an offer to settle before proceedings are begun which complies with the provisions of this rule, the court will take that offer into account when making any order as to costs.
(2) The offer must—
(a) be expressed to be open for at least 21 days after the date it was made;

(b) if made by a person who would be a defendant were proceedings commenced, include an offer to pay the costs of the offeree incurred up to the date 21 days after the date it was made; and

(c) otherwise comply with this Part.

(3) Subject to paragraph (3A), if the offeror is a defendant to a money claim—

(a) he must make a Part 36 payment within 14 days of service of the claim form; and

(b) the amount of the payment must be not less than the sum offered before proceedings began.

(3A) In a claim to which rule 36.2A applies, if the offeror is a defendant who wishes to offer to pay the whole or part of any damages in the form of a lump sum—

(a) he must make a Part 36 payment within 14 days of service of the claim form; and

(b) the amount of the payment must be not less than the lump sum offered before proceedings began.

(4) An offeree may not, after proceedings have begun, accept—

(a) an offer made under paragraph (2); or

(b) a Part 36 payment made under paragraph (3) or (3A),

without the permission of the court.

(5) An offer under this rule is made when it is received by the offeree.

36.11 Time for acceptance of a defendant's Part 36 offer or Part 36 payment

(1) A claimant may accept a Part 36 offer or a Part 36 payment made not less than 21 days before the start of the trial without needing the court's permission if he gives the defendant written notice of acceptance not later than 21 days after the offer or payment was made.

(Rule 36.13 sets out the costs consequences of accepting a defendant's offer or payment without needing the permission of the court)

(2) If—

(a) a defendant's Part 36 offer or Part 36 payment is made less than 21 days before the start of the trial; or

(b) the claimant does not accept it within the period specified in paragraph (1)—

(i) if the parties agree the liability for costs, the claimant may accept the offer or payment without needing the permission of the court;

(ii) if the parties do not agree the liability for costs the claimant may only accept the offer or payment with the permission of the court.

(3) Where the permission of the court is needed under paragraph (2) the court will, if it gives permission, make an order as to costs.

36.12 Time for acceptance of a claimant's Part 36 offer

(1) A defendant may accept a Part 36 offer made not less than 21 days before the start of the trial without needing the court's permission if he gives the claimant written notice of acceptance not later than 21 days after the offer was made.

(Rule 36.14 sets out the costs consequences of accepting a claimant's offer without needing the permission of the court)

(2) If—
- (a) a claimant's Part 36 offer is made less than 21 days before the start of the trial; or
- (b) the defendant does not accept it within the period specified in paragraph (1)—
  - (i) if the parties agree the liability for costs, the defendant may accept the offer without needing the permission of the court;
  - (ii) if the parties do not agree the liability for costs the defendant may only accept the offer with the permission of the court.

(3) Where the permission of the court is needed under paragraph (2) the court will, if it gives permission, make an order as to costs.

36.13 Costs consequences of acceptance of a defendant's Part 36 offer or Part 36 payment

(1) Where a Part 36 offer or a Part 36 payment is accepted without needing the permission of the court the claimant will be entitled to his costs of the proceedings up to the date of serving notice of acceptance.

(2) Where—
- (a) a Part 36 offer or a Part 36 payment relates to part only of the claim; and
- (b) at the time of serving notice of acceptance the claimant abandons the balance of the claim,

the claimant will be entitled to his costs of the proceedings up to the date of serving notice of acceptance, unless the court orders otherwise.

(3) The claimant's costs include any costs attributable to the defendant's counterclaim if the Part 36 offer or the Part 36 payment notice states that it takes into account the counterclaim.

(4) Costs under this rule will be payable on the standard basis if not agreed.

36.14 Costs consequences of acceptance of a claimant's Part 36 offer

Where a claimant's Part 36 offer is accepted without needing the permission of the court the claimant will be entitled to his costs of the proceedings up to the date upon which the defendant serves notice of acceptance.

36.15 The effect of acceptance of a Part 36 offer or a Part 36 payment

(1) If a Part 36 offer or Part 36 payment relates to the whole claim and is accepted, the claim will be stayed.

(2) In the case of acceptance of a Part 36 offer which relates to the whole claim—
- (a) the stay (GL) will be upon the terms of the offer; and
- (b) either party may apply to enforce those terms without the need for a new claim.

(3) If a Part 36 offer or a Part 36 payment which relates to part only of the claim is accepted—

(a) the claim will be stayed as to that part; and
(b) unless the parties have agreed costs, the liability for costs shall be decided by the court.

(4) If the approval of the court is required before a settlement can be binding, any stay which would otherwise arise on the acceptance of a Part 36 offer or a Part 36 payment will take effect only when that approval has been given.

(5) Any stay (GL) arising under this rule will not affect the power of the court—
(a) to enforce the terms of a Part 36 offer;
(b) to deal with any question of costs (including interest on costs) relating to the proceedings;
(c) to order payment out of court of any sum paid into court.

(6) Where—
(a) a Part 36 offer has been accepted; and
(b) a party alleges that—
(i) the other party has not honoured the terms of the offer; and
(ii) he is therefore entitled to a remedy for breach of contract,
the party may claim the remedy by applying to the court without the need to start a new claim unless the court orders otherwise.

36.16 Payment out of a sum in court on the acceptance of a Part 36 payment

Where a Part 36 payment is accepted the claimant obtains payment out of the sum in court by making a request for payment in the practice form.

36.17 Acceptance of a Part 36 offer or a Part 36 payment made by one or more, but not all, defendants

(1) This rule applies where the claimant wishes to accept a Part 36 offer or a Part 36 payment made by one or more, but not all, of a number of defendants.

(2) If the defendants are sued jointly or in the alternative, the claimant may accept the offer or payment without needing the permission of the court in accordance with rule 36.11(1) if—
(a) he discontinues his claim against those defendants who have not made the offer or payment; and
(b) those defendants give written consent to the acceptance of the offer or payment.

(3) If the claimant alleges that the defendants have a several liability (GL) to him the claimant may—
(a) accept the offer or payment in accordance with rule 36.11(1); and
(b) continue with his claims against the other defendants if he is entitled to do so.

(4) In all other cases the claimant must apply to the court for—
(a) an order permitting a payment out to him of any sum in court; and
(b) such order as to costs as the court considers appropriate.

36.18 Other cases where a court order is required to enable acceptance of a Part 36 offer or a Part 36 payment

(1) Where a Part 36 offer or a Part 36 payment is made in proceedings to which rule 21.10 applies—
   (a) the offer or payment may be accepted only with the permission of the court; and
   (b) no payment out of any sum in court shall be made without a court order.

(Rule 21.10 deals with compromise etc. by or on behalf of a child or patient)

(2) Where the court gives a claimant permission to accept a Part 36 offer or payment after the trial has started—
   (a) any money in court may be paid out only with a court order; and
   (b) the court must, in the order, deal with the whole costs of the proceedings.

(3) Where a claimant accepts a Part 36 payment after a defence of tender before claim has been put forward by the defendant, the money in court may be paid out only after an order of the court.

(Rule 37.3 requires a defendant who wishes to rely on a defence of tender before claim to make a payment into court)

36.19 Restriction on disclosure of a Part 36 offer or a Part 36 payment

(1) A Part 36 offer will be treated as 'without prejudice except as to costs'.

(2) The fact that a Part 36 payment has been made shall not be communicated to the trial judge until all questions of liability and the amount of money to be awarded have been decided.

(3) Paragraph (2) does not apply—
   (a) where the defence of tender before claim (GL) has been raised;
   (b) where the proceedings have been stayed (GL) under rule 36.15 following acceptance of a Part 36 offer or Part 36 payment; or
   (c) where—
      (i) the issue of liability has been determined before any assessment of the money claimed; and
      (ii) the fact that there has or has not been a Part 36 payment may be relevant to the question of the costs of the issue of liability.

36.20 Costs consequences where a claimant fails to do better than a Part 36 offer or a Part 36 payment

(1) This rule applies where at trial a claimant—
   (a) fails to better a Part 36 payment;
   (b) fails to obtain a judgment which is more advantageous than a defendant's Part 36 offer; or
   (c) in a claim to which rule 36.2A applies, fails to obtain a judgment which is more advantageous than the Part 36 offer made under that rule.

(2) Unless it considers it unjust to do so, the court will order the claimant to pay any costs incurred by the defendant after the latest date on which the payment or offer could have been accepted without needing the permission of the court.

(Rule 36.11 sets out the time for acceptance of a defendant's Part 36 offer or Part 36 payment)

36.21 Costs and other consequences where a claimant does better than he proposed in his Part 36 offer

(1) This rule applies where at trial—
  (a) a defendant is held liable for more; or
  (b) the judgment against a defendant is more advantageous to the claimant,
  than the proposals contained in a claimant's Part 36 offer (including a Part 36 offer made under rule 36.2A).
(2) The court may order interest on the whole or part of any sum of money (excluding interest) awarded to the claimant at a rate not exceeding 10% above base rate (GL) for some or all of the period starting with the latest date on which the defendant could have accepted the offer without needing the permission of the court.
(3) The court may also order that the claimant is entitled to—
  (a) his costs on the indemnity basis from the latest date when the defendant could have accepted the offer without needing the permission of the court; and
  (b) interest on those costs at a rate not exceeding 10% above base rate (GL).
(4) Where this rule applies, the court will make the orders referred to in paragraphs (2) and (3) unless it considers it unjust to do so.

(Rule 36.12 sets out the latest date when the defendant could have accepted the offer)

(5) In considering whether it would be unjust to make the orders referred to in paragraphs (2) and (3) above, the court will take into account all the circumstances of the case including—
  (a) the terms of any Part 36 offer;
  (b) the stage in the proceedings when any Part 36 offer or Part 36 payment was made;
  (c) the information available to the parties at the time when the Part 36 offer or Part 36 payment was made; and
  (d) the conduct of the parties with regard to the giving or refusing to give information for the purposes of enabling the offer or payment into court to be made or evaluated.
(6) Where the court awards interest under this rule and also awards interest on the same sum and for the same period under any other power, the total rate of interest may not exceed 10% above base rate.

36.22 Interest

(1) Unless—
  (a) a claimant's Part 36 offer which offers to accept a sum of money; or
  (b) a Part 36 payment notice,

indicates to the contrary, any such offer or payment will be treated as inclusive of all interest until the last date on which it could be accepted without needing the permission of the court.

(2) Where a claimant's Part 36 offer or Part 36 payment notice is expressed not to be inclusive of interest, the offer or notice must state—
  (a) whether interest is offered; and
  (b) if so, the amount offered, the rate or rates offered and the period or periods for which it is offered.

36.23 Deduction of benefits

(1) This rule applies where a payment to a claimant following acceptance of a Part 36 offer or Part 36 payment into court would be a compensation payment as defined in section 1 of the Social Security (Recovery of Benefits) Act 1971.

(2) A defendant to a money claim may make an offer to settle the claim which will have the consequences set out in this Part, without making a Part 36 payment if—
  (a) at the time he makes the offer he has applied for, but not received, a certificate of recoverable benefit; and
  (b) he makes a Part 36 payment not more than 7 days after he receives the certificate.

(Section 1 of the 1997 Act defines 'recoverable benefit')

(3) A Part 36 payment notice must state—
  (a) the amount of gross compensation;
  (b) the name and amount of any benefit by which that gross amount is reduced in accordance with section 8 and Schedule 2 to the 1997 Act; and
  (c) that the sum paid in is the net amount after deduction of the amount of benefit.

(4) For the purposes of rule 36.20(1)(a), a claimant fails to better a Part 36 payment if he fails to obtain judgment for more than the gross sum specified in the Part 36 payment notice.

(4A) For the purposes of rule 36.20(1)(c), where the court is determining whether the claimant has failed to obtain a judgment which is more advantageous than the Part 36 offer made under rule 36.2A, the amount of any lump sum paid into court which it takes into account is to be the amount of the gross sum specified in the Part 36 payment notice.

(5) Where—
  (a) a Part 36 payment has been made; and
  (b) application is made for the money remaining in court to be paid out,

the court may treat the money in court as being reduced by a sum equivalent to any further recoverable benefits paid to the claimant since the date of payment into court and may direct payment out accordingly.

Part 37 Miscellaneous Provisions about Payments into Court

37.1 Money paid into court under a court order—general

(1) A party who makes a payment into court under a court order must—
  (a) serve notice of the payment on every other party; and
  (b) in relation to each such notice, file a certificate of service.
(2) Money paid into court under a court order may not be paid out without the court's permission except where—
  (a) the defendant treats the money as a Part 36 payment under rule 37.2; and
  (b) the claimant accepts the Part 36 payment without needing the permission of the court.

(Rule 36.11 sets out when the claimant can accept a Part 36 payment without needing the permission of the court)

37.2 Money paid into court may be treated as a Part 36 payment

(1) Where a defendant makes a payment into court following an order made under rule 3.1(3) or 3.1(5) he may choose to treat the whole or any part of the money paid into court as a Part 36 payment.

(Rule 36.2 defines a Part 36 payment)

(2) To do this he must file a Part 36 payment notice.

(Rule 36.6 sets out what a Part 36 payment notice must contain and provides for the court to serve it on the other parties)

(3) If he does so Part 36 applies to the money as if he had paid it into court as a Part 36 payment.

Part 40 Judgments, Orders, Sale of Land Etc

40.8 Time from which interest begins to run

(1) Where interest is payable on a judgment pursuant to section 17 of the Judgments Act 1838 or section 74 of the County Courts Act 1984, the interest shall begin to run from the date that judgment is given unless—
  (a) a rule in another Part or a practice direction makes different provision; or
  (b) the court orders otherwise.
(2) The court may order that interest shall begin to run from a date before the date that judgment is given.

40.11 Time for complying with a judgment or order

A party must comply with a judgment or order for the payment of an amount of money (including costs) within 14 days of the date of the judgment or order, unless—
  (a) the judgment or order specifies a different date for compliance (including specifying payment by instalments);

(b) any of these Rules specifies a different date for compliance; or
(c) the court has stayed the proceedings or judgment.

(Parts 12 and 14 specify different dates for complying with certain default judgments and judgments on admissions)

40.13 Cases where court gives judgment both on claim and counterclaim

(1) This rule applies where the court gives judgment for specified amounts both for the claimant on his claim and against the claimant on a counterclaim.
(2) If there is a balance in favour of one of the parties, it may order the party whose judgment is for the lesser amount to pay the balance.
(3) In a case to which this rule applies, the court may make a separate order as to costs against each party.

Part 43 Scope of Costs Rules and Definitions

43.1 Scope of this Part

This Part contains definitions and interpretation of certain matters set out in the rules about costs contained in Parts 44 to 48.

(Part 44 contains general rules about costs; Part 45 deals with fixed costs; Part 46 deals with fast track trial costs; Part 47 deals with the detailed assessment of costs and related appeals and Part 48 deals with costs payable in special cases)

43.2 Definitions and application

(1) In Parts 44 to 48, unless the context otherwise requires—
  (a) 'costs' includes fees, charges, disbursements, expenses, remuneration, reimbursement allowed to a litigant in person under rule 48.6, any additional liability incurred under a funding arrangement and any fee or reward charged by a lay representative for acting on behalf of a party in proceedings allocated to the small claims track;
  (b) 'costs judge' means a taxing master of the Supreme Court;
  (c) 'costs officer' means—
    (i) a costs judge;
    (ii) a district judge; and
    (iii) an authorised court officer;
  (d) 'authorised court officer' means any officer of—
    (i) a county court;
    (ii) a district registry;
    (iii) the Principal Registry of the Family Division; or
    (iv) the Supreme Court Costs Office, whom the Lord Chancellor has authorised to assess costs;
  (e) 'fund' includes any estate or property held for the benefit of any person or class of person and any fund to which a trustee or personal representative is entitled in his capacity as such;

(f) 'receiving party' means a party entitled to be paid costs;
(g) 'paying party' means a party liable to pay costs;
(h) 'assisted person' means an assisted person within the statutory provisions relating to legal aid;
(i) 'LSC funded client' means an individual who receives services funded by the Legal Services Commission as part of the Community Legal Service within the meaning of Part I of the Access to Justice Act 1999;
(j) 'fixed costs' means the amounts which are to be allowed in respect of solicitors' charges in the circumstances set out in Section I of Part 45;
(k) 'funding arrangement' means an arrangement where a person has—
    (i) entered into a conditional fee agreement or a collective conditional fee agreement which provides for a success fee within the meaning of section 58(2) of the Courts and Legal Services Act 1901;
    (ii) taken out an insurance policy to which section 29 of the Access to Justice Act 1999 (recovery of insurance premiums by way of costs) applies; or
    (iii) made an agreement with a membership organisation to meet his legal costs;
(l) 'percentage increase' means the percentage by which the amount of a legal representative's fee can be increased in accordance with a conditional fee agreement which provides for a success fee;
(m) 'insurance premium' means a sum of money paid or payable for insurance against the risk of incurring a costs liability in the proceedings, taken out after the event that is the subject matter of the claim;
(n) 'membership organisation' means a body prescribed for the purposes of section 30 of the Access to Justice Act 1999 (recovery where body undertakes to meet costs liabilities); and
(o) 'additional liability' means the percentage increase, the insurance premium, or the additional amount in respect of provision made by a membership organisation, as the case may be.

(2) The costs to which Parts 44 to 48 apply include—
  (a) the following costs where those costs may be assessed by the court—
    (i) costs of proceedings before an arbitrator or umpire;
    (ii) costs of proceedings before a tribunal or other statutory body; and
    (iii) costs payable by a client to his solicitor; and
  (b) costs which are payable by one party to another party under the terms of a contract, where the court makes an order for an assessment of those costs.

(3) Where advocacy or litigation services are provided to a client under a conditional fee agreement, costs are recoverable under Parts 44 to 48 notwithstanding that the client is liable to pay his legal representative's fees and expenses only to the extent that sums are recovered in respect of the proceedings, whether by way of costs or otherwise.

(4) In paragraph (3), the reference to a conditional fee agreement is to an agreement which satisfies all the conditions applicable to it by virtue of section 58 of the Courts and Legal Services Act 1990.

43.3 Meaning of summary assessment

'Summary assessment' means the procedure by which the court, when making an order about costs, orders payment of a sum of money instead of fixed costs or 'detailed assessment'.

43.4 Meaning of detailed assessment

'Detailed assessment' means the procedure by which the amount of costs is decided by a costs officer in accordance with Part 47.

Part 44 General Rules about Costs

44.1 Scope of this Part

This Part contains general rules about costs and entitlement to costs.
(The definitions contained in Part 43 are relevant to this Part)

44.2 Solicitor's duty to notify client

Where—

(a) the court makes a costs order against a legally represented party; and
(b) the party is not present when the order is made,
the party's solicitor must notify his client in writing of the costs order no later than 7 days after the solicitor receives notice of the order.

44.3 Court's discretion and circumstances to be taken into account when exercising its discretion as to costs

(1) The court has discretion as to—
  (a) whether costs are payable by one party to another;
  (b) the amount of those costs; and
  (c) when they are to be paid.
(2) If the court decides to make an order about costs—
  (a) the general rule is that the unsuccessful party will be ordered to pay the costs of the successful party; but
  (b) the court may make a different order.
(3) The general rule does not apply to the following proceedings—
  (a) proceedings in the Court of Appeal on an application or appeal made in connection with proceedings in the Family Division; or
  (b) proceedings in the Court of Appeal from a judgment, direction, decision or order given or made in probate proceedings or family proceedings.
(4) In deciding what order (if any) to make about costs, the court must have regard to all the circumstances, including—
  (a) the conduct of all the parties;

(b) whether a party has succeeded on part of his case, even if he has not been wholly successful; and
(c) any payment into court or admissible offer to settle made by a party which is drawn to the court's attention (whether or not made in accordance with Part 36).

(Part 36 contains further provisions about how the court's discretion is to be exercised where a payment into court or an offer to settle is made under that Part)

(5) The conduct of the parties includes—
(a) conduct before, as well as during, the proceedings and in particular the extent to which the parties followed any relevant pre-action protocol;
(b) whether it was reasonable for a party to raise, pursue or contest a particular allegation or issue;
(c) the manner in which a party has pursued or defended his case or a particular allegation or issue; and
(d) whether a claimant who has succeeded in his claim, in whole or in part, exaggerated his claim.

(6) The orders which the court may make under this rule include an order that a party must pay—
(a) a proportion of another party's costs;
(b) a stated amount in respect of another party's costs;
(c) costs from or until a certain date only;
(d) costs incurred before proceedings have begun;
(e) costs relating to particular steps taken in the proceedings;
(f) costs relating only to a distinct part of the proceedings; and
(g) interest on costs from or until a certain date, including a date before judgment.

(7) Where the court would otherwise consider making an order under paragraph (6)(f), it must instead, if practicable, make an order under paragraph (6)(a) or (c).

(8) Where the court has ordered a party to pay costs, it may order an amount to be paid on account before the costs are assessed.

(9) Where a party entitled to costs is also liable to pay costs the court may assess the costs which that party is liable to pay and either—
(a) set off the amount assessed against the amount the party is entitled to be paid and direct him to pay any balance; or
(b) delay the issue of a certificate for the costs to which the party is entitled until he has paid the amount which he is liable to pay.

44.3A Costs orders relating to funding arrangements

(1) The court will not assess any additional liability until the conclusion of the proceedings, or the part of the proceedings, to which the funding arrangement relates.

('Funding arrangement' and 'additional liability' are defined in rule 43.2)

(2) At the conclusion of the proceedings, or the part of the proceedings, to which the funding arrangement relates the court may—
  (a) make a summary assessment of all the costs, including any additional liability;
  (b) make an order for detailed assessment of the additional liability but make a summary assessment of the other costs; or
  (c) make an order for detailed assessment of all the costs.

(Part 47 sets out the procedure for the detailed assessment of costs)

44.3B Limits on recovery under funding arrangements

(1) A party may not recover as an additional liability—
  (a) any proportion of the percentage increase relating to the cost to the legal representative of the postponement of the payment of his fees and expenses;
  (b) any provision made by a membership organisation which exceeds the likely cost to that party of the premium of an insurance policy against the risk of incurring a liability to pay the costs of other parties to the proceedings;
  (c) any additional liability for any period in the proceedings during which he failed to provide information about a funding arrangement in accordance with a rule, practice direction or court order;
  (d) any percentage increase where a party has failed to comply with—
    (i) a requirement in the costs practice direction; or
    (ii) a court order,

  to disclose in any assessment proceedings the reasons for setting the percentage increase at the level stated in the conditional fee agreement.

(2) This rule does not apply in an assessment under rule 48.9 (assessment of a solicitor's bill to his client).

(Rule 3.9 sets out the circumstances the court will consider on an application for relief from a sanction for failure to comply with any rule, practice direction or court order)

44.4 Basis of assessment

(1) Where the court is to assess the amount of costs (whether by summary or detailed assessment) it will assess those costs—
  (a) on the standard basis; or
  (b) on the indemnity basis,

  but the court will not in either case allow costs which have been unreasonably incurred or are unreasonable in amount.

(Rule 48.3 sets out how the court decides the amount of costs payable under a contract)

(2) Where the amount of costs is to be assessed on the standard basis, the court will—
  (a) only allow costs which are proportionate to the matters in issue; and

(b) resolve any doubt which it may have as to whether costs were reasonably incurred or reasonable and proportionate in amount in favour of the paying party.

(Factors which the court may take into account are set out in rule 44.5)

(3) Where the amount of costs is to be assessed on the indemnity basis, the court will resolve any doubt which it may have as to whether costs were reasonably incurred or were reasonable in amount in favour of the receiving party.

(4) Where—
- (a) the court makes an order about costs without indicating the basis on which the costs are to be assessed; or
- (b) the court makes an order for costs to be assessed on a basis other than the standard basis or the indemnity basis, the costs will be assessed on the standard basis.

(5) ....

(6) Where the amount of a solicitor's remuneration in respect of non-contentious business is regulated by any general orders made under the Solicitors Act 1974, the amount of the costs to be allowed in respect of any such business which falls to be assessed by the court will be decided in accordance with those general orders rather than this rule and rule 44.5.

44.5 Factors to be taken into account in deciding the amount of costs

(1) The court is to have regard to all the circumstances in deciding whether costs were—
- (a) if it is assessing costs on the standard basis—
  - (i) proportionately and reasonably incurred; or
  - (ii) were proportionate and reasonable in amount, or
- (b) if it is assessing costs on the indemnity basis—
  - (i) unreasonably incurred; or
  - (ii) unreasonable in amount.

(2) In particular the court must give effect to any orders which have already been made.

(3) The court must also have regard to—
- (a) the conduct of all the parties, including in particular—
  - (i) conduct before, as well as during, the proceedings; and
  - (ii) the efforts made, if any, before and during the proceedings in order to try to resolve the dispute;
- (b) the amount or value of any money or property involved;
- (c) the importance of the matter to all the parties;
- (d) the particular complexity of the matter or the difficulty or novelty of the questions raised;
- (e) the skill, effort, specialised knowledge and responsibility involved;
- (f) the time spent on the case; and
- (g) the place where and the circumstances in which work or any part of it was done.

(Rule 35.4(4) gives the court power to limit the amount that a party may recover with regard to the fees and expenses of an expert)

44.6 Fixed costs

A party may recover the fixed costs specified in Part 45 in accordance with that Part.

44.7 Procedure for assessing costs

Where the court orders a party to pay costs to another party (other than fixed costs) it may either—

(a) make a summary assessment of the costs; or

(b) order detailed assessment of the costs by a costs officer,

unless any rule, practice direction or other enactment provides otherwise.

(The costs practice direction sets out the factors which will affect the court's decision under this rule)

44.8 Time for complying with an order for costs

A party must comply with an order for the payment of costs within 14 days of—

(a) the date of the judgment or order if it states the amount of those costs;

(b) if the amount of those costs (or part of them) is decided later in accordance with Part 47, the date of the certificate which states the amount; or

(c) in either case, such later date as the court may specify.

(Part 47 sets out the procedure for detailed assessment of costs)

44.9 Costs on the small claims track and fast track

(1) Part 27 (small claims) and Part 46 (fast track trial costs) contain special rules about—

(a) liability for costs;

(b) the amount of costs which the court may award; and

(c) the procedure for assessing costs.

(2) Once a claim is allocated to a particular track, those special rules shall apply to the period before, as well as after, allocation except where the court or a practice direction provides otherwise.

44.10 Limitation on amount court may allow where a claim allocated to the fast track settles before trial

(1) Where the court—

(a) assesses costs in relation to a claim which—

(i) has been allocated to the fast track; and

(ii) settles before the start of the trial; and

(b) is considering the amount of costs to be allowed in respect of a party's advocate for preparing for the trial,

it may not allow, in respect of those advocate's costs, an amount that exceeds the amount of fast track trial costs which would have been payable in relation to the claim had the trial taken place.

(2) When deciding the amount to be allowed in respect of the advocate's costs, the court shall have regard to—
   (a) when the claim was settled; and
   (b) when the court was notified that the claim had settled.

(3) In this rule, 'advocate' and 'fast track trial costs' have the meanings given to them by Part 46.

(Part 46 sets out the amount of fast track trial costs which may be awarded)

44.11 Costs following allocation and re-allocation

(1) Any costs orders made before a claim is allocated will not be affected by allocation.

(2) Where—
   (a) a claim is allocated to a track; and
   (b) the court subsequently re-allocates that claim to a different track, then unless the court orders otherwise, any special rules about costs applying—
      (i) to the first track, will apply to the claim up to the date of re-allocation; and
      (ii) to the second track, will apply from the date of re-allocation.

(Part 26 deals with the allocation and re-allocation of claims between tracks)

44.12 Cases where costs orders deemed to have been made

(1) Where a right to costs arises under—
   (a) rule 3.7 (defendant's right to costs where claim struck out for non-payment of fees);
   (b) rule 36.13(1) (claimant's right to costs where he accepts defendant's Part 36 offer or Part 36 payment);
   (c) rule 36.14 (claimant's right to costs where defendant accepts the claimant's Part 36 offer); or
   (d) rule 38.6 (defendant's right to costs where claimant discontinues), a costs order will be deemed to have been made on the standard basis.

(2) Interest payable pursuant to section 17 of the Judgments Act 1838 or section 74 of the County Courts Act 1984 on the costs deemed to have been ordered under paragraph (1) shall begin to run from the date on which the event which gave rise to the entitlement to costs occurred.

44.13 Special situations

(1) Where the court makes an order which does not mention costs—
   (a) subject to paragraphs (1A) and (1B), the general rule is that no party is entitled to costs in relation to that order; but
   (b) this does not affect any entitlement of a party to recover costs out of a fund held by him as trustee or personal representative, or pursuant to any lease, mortgage or other security.

(1A) Where the court makes—
   (a) an order granting permission to appeal;
   (b) an order granting permission to apply for judicial review; or

(c) any other order or direction sought by a party on an application without notice, and its order does not mention costs, it will be deemed to include an order for applicant's costs in the case.

(1B) Any party affected by a deemed order for costs under paragraph (1A) may apply at any time to vary the order.

(2) The court hearing an appeal may, unless it dismisses the appeal, make orders about the costs of the proceedings giving rise to the appeal as well as the costs of the appeal.

(3) Where proceedings are transferred from one court to another, the court to which they are transferred may deal with all the costs, including the costs before the transfer.

(4) Paragraph (3) is subject to any order of the court which ordered the transfer.

44.14 Court's powers in relation to misconduct

(1) The court may make an order under this rule where—

(a) a party or his legal representative, in connection with a summary or detailed assessment, fails to comply with a rule, practice direction or court order; or

(b) it appears to the court that the conduct of a party or his legal representative, before or during the proceedings which gave rise to the assessment proceedings, was unreasonable or improper.

(2) Where paragraph (1) applies, the court may—

(a) disallow all or part of the costs which are being assessed; or

(b) order the party at fault or his legal representative to pay costs which he has caused any other party to incur.

(3) Where—

(a) the court makes an order under paragraph (2) against a legally represented party; and

(b) the party is not present when the order is made,

the party's solicitor must notify his client in writing of the order no later than 7 days after the solicitor receives notice of the order.

44.15 Providing information about funding arrangements

(1) A party who seeks to recover an additional liability must provide information about the funding arrangement to the court and to other parties as required by a rule, practice direction or court order.

(2) Where the funding arrangement has changed, and the information a party has previously provided in accordance with paragraph (1) is no longer accurate, that party must file notice of the change and serve it on all other parties within 7 days.

(3) Where paragraph (2) applies, and a party has already filed—

(a) an allocation questionnaire; or

(b) a pre-trial check list (listing questionnaire)

he must file and serve a new estimate of costs with the notice.

(The costs practice direction sets out—
- the information to be provided when a party issues or responds to a claim form, files an allocation questionnaire, a pre-trial check list, and a claim for costs;
- the meaning of estimate of costs and the information required in it)

(Rule 44.3B sets out situations where a party will not recover a sum representing any additional liability)

44.16 Adjournment where legal representative seeks to challenge disallowance of any amount of percentage increase

Where—
(a) the court disallows any amount of a legal representative's percentage increase in summary or detailed assessment proceedings; and
(b) the legal representative applies for an order that the disallowed amount should continue to be payable by his client,

the court may adjourn the hearing to allow the client to be—
(i) notified of the order sought; and
(ii) separately represented.

(Regulation 3(2)(b) of the Conditional Fee Agreements Regulations 2000 provides that a conditional fee agreement which provides for a success fee must state that any amount of a percentage increase disallowed on assessment ceases to be payable unless the court is satisfied that it should continue to be so payable. Regulation 5(2)(b) of the Collective Conditional Fee Agreements Regulations 2000 makes similar provision in relation to collective conditional fee agreements)

44.17 Application of costs rules

This Part and Part 45 (fixed costs), Part 46 (fast track trial costs), Part 47 (procedure for detailed assessment of costs and default provisions) and Part 48 (special cases), do not apply to the assessment of costs in proceedings to the extent that
(a) section 11 of the Access to Justice Act 1999, and provisions made under that Act, or
(b) regulations made under the Legal Aid Act 1988,

make different provision.

(The costs practice direction sets out the procedure to be followed where a party was wholly or partially funded by the Legal Services Commission)

Part 45 Fixed Costs

I Fixed Costs

45.1 Scope of this Section

(1) This Section sets out the amounts which, unless the court orders otherwise, are to be allowed in respect of solicitors' charges in the cases to which this Section applies.

(2) This Section applies where—
   (a) the only claim is a claim for a specified sum of money where the value of the claim exceeds £25 and—
      (i) judgment in default is obtained under rule 12.4(1);
      (ii) judgment on admission is obtained under rule 14.4(3);
      (iii) judgment on admission on part of the claim is obtained under rule 14.5(6);
      (iv) summary judgment is given under Part 24;
      (v) the court has made an order to strike out (GL) a defence under rule 3.4(2)(a) as disclosing no reasonable grounds for defending the claim; or
      (vi) rule 45.3 applies;
   (b) the only claim is a claim where the court gave a fixed date for the hearing when it issued the claim and judgment is given for the delivery of goods, and the value of the claim exceeds £25;
   (c) the claim is for the recovery of land, including a possession claim under Part 55, whether or not the claim includes a claim for a sum of money and the defendant gives up possession, pays the amount claimed, if any, and the fixed commencement costs stated in the claim form;
   (d) the claim is for the recovery of land, including a possession claim under Part 55, where one of the grounds for possession is arrears of rent, for which the court gave a fixed date for the hearing when it issued the claim and judgment is given for the possession of land (whether or not the order for possession is suspended on terms) and the defendant—
      (i) has neither delivered a defence, or counterclaim, nor otherwise denied liability; or
      (ii) has delivered a defence which is limited to specifying his proposals for the payment of arrears of rent;
   (e) the claim is a possession claim under Section II of Part 55 (accelerated possession claims of land let on an assured shorthold tenancy) and a possession order is made where the defendant has neither delivered a defence, or counterclaim, nor otherwise denied liability;
   (f) the claim is a demotion claim under Section III of Part 65 or a demotion claim is made in the same claim form in which a claim for possession is made under Part 55 and that demotion claim is successful; or
   (g) a judgment creditor has taken steps under Parts 70 to 73 to enforce a judgment or order.

(The practice direction supplementing rule 7.9 sets out the types of case where a court will give a fixed date for a hearing when it issues a claim)

(3) Any appropriate court fee will be allowed in addition to the costs set out in this Section.

(4) The claim form may include a claim for fixed commencement costs.

II Road Traffic Accidents—Fixed Recoverable Costs

45.7 Scope and interpretation

(1) This Section sets out the costs which are to be allowed in—
   (a) costs-only proceedings under the procedure set out in rule 44.12A; or
   (b) proceedings for approval of a settlement or compromise under rule 21.10(2), in cases to which this Section applies.

(2) This Section applies where—
   (a) the dispute arises from a road traffic accident;
   (b) the agreed damages include damages in respect of personal injury, damage to property, or both;
   (c) the total value of the agreed damages does not exceed £10,000; and
   (d) if a claim had been issued for the amount of the agreed damages, the small claims track would not have been the normal track for that claim.

(3) This Section does not apply where the claimant is a litigant in person.

(Rule 2.3 defines 'personal injuries' as including any disease and any impairment of a person's physical or mental condition)

(Rule 26.6 provides for when the small claims track is the normal track)

(4) In this Section—
   (a) 'road traffic accident' means an accident resulting in bodily injury to any person or damage to property caused by, or arising out of, the use of a motor vehicle on a road or other public place in England and Wales;
   (b) 'motor vehicle' means a mechanically propelled vehicle intended for use on roads; and
   (c) 'road' means any highway and any other road to which the public has access and includes bridges over which a road passes.

45.8 Application of fixed recoverable costs

Subject to rule 45.12, the only costs which are to be allowed are—
   (a) fixed recoverable costs calculated in accordance with rule 45.9;
   (b) disbursements allowed in accordance with rule 45.10; and
   (c) a success fee allowed in accordance with rule 45.11.

(Rule 45.12 provides for where a party issues a claim for more than the fixed recoverable costs)

45.9 Amount of fixed recoverable costs

(1) Subject to paragraphs (2) and (3), the amount of fixed recoverable costs is the total of—
   (a) £800;
   (b) 20% of the damages agreed up to £5,000; and
   (c) 15% of the damages agreed between £5,000 and £10,000.

(2) Where the claimant—
   (a) lives or works in an area set out in the relevant practice direction; and
   (b) instructs a solicitor or firm of solicitors who practise in that area,

the fixed recoverable costs shall include, in addition to the costs specified in paragraph (1), an amount equal to 12.5% of the costs allowable under that paragraph.

(3) Where appropriate, value added tax (VAT) may be recovered in addition to the amount of fixed recoverable costs and any reference in this Section to fixed recoverable costs is a reference to those costs net of any such VAT.

45.10 Disbursements

(1) The court—
    (a) may allow a claim for a disbursement of a type mentioned in paragraph (2); but
    (b) must not allow a claim for any other type of disbursement.

(2) The disbursements referred to in paragraph (1) are—
    (a) the cost of obtaining—
        (i) medical records;
        (ii) a medical report;
        (iii) a police report;
        (iv) an engineer's report; or
        (v) a search of the records of the Driver Vehicle Licensing Authority;
    (b) the amount of an insurance premium; or, where a membership organization undertakes to meet liabilities incurred to pay the costs of other parties to proceedings, a sum not exceeding such additional amount of costs as would be allowed under section 30 in respect of provision made against the risk of having to meet such liabilities ('membership organisation' is defined in rule 43.2(1)(n));
    (c) where they are necessarily incurred by reason of one or more of the claimants being a child or patient as defined in Part 21—
        (i) fees payable for instructing counsel; or
        (ii) court fees payable on an application to the court;
    (d) any other disbursement that has arisen due to a particular feature of the dispute.

    ('Insurance premium' is defined in rule 43.2)

45.11 Success fee

(1) A claimant may recover a success fee if he has entered into a funding arrangement of a type specified in rule 43.2(k)(i).

(2) The amount of the success fee shall be 12.5% of the fixed recoverable costs calculated in accordance with rule 45.9(1), disregarding any additional amount which may be included in the fixed recoverable costs by virtue of rule 45.9(2).

(Rule 43.2(k)(i) defines a funding arrangement as including a conditional fee agreement or collective conditional fee agreement which provides for a success fee)

45.12 Claims for an amount of costs exceeding fixed recoverable costs

(1) The court will entertain a claim for an amount of costs (excluding any success fee or disbursements) greater than the fixed recoverable costs but only if it considers that there are exceptional circumstances making it appropriate to do so.
(2) If the court considers such a claim appropriate, it may—
   (a) assess the costs; or
   (b) make an order for the costs to be assessed.
(3) If the court does not consider the claim appropriate, it must make an order for fixed recoverable costs only.

45.13 Failure to achieve costs greater than fixed recoverable costs

(1) This rule applies where—
   (a) costs are assessed in accordance with rule 45.12(2); and
   (b) the court assesses the costs (excluding any VAT) as being an amount which is less than 20% greater than the amount of the fixed recoverable costs.
(2) The court must order the defendant to pay to the claimant the lesser of—
   (a) the fixed recoverable costs; and
   (b) the assessed costs.

45.14 Costs of the costs-only proceedings or the detailed assessment

Where—
(a) the court makes an order for fixed recoverable costs in accordance with rule 45.12(3); or
(b) rule 45.13 applies,
the court must—
   (i) make no award for the payment of the claimant's costs in bringing the proceedings under rule 44.12A; and
   (ii) order that the claimant pay the defendant's costs of defending those proceedings.

III Fixed Percentage Increase in Road Traffic Accident Claims

45.15 Scope and interpretation

(1) This Section sets out the percentage increase which is to be allowed in the cases to which this Section applies.
(Rule 43.2(1)(l) defines 'percentage increase' as the percentage by which the amount of a legal representative's fee can be increased in accordance with a conditional fee agreement which provides for a success fee)
(2) This Section applies where—
   (a) the dispute arises from a road traffic accident; and
   (b) the claimant has entered into a funding arrangement of a type specified in rule 43.2(k)(i).

(Rule 43.2(k)(i) defines a funding arrangement as including an arrangement where a person has entered into a conditional fee agreement or collective conditional fee agreement which provides for a success fee)

(3) This Section does not apply if the proceedings are costs-only proceedings to which Section II of this Part applies.

(4) This Section does not apply—
- (a) to a claim which has been allocated to the small claims track;
- (b) to a claim not allocated to a track, but for which the small claims track is the normal track; or
- (c) where the road traffic accident which gave rise to the dispute occurred before 6th October 2003.

(5) The definitions in rule 45.7(4) apply to this Section as they apply to Section II.

(6) In this Section—
- (a) a reference to 'fees' is a reference to fees for work done under a conditional fee agreement or collective conditional fee agreement;
- (b) a reference to 'trial' is a reference to the final contested hearing or to the contested hearing of any issue ordered to be tried separately;
- (c) a reference to a claim concluding at trial is a reference to a claim concluding by settlement after the trial has commenced or by judgment; and
- (d) 'trial period' means a period of time fixed by the court within which the trial is to take place and where the court fixes more than one such period in relation to a claim, means the most recent period to be fixed.

45.16 Percentage increase of solicitors' fees

Subject to rule 45.18, the percentage increase which is to be allowed in relation to solicitors' fees is—
- (a) 100% where the claim concludes at trial; or
- (b) 12.5% where—
  - (i) the claim concludes before a trial has commenced; or
  - (ii) the dispute is settled before a claim is issued.

45.17 Percentage increase of counsel's fees

(1) Subject to rule 45.18, the percentage increase which is to be allowed in relation to counsel's fees is—
- (a) 100% where the claim concludes at trial;
- (b) if the claim has been allocated to the fast track—
  - (i) 50% if the claim concludes 14 days or less before the date fixed for the commencement of the trial; or
  - (ii) 12.5% if the claim concludes more than 14 days before the date fixed for the commencement of the trial or before any such date has been fixed;
- (c) if the claim has been allocated to the multi-track—
  - (i) 75% if the claim concludes 21 days or less before the date fixed for the commencement of the trial; or

(ii) 12.5% if the claim concludes more than 21 days before the date fixed for the commencement of the trial or before any such date has been fixed;

(d) 12.5% where—

(i) the claim has been issued but concludes before it has been allocated to a track; or

(ii) in relation to costs-only proceedings, the dispute is settled before a claim is issued.

(2) Where a trial period has been fixed, if—

(a) the claim concludes before the first day of that period; and

(b) no trial date has been fixed within that period before the claim concludes,

the first day of that period is treated as the date fixed for the commencement of the trial for the purposes of paragraph (1).

(3) Where a trial period has been fixed, if—

(a) the claim concludes before the first day of that period; but

(b) before the claim concludes, a trial date had been fixed within that period,

the trial date is the date fixed for the commencement of the trial for the purposes of paragraph (1).

(4) Where a trial period has been fixed and the claim concludes—

(a) on or after the first day of that period; but

(b) before commencement of the trial,

the percentage increase in paragraph (1)(b)(i) or (1)(c)(i) shall apply as appropriate, whether or not a trial date has been fixed within that period.

(5) For the purposes of this rule, in calculating the periods of time, the day fixed for the commencement of the trial (or the first day of the trial period, where appropriate) is not included.

45.18 Application for an alternative percentage increase where the fixed increase is 12.5%

(1) This rule applies where the percentage increase to be allowed—

(a) in relation to solicitors' fees under the provisions of rule 45.16; or

(b) in relation to counsel's fees under rule 45.17, is 12.5%.

(2) A party may apply for a percentage increase greater or less than that amount if—

(a) the parties agree damages of an amount greater than £500,000 or the court awards damages of an amount greater than £500,000; or

(b) the court awards damages of £500,000 or less but would have awarded damages greater than £500,000 if it had not made a finding of contributory negligence; or

(c) the parties agree damages of £500,000 or less and it is reasonable to expect that if the court had made an award of damages, it would have awarded damages greater than £500,000, disregarding any reduction the court may have made in respect of contributory negligence.

(3) In paragraph (2), a reference to a lump sum of damages includes a reference to periodical payments of equivalent value.

(4) If the court is satisfied that the circumstances set out in paragraph (2) apply it must—
  (a) assess the percentage increase; or
  (b) make an order for the percentage increase to be assessed.

45.19 Assessment of alternative percentage increase

(1) This rule applies where the percentage increase of fees is assessed under rule 45.18(4).

(2) If the percentage increase is assessed as greater than 20% or less than 7.5%, the percentage increase to be allowed shall be that assessed by the court.

(3) If the percentage increase is assessed as no greater than 20% and no less than 7.5%—
  (a) the percentage increase to be allowed shall be 12.5%; and
  (b) the costs of the application and assessment shall be paid by the applicant.

IV Fixed Percentage Increase in Employers Liability Claims

45.20 Scope and interpretation

(1) Subject to paragraph (2), this Section applies where—
  (a) the dispute is between an employee and his employer arising from a bodily injury sustained by the employee in the course of his employment; and
  (b) the claimant has entered into a funding arrangement of a type specified in rule 43.2(1)(k)(i).

(2) This Section does not apply—
  (a) where the dispute—
    (i) relates to a disease;
    (ii) relates to an injury sustained before 1st October 2004; or
    (iii) arises from a road traffic accident (as defined in rule 45.7(4)(a)); or
    (iv) relates to an injury to which Section V of this Part applies; or
  (b) to a claim—
    (i) which has been allocated to the small claims track; or
    (ii) not allocated to a track, but for which the small claims track is the normal track.

(3) For the purposes of this Section—
  (a) 'employee' has the meaning given to it by section 2(1) of the Employers' Liability (Compulsory Insurance) Act 1969; and
  (b) a reference to 'fees' is a reference to fees for work done under a conditional fee agreement or collective conditional fee agreement.

45.21 Percentage increase of solicitors' and counsel's fees

In the cases to which this Section applies, subject to rule 45.22 the percentage increase which is to be allowed in relation to solicitors' and counsel's fees is to be determined in accordance with rules 45.16 and 45.17, subject to the modifications that—

(a) the percentage increase which is to be allowed in relation to solicitors' fees under rule 45.16(b) is—
   (i) 27.5% if a membership organisation has undertaken to meet the claimant's liabilities for legal costs in accordance with section 30 of the Access to Justice Act 1999; and
   (ii) 25% in any other case; and
(b) the percentage increase which is to be allowed in relation to counsel's fees under rule 45.17(1)(b)(ii), (1)(c)(ii) or (1)(d) is 25%. ('membership organisation' is defined in rule 43.2(1)(n))

45.22 Alternative percentage increase

(1) In the cases to which this Section applies, rule 45.18(2)–(4) applies where—
   (a) the percentage increase of solicitors' fees to be allowed in accordance with rule 45.21 is 25% or 27.5%; or
   (b) the percentage increase of counsel's fees to be allowed is 25%.
(2) Where the percentage increase of fees is assessed by the court under rule 45.18(4) as applied by paragraph (1) above—
   (a) if the percentage increase is assessed as greater than 40% or less than 15%, the percentage increase to be allowed shall be that assessed by the court; and
   (b) if the percentage increase is assessed as no greater than 40% and no less than 15%—
      (i) the percentage increase to be allowed shall be 25% or 27.5% (as the case may be); and
      (ii) the costs of the application and assessment shall be paid by the applicant.

V Fixed Recoverable Success Fees in Employer's Liability Disease Claims

45.23 Scope and interpretation

(1) Subject to paragraph (2), this Section applies where—
   (a) the dispute is between an employee (or, if the employee is deceased, the employee's estate or dependants) and his employer (or a person alleged to be liable for the employer's alleged breach of statutory or common law duties of care); and
   (b) the dispute relates to a disease with which the employee is diagnosed that is alleged to have been contracted as a consequence of the employer's alleged breach of statutory or common law duties of care in the course of the employee's employment; and
   (c) the claimant has entered into a funding arrangement of a type specified in rule 43.2(1)(k)(i).

(2) This Section does not apply where—
  (a) the claimant sent a letter of claim to the defendant containing a summary of the facts on which the claim is based and main allegations of fault before 1st October 2005; or
  (b) rule 45.20(2)(b) applies.

(3) For the purposes of this Section—
  (a) rule 45.15(6) applies;
  (b) 'employee' has the meaning given to it by section 2(1) of the Employers' Liability (Compulsory Insurance) Act 1969;
  (c) 'Type A claim' means a claim relating to a disease or physical injury alleged to have been caused by exposure to asbestos;
  (d) 'Type B claim' means a claim relating to—
    (i) a psychiatric injury alleged to have been caused by work-related psychological stress;
    (ii) a work-related upper limb disorder which is alleged to have been caused by physical stress or strain, excluding hand/arm vibration injuries; and
  (e) 'Type C claim' means a claim relating to a disease not falling within either type A or type B.

(The Table annexed to the Practice Direction supplementing Part 45 contains a non-exclusive list of diseases within Type A and Type B)

45.24 Percentage increase of solicitors' fees

(1) In the cases to which this Section applies, subject to rule 45.26, the percentage increase which is to be allowed in relation to solicitors' fees is—
  (a) 100% if the claim concludes at trial; or
  (b) where—
    (i) the claim concludes before a trial has commenced; or
    (ii) the dispute is settled before a claim is issued,

  to be determined by rule 45.24(2).

(2) Where rule 45.24(1)(b) applies, the percentage increase which is to be allowed in relation to solicitors' fees is—
  (a) in type A claims—
    (i) 30% if a membership organisation has undertaken to meet the claimant's liabilities for legal costs in accordance with section 30 of the Access to Justice Act 1999; and
    (ii) 27.5% in any other case;
  (b) in type B claims, 100%; and
  (c) in type C claims—
    (i) 70% if a membership organisation has undertaken to meet the claimant's liabilities for legal costs in accordance with section 30 of the Access to Justice Act 1999; and
    (ii) 62.5% in any other case.

('Membership organisation' is defined in rule 43.2(1)(n))

45.25 Percentage increase of counsel's fees

(1) In the cases to which this Section applies, subject to rule 45.26, the percentage increase which is to be allowed in relation to counsel's fees is—
  (a) 100% if the claim concludes at trial; or
  (b) where—
    (i) the claim concludes before a trial has commenced; or
    (ii) the dispute is settled before a claim is issued,
    to be determined by rule 45.25(2).

(2) Where rule 45.25(1)(b) applies, the percentage increase which is to be allowed in relation to counsel's fees is—
  (a) if the claim has been allocated to the fast track, the amount shown in Table 6; and
  (b) if the claim has been allocated to the multi-track, the amount shown in Table 7.

(3) Where a trial period has been fixed, rules 45.17(2) to 45.17(5) apply for the purposes of determining the date fixed for the commencement of the trial.

45.26 Alternative percentage increase

(1) In cases to which this Section applies and subject to paragraph (2) below, rules 45.18(2) to (4) apply where the percentage increase is the amount allowed under rules 45.24 and 45.25.

Table 6 Claims allocated to the fast track

	If the claim concludes 14 days or less before the date fixed for the commencement of the trial	If the claim concludes more than 14 days before the date fixed for the commencement of the trial or before any such date has been fixed
Type A Claim	75%	27.5%
Type B Claim	100%	100%
Type C Claim	75%	62.5%

Table 7 Claims allocated to the multi-track

	If the claim concludes 21 days or less before the date fixed for the commencement of the trial	If the claim concludes more than 21 days before the date fixed for the commencement of the trial or before any such date has been fixed
Type A Claim	50%	27.5%
Type B Claim	100%	100%
Type C Claim	62.5%	62.5%

(2) For the purposes of this section, the sum of £250,000 shall be substituted for the sum of £500,000 in rules 45.18(2)(a) to (c).

(3) Where the percentage increase of fees is assessed by the court under rule 45.18(4), as applied by paragraph 1 above, the percentage increase to be allowed shall be the amount shown in Table 8.

(4) The percentage increase cannot be varied where the case concludes at trial.

Table 8 Percentage increase allowed under rule 45.18(4)

Type of claim	Amount allowed	
A	If the percentage increase is assessed as greater than 40% or less than 15%, the percentage increase that is assessed by the court	If the percentage increase is assessed as no greater than 40% and no less than 15%— (i) 27.5%; and (ii) the costs of the application and the assessment shall be paid by the applicant.
B	If the percentage increase is assessed as less than 75%, the percentage increase that is assessed by the court	If the percentage increase is assessed as no less than 75%— (i) 100%; and (ii) the costs of the application and the assessment shall be paid by the applicant.
C	If the percentage increase is assessed as greater than 75% or less than 50%, the percentage increase is assessed by the court	If the percentage increase is assessed as no greater than 75% and no less than 50%— (i) 62.5%; and (ii) the costs of the application and the assessment shall be paid by the applicant.

Part 46 Fast Track Trial Costs

46.1 Scope of this Part

(1) This Part deals with the amount of costs which the court may award as the costs of an advocate for preparing for and appearing at the trial of a claim in the fast track (referred to in this rule as 'fast track trial costs').

(2) For the purposes of this Part—

(a) 'advocate' means a person exercising a right of audience as a representative of, or on behalf of, a party;

(b) 'fast track trial costs' means the costs of a party's advocate for preparing for and appearing at the trial, but does not include—
   (i) any other disbursements; or
   (ii) any value added tax payable on the fees of a party's advocate; and
(c) 'trial' includes a hearing where the court decides an amount of money or the value of goods following a judgment under Part 12 (default judgment) or Part 14 (admissions) but does not include—
   (i) the hearing of an application for summary judgment under Part 24; or
   (ii) the court's approval of a settlement or other compromise under rule 21.10.

(Part 21 deals with claims made by or on behalf of, or against, children and patients)

46.2 Amount of fast track trial costs

(1) The following table shows the amount of fast track trial costs which the court may award (whether by summary or detailed assessment).

Value of the claim	Amount of fast track trial costs which the court may award
Up to £3000	£350
More than £3,000 but not more than £10,000	£500
More than £10,000	£750

(2) The court may not award more or less than the amount shown in the table except where—
   (a) it decides not to award any fast track trial costs; or
   (b) rule 46.3 applies,

   but the court may apportion the amount awarded between the parties to reflect their respective degrees of success on the issues at trial.

(3) Where the only claim is for the payment of money—
   (a) for the purpose of quantifying fast track trial costs awarded to a claimant, the value of the claim is the total amount of the judgment excluding—
      (i) interest and costs; and
      (ii) any reduction made for contributory negligence.
   (b) for the purpose of the quantifying fast track trial costs awarded to a defendant, the value of the claim is—
      (i) the amount specified in the claim form (excluding interest and costs);
      (ii) if no amount is specified, the maximum amount which the claimant reasonably expected to recover according to the statement of value included in the claim form under rule 16.3; or
      (iii) more than £10,000, if the claim form states that the claimant cannot reasonably say how much he expects to recover.

(4) Where the claim is only for a remedy other than the payment of money the value of the claim is deemed to be more than £3,000 but not more than £10,000, unless the court orders otherwise.

(5) Where the claim includes both a claim for the payment of money and for a remedy other than the payment of money, the value of the claim is deemed to be the higher of—

(a) the value of the money claim decided in accordance with paragraph (3); or

(b) the deemed value of the other remedy decided in accordance with paragraph (4),

unless the court orders otherwise.

(6) Where—

(a) a defendant has made a counterclaim against the claimant;

(b) the counterclaim has a higher value than the claim; and

(c) the claimant succeeds at trial both on his claim and the counterclaim,

for the purpose of quantifying fast track trial costs awarded to the claimant, the value of the claim is the value of the defendant's counterclaim calculated in accordance with this rule.

(Rule 20.4 sets out how a defendant may make a counterclaim)

46.3 Power to award more or less than the amount of fast track trial costs

(1) This rule sets out when a court may award—

(a) an additional amount to the amount of fast track trial costs shown in the table in rule 46.2(1); and

(b) less than those amounts.

(2) If—

(a) in addition to the advocate, a party's legal representative attends the trial;

(b) the court considers that it was necessary for a legal representative to attend to assist the advocate; and

(c) the court awards fast track trial costs to that party,

the court may award an additional £250 in respect of the legal representative's attendance at the trial.

('Legal representative' is defined in rule 2.3)

(2A) The court may in addition award a sum representing an additional liability.

(The requirements to provide information about a funding arrangement where a party wishes to recover any additional liability under a funding arrangement are set out in the costs practice direction)

('Additional liability' is defined in rule 43.2)

(3) If the court considers that it is necessary to direct a separate trial of an issue then the court may award an additional amount in respect of the separate trial but that amount is limited in accordance with paragraph (4) of this rule.

(4) The additional amount the court may award under paragraph 3 must not exceed two-thirds of the amount payable for that claim, subject to a minimum award of £350.

(5) Where the party to whom fast track trial costs are to be awarded is a litigant in person, the court will award—

(a) if the litigant in person can prove financial loss, two-thirds of the amount that would otherwise be awarded; or

(b) if the litigant in person fails to prove financial loss, an amount in respect of the time spent reasonably doing the work at the rate specified in the costs practice direction.

(6) Where a defendant has made a counterclaim against the claimant, and—

(a) the claimant has succeeded on his claim; and

(b) the defendant has succeeded on his counterclaim,

the court will quantify the amount of the award of fast track trial costs to which—

(i) but for the counterclaim, the claimant would be entitled for succeeding on his claim; and

(ii) but for the claim, the defendant would be entitled for succeeding on his counterclaim,

and make one award of the difference, if any, to the party entitled to the higher award of costs.

(7) Where the court considers that the party to whom fast track trial costs are to be awarded has behaved unreasonably or improperly during the trial, it may award that party an amount less than would otherwise be payable for that claim, as it considers appropriate.

(8) Where the court considers that the party who is to pay the fast track trial costs has behaved improperly during the trial the court may award such additional amount to the other party as it considers appropriate.

46.4 Fast track trial costs where there is more than one claimant or defendant

(1) Where the same advocate is acting for more than one party—

(a) the court may make only one award in respect of fast track trial costs payable to that advocate; and

(b) the parties for whom the advocate is acting are jointly entitled to any fast track trial costs awarded by the court.

(2) Where—

(a) the same advocate is acting for more than one claimant; and

(b) each claimant has a separate claim against the defendant,

the value of the claim, for the purpose of quantifying the award in respect of fast track trial costs is to be ascertained in accordance with paragraph (3).

(3) The value of the claim in the circumstances mentioned in paragraph (2) is—

(a) where the only claim of each claimant is for the payment of money—

(i) if the award of fast track trial costs is in favour of the claimants, the total amount of the judgment made in favour of all the claimants jointly represented; or

(ii) if the award is in favour of the defendant, the total amount claimed by the claimants,

and in either case, quantified in accordance with rule 46.2(3);

(b) where the only claim of each claimant is for a remedy other than the payment of money, deemed to be more than £3,000 but not more than £10,000; and

(c) where claims of the claimants include both a claim for the payment of money and for a remedy other than the payment of money, deemed to be—

(i) more than £3,000 but not more than £10,000; or

(ii) if greater, the value of the money claims calculated in accordance with sub-paragraph (a) above.

(4) Where—

(a) there is more than one defendant; and

(b) any or all of the defendants are separately represented,

the court may award fast track trial costs to each party who is separately represented.

(5) Where—

(a) there is more than one claimant; and

(b) a single defendant,

the court may make only one award to the defendant of fast track trial costs, for which the claimants are jointly and severally liable (GL).

(6) For the purpose of quantifying the fast track trial costs awarded to the single defendant under paragraph (5), the value of the claim is to be calculated in accordance with paragraph (3) of this rule.

Rule 48 Special Cases

48.2 Costs orders in favour of or against non-parties

(1) Where the court is considering whether to exercise its power under section 51 of the Supreme Court Act 1981 (costs are in the discretion of the court) to make a costs order in favour of or against a person who is not a party to proceedings—

(a) that person must be added as a party to the proceedings for the purposes of costs only; and

(b) he must be given a reasonable opportunity to attend a hearing at which the court will consider the matter further.

(2) This rule does not apply—

(a) where the court is considering whether to—

(i) make an order against the Legal Services Commission;

(ii) make a wasted costs order (as defined in 48.7); and

(b) in proceedings to which rule 48.1 applies (pre-commencement disclosure and orders for disclosure against a person who is not a party).

48.3 Amount of costs where costs are payable pursuant to a contract

(1) Where the court assesses (whether by the summary or detailed procedure) costs which are payable by the paying party to the receiving party under the terms of a contract, the costs payable under those terms are, unless the contract expressly provides otherwise, to be presumed to be costs which—
(a) have been reasonably incurred; and
(b) are reasonable in amount, and the court will assess them accordingly.

(The costs practice direction sets out circumstances where the court may order otherwise)

(2) This rule does not apply where the contract is between a solicitor and his client.

48.5 Costs where money is payable by or to a child or patient

(1) This rule applies to any proceedings where a party is a child or patient and—
(a) money is ordered or agreed to be paid to, or for the benefit of, that party; or
(b) money is ordered to be paid by him or on his behalf.

('Child' and 'patient' are defined in rule 2.3)

(2) The general rule is that—
(a) the court must order a detailed assessment of the costs payable by, or out of money belonging to, any party who is a child or patient; and
(b) on an assessment under paragraph (a), the court must also assess any costs payable to that party in the proceedings, unless—
(i) the court has issued a default costs certificate in relation to those costs under rule 47.11; or
(ii) the costs are payable in proceedings to which Section II of Part 45 applies.

(3) The court need not order detailed assessment of costs in the circumstances set out in the costs practice direction.

(4) Where—
(a) a claimant is a child or patient; and
(b) a detailed assessment has taken place under paragraph (2)(a), the only amount payable by the child or patient is the amount which the court certifies as payable.

(This rule applies to a counterclaim by or on behalf of a child or patient by virtue of rule 20.3)

48.6 Litigants in person

(1) This rule applies where the court orders (whether by summary assessment or detailed assessment) that the costs of a litigant in person are to be paid by any other person.

(2) The costs allowed under this rule must not exceed, except in the case of a disbursement, two thirds of the amount which would have been allowed if the litigant in person had been represented by a legal representative.

(3) The litigant in person shall be allowed—
   (a) costs for the same categories of—
      (i) work; and
      (ii) disbursements,
      which would have been allowed if the work had been done or the disbursements had been made by a legal representative on the litigant in person's behalf;
   (b) the payments reasonably made by him for legal services relating to the conduct of the proceedings; and
   (c) the costs of obtaining expert assistance in assessing the costs claim.
(4) The amount of costs to be allowed to the litigant in person for any item of work claimed shall be—
   (a) where the litigant can prove financial loss, the amount that he can prove he has lost for time reasonably spent on doing the work; or
   (b) where the litigant cannot prove financial loss, an amount for the time reasonably spent on doing the work at the rate set out in the practice direction.
(5) A litigant who is allowed costs for attending at court to conduct his case is not entitled to a witness allowance in respect of such attendance in addition to those costs.
(6) For the purposes of this rule, a litigant in person includes—
   (a) a company or other corporation which is acting without a legal representative; and
   (b) a barrister, solicitor, solicitor's employee or other authorised litigator (as defined in the Courts and Legal Services Act 1990) who is acting for himself.

II Costs Relating to Solicitors and other Legal Representatives

48.7 Personal liability of legal representative for costs—wasted costs orders

(1) This rule applies where the court is considering whether to make an order under section 51(6) of the Supreme Court Act 1981 (court's power to disallow or (as the case may be) order a legal representative to meet, 'wasted costs').
(2) The court must give the legal representative a reasonable opportunity to attend a hearing to give reasons why it should not make such an order.
(3) Omitted.
(4) When the court makes a wasted costs order, it must—
   (a) specify the amount to be disallowed or paid; or
   (b) direct a costs judge or a district judge to decide the amount of costs to be disallowed or paid.
(5) The court may direct that notice must be given to the legal representative's client, in such manner as the court may direct—
   (a) of any proceedings under this rule; or
   (b) of any order made under it against his legal representative.

(6) Before making a wasted costs order, the court may direct a costs judge or a district judge to inquire into the matter and report to the court.
(7) The court may refer the question of wasted costs to a costs judge or a district judge, instead of making a wasted costs order.

Part 52 Appeals

52.1 Scope and interpretation

(1) The rules in this Part apply to appeals to—
 (a) the civil division of the Court of Appeal;
 (b) the High Court; and
 (c) a county court.
(2) This Part does not apply to an appeal in detailed assessment proceedings against a decision of an authorised court officer.

(Rules 47.21 to 47.26 deal with appeals against a decision of an authorised court officer in detailed assessment proceedings)

(3) In this Part—
 (a) 'appeal' includes an appeal by way of case stated;
 (b) 'appeal court' means the court to which an appeal is made;
 (c) 'lower court' means the court, tribunal or other person or body from whose decision an appeal is brought;
 (d) 'appellant' means a person who brings or seeks to bring an appeal;
 (e) 'respondent' means—
  (i) a person other than the appellant who was a party to the proceedings in the lower court and who is affected by the appeal; and
  (ii) a person who is permitted by the appeal court to be a party to the appeal; and
 (f) 'appeal notice' means an appellant's or respondent's notice.
(4) This Part is subject to any rule, enactment or practice direction which sets out special provisions with regard to any particular category of appeal.

52.11 Hearing of appeals

(1) Every appeal will be limited to a review of the decision of the lower court unless—
 (a) a practice direction makes different provision for a particular category of appeal; or
 (b) the court considers that in the circumstances of an individual appeal it would be in the interests of justice to hold a re-hearing.
(2) Unless it orders otherwise, the appeal court will not receive—
 (a) oral evidence; or
 (b) evidence which was not before the lower court.

(3) The appeal court will allow an appeal where the decision of the lower court was—
  (a) wrong; or
  (b) unjust because of a serious procedural or other irregularity in the proceedings in the lower court.

(4) The appeal court may draw any inference of fact which it considers justified on the evidence.

(5) At the hearing of the appeal a party may not rely on a matter not contained in his appeal notice unless the appeal court gives permission.

52.12 Non-disclosure of Part 36 offers and payments

(1) The fact that a Part 36 offer or Part 36 payment has been made must not be disclosed to any judge of the appeal court who is to hear or determine—
  (a) an application for permission to appeal; or
  (b) an appeal,

  until all questions (other than costs) have been determined.

(2) Paragraph (1) does not apply if the Part 36 offer or Part 36 payment is relevant to the substance of the appeal.

(3) Paragraph (1) does not prevent disclosure in any application in the appeal proceedings if disclosure of the fact that a Part 36 offer or Part 36 payment has been made is properly relevant to the matter to be decided.

APPENDIX E

Extracts from Practice Directions to the Civil Procedure Rules 1998 (as amended)

PD 36 Practice Direction—Offers to Settle and Payments into Court

Part 36 offers and Part 36 payments

1.1 A written offer to settle a claim or part of a claim or any issue that arises in it made in accordance with the provisions of Part 36 is called:
(1) if made by way of a payment into court, a Part 36 payment; or
(2) if made otherwise, a Part 36 offer (including an offer under rule 36.2A).

1.2 A Part 36 offer or Part 36 payment has the costs and other consequences set out in rules 36.13, 36.14, 36.20 and 36.21.

1.3 An offer to settle which is not made in accordance with Part 36 will only have the consequences specified in that Part if the court so orders and will be given such weight on any issue as to costs as the court thinks appropriate.

Parties and Part 36 offers

2.1 A Part 36 offer, subject to paragraph 3 below, may be made by any party.

2.2 The party making an offer is the 'offeror' and the party to whom it is made is the 'offeree'.

2.3 A Part 36 offer may consist of a proposal to settle for a specified sum or for some other remedy.

2.4 A Part 36 offer is made when received by the offeree.

2.5 An improvement to a Part 36 offer is effective when its details are received by the offeree.

Parties and Part 36 payments

3.1 An offer to settle for a specified sum made by a defendant must, in order to comply with Part 36, be made by way of a Part 36 payment into court.

3.2 A Part 36 payment is made when the Part 36 payment notice is served on the claimant.

3.3 An increase to a Part 36 payment will be effective when notice of the increase is served on the claimant.

(For service of the Part 36 payment notice see rule 36.6(3) and (4))

3.4 A defendant who wishes to withdraw or reduce a Part 36 payment must obtain the court's permission to do so.

3.5 Permission may be obtained by making an application in accordance with Part 23 stating the reasons giving rise to the wish to withdraw or reduce the Part 36 payment.

Making a Part 36 payment

4.1 Except where paragraph 4.2 applies, to make a Part 36 payment in any court the defendant must—
(1) serve the Part 36 payment notice on the offeree;
(2) file at the court—
(a) a copy of the payment notice; and
(b) a certificate of service confirming service on the offeree; and
(3) send to the Court Funds Office—
(a) the payment, usually a cheque made payable to the Accountant General of the Supreme Court;
(b) a sealed copy of the claim form; and
(c) Court Funds Office form 100.

4.2 A litigant in person without a current account may, in a claim proceeding in a county court or District Registry, make a Part 36 payment by—
(1) lodging the payment in cash with the court;
(2) filing at the court—
(a) the Part 36 payment notice; and
(b) Court Funds Office form 100.

Part 36 offers and Part 36 payments—general provisions

5.1 A Part 36 offer or a Part 36 payment notice must:
(1) state that it is a Part 36 offer or that the payment into court is a Part 36 payment; and
(2) be signed by the offeror or his legal representative.

5.2 The contents of a Part 36 offer must also comply with the requirements of rule 36.5(3), (5) and (6).

5.3 The contents of a Part 36 payment notice must comply with rule 36.6(2) and, if rule 36.23 applies, with rule 36.23(3).

5.3A The contents of a Part 36 offer to which rule 36.2A applies must comply with the requirements of rule 36.2A(5).

5.4 A Part 36 offer or Part 36 payment will be taken to include interest unless it is expressly stated in the offer or the payment notice that interest is not included, in which case the details set out in rule 36.22(2) must be given.

5.5 Where a Part 36 offer is made by a company or other corporation, a person holding a senior position in the company or corporation may sign the offer on the offeror's behalf, but must state the position he holds.

5.6 Each of the following persons is a person holding a senior position:
(1) in respect of a registered company or corporation, a director, the treasurer, secretary, chief executive, manager or other officer of the company or corporation; and

(2) in respect of a corporation which is not a registered company, in addition to those persons set out in (1), the mayor, chairman, president, town clerk or similar officer of the corporation.

Clarification of Part 36 offer or payment

6.1 An offeree may apply to the court for an order requiring the offeror to clarify the terms of a Part 36 offer or Part 36 payment notice (a clarification order) where the offeror has failed to comply within 7 days with a request for clarification.

6.2 An application for a clarification order should be made in accordance with Part 23.

6.3 The application notice should state the respects in which the terms of the Part 36 offer or Part 36 payment notice, as the case may be, are said to need clarification.

Acceptance of a Part 36 offer or payment

7.1 The times for accepting a Part 36 offer or a Part 36 payment are set out in rules 36.11 and 36.12.

7.2 The general rule is that a Part 36 offer or Part 36 payment made more than 21 days before the start of the trial may be accepted within 21 days after it was made without the permission of the court. The costs consequences set out in rules 36.13 and 36.14 will then come into effect.

7.2A Where a Part 36 payment is made as part of a Part 36 offer made under rule 36.2A, the payment is ignored for the purposes of determining the times set out in rules 36.11 and 36.13.

7.3 A Part 36 offer or Part 36 payment made less than 21 days before the start of the trial cannot be accepted without the permission of the court unless the parties agree what the costs consequences of acceptance will be.

7.4 The permission of the court may be sought:

(1) before the start of the trial, by making an application in accordance with Part 23; and

(2) after the start of the trial, by making an application to the trial judge.

7.5 If the court gives permission it will make an order dealing with costs and may order that, in the circumstances, the costs consequences set out in rules 36.13 and 36.14 will apply.

7.6 Where a Part 36 offer or Part 36 payment is accepted in accordance with rule 36.11(1) or rule 36.12(1) the notice of acceptance must be sent to the offeror and filed with the court.

7.7 The notice of acceptance:

(1) must set out—

(a) the claim number; and

(b) the title of the proceedings,

(2) must identify the Part 36 offer or Part 36 payment notice to which it relates; and

(3) must be signed by the offeree or his legal representative (see paragraphs 5.5 and 5.6 above).

7.8 Where:

(1) the court's approval; or

(2) an order for payment of money out of court; or

(3) an order apportioning money in court—

(a) between the Fatal Accidents Act 1976 and the Law Reform (Miscellaneous Provisions) Act 1934; or

(b) between the persons entitled to it under the Fatal Accidents Act 1976, is required for acceptance of a Part 36 offer or Part 36 payment, application for the approval or the order should be made in accordance with Part 23.

7.9 The court will include in any order made under paragraph 7.8 above a direction for:

(1) the payment out of the money in court; and

(2) the payment of interest.

7.10 Unless the parties have agreed otherwise:

(1) interest accruing up to the date of acceptance will be paid to the offeror; and

(2) interest accruing as from the date of acceptance until payment out will be paid to the offeree.

7.11 A claimant may not accept a Part 36 payment or Part 36 offer made under rule 36.2A which is part of a defendant's offer to settle the whole of a claim consisting of both a money and a non-money claim unless at the same time he accepts the offer to settle the whole of the claim.

Therefore:

(1) if a claimant accepts a Part 36 payment or Part 36 offer made under rule 36.2A which is part of a defendant's offer to settle the whole of the claim; or

(2) if a claimant accepts a Part 36 offer which is part of a defendant's offer to settle the whole of the claim, the claimant will be deemed to have accepted the offer to settle the whole of the claim.

(See paragraph 8 below for the method of obtaining money out of court)

Payment out of court

8.1 To obtain money out of court following acceptance of a Part 36 payment, the claimant should—

(1) file a request for payment in Court Funds Office form 201 with the Court Funds Office; and

(2) file a copy of form 201 at the court.

8.2 The request for payment should contain the following details:

(1) where the party receiving the payment—

(a) is legally represented—

(i) the name, business address and reference of the legal representative; and
(ii) the name of the bank and the sort code number, the title of the account and the account number where the payment is to be transmitted, and

(2) where the party is acting in person—
(a) his name and address; and
(b) his bank account details as in (ii) above.

8.3 Where a trial is to take place at a different court to that where the case is proceeding, the claimant must also file notice of request for payment with the court where the trial is to take place.

8.4 Subject to paragraph 8.5(1) and (2), if a party does not wish the payment to be transmitted into his bank account or if he does not have a bank account, he may send a written request to the Accountant-General for the payment to be made to him by cheque.

8.5 Where a party seeking payment out of court has provided the necessary information, the payment:
(1) where a party is legally represented, must be made to the legal representative;
(2) if the party is not legally represented but is, or has been, in receipt of legal aid in respect of the proceedings and a notice to that effect has been filed, should be made to the Legal Aid Board by direction of the court;
(3) where a person entitled to money in court dies without having made a will and the court is satisfied—
(a) that no grant of administration of his estate has been made; and
(b) that the assets of his estate, including the money in court, do not exceed in value the amount specified in any order in force under section 6 of the Administration of Estates (Small Payments) Act 1965, may be ordered to be made to the person appearing to have the prior right to a grant of administration of the estate of the deceased, e.g. a widower, widow, child, father, mother, brother or sister of the deceased.

Foreign currency

9.1 Money may be paid into court in a foreign currency:
(1) where it is a Part 36 payment and the claim is in a foreign currency, or
(2) under a court order.

9.2 The court may direct that the money be placed in an interest bearing account in the currency of the claim or any other currency.

9.3 Where a Part 36 payment is made in a foreign currency and has not been accepted within 21 days, the defendant may apply for an order that the money be placed in an interest bearing account.

9.4 The application should be made in accordance with Part 23 and should state:
(1) that the payment has not been accepted in accordance with rule 36.11; and
(2) the type of currency on which interest is to accrue.

Compensation recovery

10.1 Where a defendant makes a Part 36 payment in respect of a claim for a sum or part of a sum:
(1) which falls under the heads of damage set out in column 1 of Schedule 2 of the Social Security (Recovery of Benefits) Act 1997 in respect of recoverable benefits received by the claimant as set out in column 2 of that Schedule; and
(2) where the defendant is liable to pay recoverable benefits to the Secretary of State, the defendant should obtain from the Secretary of State a certificate of recoverable benefits and file the certificate with the Part 36 payment notice.

10.2 If a defendant wishes to offer to settle a claim where he has applied for but not yet received a certificate of recoverable benefits, he may, provided that he makes a Part 36 payment not more than 7 days after he has received the certificate, make a Part 36 offer which will have the costs and other consequences set out in rules 36.13 and 36.20.

10.3 The Part 36 payment notice should state in addition to the requirements set out in rule 36.6(2):
(1) the total amount represented by the Part 36 payment (the gross compensation);
(2) that the defendant has reduced this sum by £ , in accordance with section 8 of and Schedule 2 to the Social Security (Recovery of Benefits) Act 1997, which was calculated as follows:
Name of benefit Amount
and
(3) that the amount paid in, being the sum of £ is the net amount after the deduction of the amount of benefit.

10.4 On acceptance of a Part 36 payment to which this paragraph relates, a claimant will receive the sum in court which will be net of the recoverable benefits.

10.5 In establishing at trial whether a claimant has bettered or obtained a judgment more advantageous than a Part 36 payment to which this paragraph relates, the court will base its decision on the gross sum specified in the Part 36 payment notice.

General

11.1 Where a party on whom a Part 36 offer, a Part 36 payment notice or a notice of acceptance is to be served is legally represented, the Part 36 offer, Part 36 payment notice and notice of acceptance must be served on the legal representative.

11.2 In a claim arising out of an accident involving a motor vehicle on a road or in a public place:
(1) where the damages claimed include a sum for hospital expenses; and
(2) the defendant or his insurer pays that sum to the hospital under section 157 of the Road Traffic Act 1988, the defendant must give notice of that payment to the court and all the other parties to the proceedings.

11.3 Money paid into court:
(1) as a Part 36 payment which is not accepted by the claimant; or
(2) under a court order;
will be placed after 21 days in a basic account (subject to paragraph 11.4 below) for interest to accrue.

11.4 Where money referred to in paragraph 11.3 above is paid in respect of a child or patient it will be placed in a special investment account for interest to accrue.
(A practice direction supplementing Part 21 contains information about the investment of money in court in respect of a child or patient)
(Practice directions supplementing Part 40 contain information about adjustment of the judgment sum in respect of recoverable benefits, and about structured settlements)
(A practice direction supplementing Part 41 contains information about provisional damages awards)

Personal injury claims for future pecuniary loss

12.1 A Part 36 offer to settle a claim for damages (whether in the form of a lump sum, periodical payments or both) for personal injury which includes a claim for future pecuniary loss must contain the details of the offer which are set out in rule 36.2A.

12.2 Section 2(4) of the Damages Act 1996 sets out the circumstances in which the continuity of periodical payments will be taken to be secure. Section 2(8) and (9) of the Act deal with the index-linking of periodical payments.

12.3 Except where otherwise stated in this Practice Direction, the rules in Part 36 will apply to offers to settle made under rule 36.2A as they apply to other Part 36 payments and to Part 36 offers.

PD 43–48 Practice Direction about Costs

Section 1 Introduction

1.1 This Practice Direction supplements Parts 43 to 48 of the Civil Procedure Rules. It applies to all proceedings to which those Parts apply.

1.2 Paragraphs 57.1 to 57.9 of this Practice Direction deal with various transitional provisions affecting proceedings about costs.

1.3 Attention is drawn to the powers to make orders about costs conferred on the Supreme Court and any county court by Section 51 of the Supreme Court Act 1981.

1.4 In these Directions:

'counsel' means a barrister or other person with a right of audience in relation to proceedings in the High Court or in the County Courts in which he is instructed to act.

'LSC' means Legal Services Commission.

'solicitor' means a solicitor of the Supreme Court or other person with a right of audience in relation to proceedings, who is conducting the claim or defence (as the case may be) on behalf of a party to the proceedings and, where the context admits, includes a patent agent.

1.5 In respect of any document which is required by these Directions to be signed by a party or his legal representative the Practice Direction supplementing Part 22 will apply as if the document in question was a statement of truth. (The Practice Direction supplementing Part 22 makes provision for cases in which a party is a child, a patient or a company or other corporation and cases in which a document is signed on behalf of a partnership.)

Section 2 Scope of costs rules and definitions

Rule 43.2 Definitions and application

2.1 Where the court makes an order for costs and the receiving party has entered into a funding arrangement as defined in rule 43.2, the costs payable by the paying party include any additional liability (also defined in rule 43.2) unless the court orders otherwise.

2.2 In the following paragraphs—

'funding arrangement', 'percentage increase', 'insurance premium', 'membership organisation' and 'additional liability' have the meanings given to them by rule 43.2.

A 'conditional fee agreement' is an agreement with a person providing advocacy or litigation services which provides for his fees and expenses, or part of them, to be payable only in specified circumstances, whether or not it provides for a success fee as mentioned in section 58(2)(b) of the Courts and Legal Services Act 1990.

'base costs' means costs other than the amount of any additional liability.

2.3 Rule 44.3A(1) provides that the court will not assess any additional liability until the conclusion of the proceedings or the part of the proceedings to which the funding arrangement relates. (As to the time when detailed assessment may be carried out see paragraph 27.1 below.)

2.4 For the purposes of the following paragraphs of this practice direction and rule 44.3A proceedings are concluded when the court has finally determined the matters in issue in the claim, whether or not there is an appeal. The making of an award of provisional damages under Part 41 will also be treated as a final determination of the matters in issue.

2.5 The court may order or the parties may agree in writing that, although the proceedings are continuing, they will nevertheless be treated as concluded.

Section 3 Model forms for claims for costs

Rule 43.3 Meaning of summary assessment

3.1 Rule 43.3 defines summary assessment. When carrying out a summary assessment of costs where there is an additional liability the court may assess the base costs alone, or the base costs and the additional liability.

3.2 Form N260 is a model form of Statement of Costs to be used for summary assessments.

3.3 Further details about Statements of Costs are given in paragraph 13.5 below.

Rule 43.4 Meaning of detailed assessment

3.4 Rule 43.4 defines detailed assessment. When carrying out a detailed assessment of costs where there is an additional liability the court will assess both the base costs and the additional liability, or, if the base costs have already been assessed, the additional liability alone.

3.6 Further details about bills of costs are given in the next section of these Directions and in paragraphs 28.1 to 49.1, below.

3.7 Precedents A, B, C and D in the Schedule of Costs Precedents and the next section of this Practice Direction all refer to a model form of bill of costs. The use of a model form is not compulsory, but is encouraged. A party wishing to rely upon a bill which departs from the model form should include in the background information of the bill an explanation for that departure.

3.8 In any order of the court (whether made before or after 26 April 1999) the word 'taxation' will be taken to mean 'detailed assessment' and the words 'to be taxed' will be taken to mean 'to be decided by detailed assessment' unless in either case the context otherwise requires.

Section 4 Form and contents of bills of costs

4.1 A bill of costs may consist of such of the following sections as may be appropriate:

(1) title page;
(2) background information;
(3) items of costs claimed under the headings specified in paragraph 4.6;
(4) summary showing the total costs claimed on each page of the bill;
(5) schedules of time spent on non-routine attendances; and
(6) the certificates referred to in paragraph 4.15.

4.2 Where it is necessary or convenient to do so, a bill of costs may be divided into two or more parts, each part containing sections (2), (3) and (4) above. A division into parts will be necessary or convenient in the following circumstances:

(1) Where the receiving party acted in person during the course of the proceedings (whether or not he also had a legal representative at that

time) the bill should be divided into different parts so as to distinguish between:

(a) the costs claimed for work done by the legal representative; and

(b) the costs claimed for work done by the receiving party in person.

(2) Where the receiving party was represented by different solicitors during the course of the proceedings, the bill should be divided into different parts so as to distinguish between the costs payable in respect of each solicitor.

(3) Where the receiving party obtained legal aid or LSC funding in respect of all or part of the proceedings the bill should be divided into separate parts so as to distinguish between:

(a) costs claimed before legal aid or LSC funding was granted;

(b) costs claimed after legal aid or LSC funding was granted; and

(c) any costs claimed after legal aid or LSC funding ceased.

(4) Where value added tax (VAT) is claimed and there was a change in the rate of VAT during the course of the proceedings, the bill should be divided into separate parts so as to distinguish between:

(a) costs claimed at the old rate of VAT; and

(b) costs claimed at the new rate of VAT.

(5) Where the bill covers costs payable under an order or orders under which there are different paying parties the bill should be divided into parts so as to deal separately with the costs payable by each paying party.

(6) Where the bill covers costs payable under an order or orders, in respect of which the receiving party wishes to claim interest from different dates, the bill should be divided to enable such interest to be calculated.

4.3 Where a party claims costs against another party and also claims costs against the LSC only for work done in the same period, the costs claimed against the LSC only can be claimed either in a separate part of the bill or in additional columns in the same part of the bill. Precedents C and D in the Schedule of Costs Precedents annexed to this Practice Direction show how bills should be drafted when costs are claimed against the LSC only.

4.4 The title page of the bill of costs must set out:

(1) the full title of the proceedings;

(2) the name of the party whose bill it is and a description of the document showing the right to assessment (as to which see paragraph 40.4, below);

(3) if VAT is included as part of the claim for costs, the VAT number of the legal representative or other person in respect of whom VAT is claimed;

(4) details of all legal aid certificates, LSC certificates and relevant amendment certificates in respect of which claims for costs are included in the bill.

4.5 The background information included in the bill of costs should set out:

(1) a brief description of the proceedings up to the date of the notice of commencement;

(2) a statement of the status of the solicitor or solicitor's employee in respect of whom costs are claimed and (if those costs are calculated on the basis of hourly rates) the hourly rates claimed for each such person. It should be noted that 'legal executive' means a Fellow of the Institute of Legal Executives. Other clerks, who are fee earners of equivalent experience, may be entitled to similar rates. It should be borne in mind that Fellows of the Institute of Legal Executives will have spent approximately 6 years in practice, and taken both general and specialist examinations. The Fellows have therefore acquired considerable practical and academic experience. Clerks without the equivalent experience of legal executives will normally be treated as being the equivalent of trainee solicitors and para-legals.

(3) a brief explanation of any agreement or arrangement between the receiving party and his solicitors, which affects the costs claimed in the bill.

4.6 The bill of costs may consist of items under such of the following heads as may be appropriate:

(1) attendances on the court and counsel up to the date of the notice of commencement;

(2) attendances on and communications with the receiving party;

(3) attendances on and communications with witnesses, including any expert witness;

(4) attendances to inspect any property or place for the purposes of the proceedings;

(5) attendances on and communications with other persons, including offices of public records;

(6) communications with the court and with counsel;

(7) work done on documents: preparing and considering documentation, including documentation relating to pre-action protocols where appropriate, work done in connection with arithmetical calculations of compensation and/or interest and time spent collating documents;

(8) work done in connection with negotiations with a view to settlement if not already covered in the heads listed above;

(9) attendances on and communications with London and other agents and work done by them;

(10) other work done which was of or incidental to the proceedings and which is not already covered in the heads listed above.

4.7 In respect of each of the heads of costs:

(1) 'communications' means letters out and telephone calls;

(2) communications, which are not routine communications, must be set out in chronological order;

(3) routine communications should be set out as a single item at the end of each head;

4.8 Routine communications are letters out, e-mails out and telephone calls which because of their simplicity should not be regarded as letters or e-mails of substance or telephone calls which properly amount to an attendance.

4.9 Each item claimed in the bill of costs must be consecutively numbered.

4.10 In each part of the bill of costs which claims items under head (1) (attendances on court and counsel) a note should be made of:

(1) all relevant events, including events which do not constitute chargeable items;

(2) any orders for costs which the court made (whether or not a claim is made in respect of those costs in this bill of costs).

4.11 The numbered items of costs may be set out on paper divided into columns. Precedents A, B, C and D in the Schedule of Costs Precedents annexed to this Practice Direction illustrate various model forms of bills of costs.

4.12 In respect of heads (2) to (10) in paragraph 4.6 above, if the number of attendances and communications other than routine communications is twenty or more, the claim for the costs of those items in that section of the bill of costs should be for the total only and should refer to a schedule in which the full record of dates and details is set out. If the bill of costs contains more than one schedule each schedule should be numbered consecutively.

4.13 The bill of costs must not contain any claims in respect of costs or court fees which relate solely to the detailed assessment proceedings other than costs claimed for preparing and checking the bill.

4.14 The summary must show the total profit costs and disbursements claimed separately from the total VAT claimed. Where the bill of costs is divided into parts the summary must also give totals for each part. If each page of the bill gives a page total the summary must also set out the page totals for each page.

4.15 The bill of costs must contain such of the certificates the texts of which are set out in Precedent F of the Schedule of Costs Precedents annexed to this Practice Direction, as are appropriate.

4.16 The following provisions relate to work done by solicitors:

(1) Routine letters out and routine telephone calls will in general be allowed on a unit basis of 6 minutes each, the charge being calculated by reference to the appropriate hourly rate. The unit charge for letters out will include perusing and considering the relevant letters in and no separate charge should be made for in-coming letters.

(2) E-mails received by solicitors will not normally be allowed. The court may, in its discretion, allow an actual time charge for preparation of e-mails sent by solicitors, which properly amount to attendances provided that the time taken has been recorded. The court may also, in its discretion, allow a sum in respect of routine e-mails sent to the client or others on a unit basis of 6 minutes each, the charge being calculated by reference to the appropriate hourly rate.

(3) Local travelling expenses incurred by solicitors will not be allowed. The definition of 'local' is a matter for the discretion of the court. While no

absolute rule can be laid down, as a matter of guidance, 'local' will, in general, be taken to mean within a radius of 10 miles from the court dealing with the case at the relevant time. Where travelling and waiting time is claimed, this should be allowed at the rate agreed with the client unless this is more than the hourly rate on the assessment.

(4) The cost of postage, couriers, out-going telephone calls, fax and telex messages will in general not be allowed but the court may exceptionally in its discretion allow such expenses in unusual circumstances or where the cost is unusually heavy.

(5) The cost of making copies of documents will not in general be allowed but the court may exceptionally in its discretion make an allowance for copying in unusual circumstances or where the documents copied are unusually numerous in relation to the nature of the case. Where this discretion is invoked the number of copies made, their purpose and the costs claimed for them must be set out in the bill.

(6) Agency charges as between a principal solicitor and his agent will be dealt with on the principle that such charges, where appropriate, form part of the principal solicitor's charges. Where these charges relate to head (1) in paragraph 4.6 (attendances at court and on counsel) they should be included in their chronological order in that head. In other cases they should be included in head (9) (attendances on London and other agents).

4.17 (1) Where a claim is made for a percentage increase in addition to an hourly rate or base fee, the amount of the increase must be shown separately, either in the appropriate arithmetic column or in the narrative column.

(2) Where a claim is made against the LSC only and includes enhancement and where a claim is made in family proceedings and includes a claim for uplift or general care and conduct, the amount of enhancement uplift and general care and conduct must be shown, in respect of each item upon which it is claimed, as a separate amount either in the appropriate arithmetic column or in the narrative column.

'Enhancement' means the increase in prescribed rates which may be allowed by a costs officer in accordance with the Legal Aid in Civil Proceedings (Remuneration) Regulations 1994 or the Legal Aid in Family Proceedings Regulations 1991.

Costs of preparing the bill

4.18 A claim may be made for the reasonable costs of preparing and checking the bill of costs.

Section 5 Special provisions relating to VAT

5.1 This section deals with claims for value added tax (VAT) which are made in respect of costs being dealt with by way of summary assessment or detailed assessment.

VAT registration number

5.2 The number allocated by HM Revenue and Customs to every person registered under the Value Added Tax Act 1983 (except a Government Department) must appear in a prominent place at the head of every statement, bill of costs, fee sheet, account or voucher on which VAT is being included as part of a claim for costs.

Entitlement to VAT on costs

5.3 VAT should not be included in a claim for costs if the receiving party is able to recover the VAT as input tax. Where the receiving party is able to obtain credit from HM Revenue and Customs for a proportion of the VAT as input tax, only that proportion which is not eligible for credit should be included in the claim for costs.

5.4 The receiving party has responsibility for ensuring that VAT is claimed only when the receiving party is unable to recover the VAT or a proportion thereof as input tax.

5.5 Where there is a dispute as to whether VAT is properly claimed the receiving party must provide a certificate signed by the solicitors or the auditors of the receiving party substantially in the form illustrated in Precedent F in the Schedule of Costs Precedents annexed to this Practice Direction. Where the receiving party is a litigant in person who is claiming VAT, reference should be made by him to HM Revenue and Customs and wherever possible a Statement to similar effect produced at the hearing at which the costs are assessed.

5.6 Where there is a dispute as to whether any service in respect of which a charge is proposed to be made in the bill is zero rated or exempt, reference should be made to HM Revenue and Customs and wherever possible the view of HM Revenue and Customs obtained and made known at the hearing at which the costs are assessed. Such application should be made by the receiving party. In the case of a bill from a solicitor to his own client, such application should be made by the client.

Form of bill of costs where VAT rate changes

5.7 Where there is a change in the rate of VAT, suppliers of goods and services are entitled by ss.88 (1) and 88(2) of the VAT Act 1994 in most circumstances to elect whether the new or the old rate of VAT should apply to a supply where the basic and actual tax points span a period during which there has been a change in VAT rates.

5.8 It will be assumed, unless a contrary indication is given in writing, that an election to take advantage of the provisions mentioned in paragraph 5.7 above and to charge VAT at the lower rate has been made. In any case in which an election to charge at the lower rate is not made, such a decision must be justified to the court assessing the costs.

Apportionment

5.9 All bills of costs, fees and disbursements on which VAT is included must be divided into separate parts so as to show work done before, on and after the date or dates from which any change in the rate of VAT takes effect. Where, however, a lump sum charge is made for work which spans a period during which there has been a change in VAT rates, and paragraphs 5.7 and 5.8 above do not apply, reference should be made to paragraphs 8 and 9 of Appendix F of Customs' Notice 700 (or any revised edition of that notice), a copy of which should be in the possession of every registered trader. If necessary, the lump sum should be apportioned. The totals of profit costs and disbursements in each part must be carried separately to the summary.

5.10 Should there be a change in the rate between the conclusion of a detailed assessment and the issue of the final costs certificate, any interested party may apply for the detailed assessment to be varied so as to take account of any increase or reduction in the amount of tax payable. Once the final costs certificate has been issued, no variation under this paragraph will be permitted.

Disbursements

5.11 Petty (or general) disbursements such as postage, fares etc which are normally treated as part of a solicitor's overheads and included in his profit costs should be charged with VAT even though they bear no tax when the solicitor incurs them. The cost of travel by public transport on a specific journey for a particular client where it forms part of the service rendered by a solicitor to his client and is charged in his bill of costs, attracts VAT.

5.12 Reference is made to the criteria set out in the VAT Guide (Customs and Excise Notice 700—1st August 1991 edition paragraph 83, or any revised edition of that Notice), as to expenses which are not subject to VAT. Charges for the cost of travel by public transport, postage, telephone calls and telegraphic transfers where these form part of the service rendered by the solicitor to his client are examples of charges which do not satisfy these criteria and are thus liable to VAT at the standard rate.

Legal Aid/LSC Funding

5.13 (1) VAT will be payable in respect of every supply made pursuant to a legal aid/LSC certificate where—
- (a) the person making the supply is a taxable person; and
- (b) the assisted person/LSC funded client—
  - (i) belongs in the United Kingdom or another member state of the European Union; and
  - (ii) is a private individual or receives the supply for non-business purposes.

(2) Where the assisted person/LSC funded client belongs outside the European Union, VAT is generally not payable unless the supply relates to land in the United Kingdom.

(3) For the purpose of sub-paragraphs (1) and (2), the place where a person belongs is determined by section 9 of the Value Added Tax Act 1994.

(4) Where the assisted person/LSC funded client is registered for VAT and the legal services paid for by the LSC are in connection with that person's business, the VAT on those services will be payable by the LSC only.

5.14 Any summary of costs payable by the LSC must be drawn so as to show the total VAT on Counsel's fees as a separate item from the VAT on other disbursements and the VAT on profit costs.

Tax invoice

5.15 A bill of costs filed for detailed assessment is always retained by the Court. Accordingly if a solicitor waives his solicitor and client costs and accepts the costs certified by the court as payable by the unsuccessful party in settlement, it will be necessary for a short statement as to the amount of the certified costs and the VAT thereon to be prepared for use as the tax invoice.

Vouchers

5.16 Where receipted accounts for disbursements made by the solicitor or his client are retained as tax invoices a photostat copy of any such receipted account may be produced and will be accepted as sufficient evidence of payment when disbursements are vouched.

Certificates

5.17 In a costs certificate payable by the LSC, the VAT on solicitor's costs, Counsel's fees and disbursements will be shown separately.

Litigants acting in person

5.18 Where a litigant acts in litigation on his own behalf he is not treated for the purposes of VAT as having supplied services and therefore no VAT is chargeable in respect of work done by that litigant (even where, for example, that litigant is a solicitor or other legal representative).

5.19 Consequently in the circumstances described in the preceding paragraph, a bill of costs presented for agreement or assessment should not claim any VAT which will not be allowed on assessment.

Government departments

5.20 On an assessment between parties, where costs are being paid to a Government department in respect of services rendered by its legal staff, VAT should not be added.

Section 6 Estimates of costs

6.1 This section sets out certain steps which parties and their legal representatives must take in order to keep the parties informed about their potential liability in respect of costs and in order to assist the court to decide what, if any, order to make about costs and about case management.

6.2 (1) In this section an 'estimate of costs' means—

(a) an estimate of base costs (including disbursements) already incurred; and

(b) an estimate of base costs (including disbursements) to be incurred, which a party intends to seek to recover from any other party under an order for costs if he is successful in the case.

('Base costs' are defined in paragraph 2.2 of this Practice Direction)

(2) A party who intends to recover an additional liability (defined in rule 43.2) need not reveal the amount of that liability in the estimate.

6.3 The court may at any stage in a case order any party to file an estimate of costs and to serve copies of the estimate on all other parties. The court may direct that the estimate be prepared in such a way as to demonstrate the likely effects of giving or not giving a particular case management direction which the court is considering, for example a direction for a split trial or for the trial of a preliminary issue. The court may specify a time limit for filing and serving the estimate. However, if no time limit is specified the estimate should be filed and served within 28 days of the date of the order.

6.4 (1) When—

(a) a party to a claim which is outside the financial scope of the small claims track files an allocation questionnaire; or

(b) a party to a claim which is being dealt with on the fast track or the multi track, or under Part 8, files a pre-trial check list (listing questionnaire), he must also file an estimate of costs and serve a copy of it on every other party, unless the court otherwise directs. Where a party is represented, the legal representative must in addition serve an estimate on the party he represents.

(2) Where a party is required to file and serve a new estimate of costs in accordance with Rule 44.15(3), if that party is represented the legal representative must in addition serve the new estimate on the party he represents.

(3) This paragraph does not apply to litigants in person.

6.5 An estimate of costs should be substantially in the form illustrated in Precedent H in the Schedule of Costs Precedents annexed to the Practice Direction.

6.5A (1) If there is a difference of 20% or more between the base costs claimed by a receiving party on detailed assessment and the costs shown in an estimate of costs filed by that party, the receiving party must provide a statement of the reasons for the difference with his bill of costs.

(2) If a paying party—

(a) claims that he reasonably relied on an estimate of costs filed by a receiving party; or

(b) wishes to rely upon the costs shown in the estimate in order to dispute the reasonableness or proportionality of the costs claimed.

The paying party must serve a statement setting out his case in this regard in his points of dispute.

('Relevant person' is defined in paragraph 32.10(1) of the Costs Practice Direction)

6.6 (1) On an assessment of the costs of a party, the court may have regard to any estimate previously filed by that party, or by any other party in the same proceedings. Such an estimate may be taken into account as a factor among others, when assessing the reasonableness and proportionality of any costs claimed.

(2) In particular, where—

(a) there is a difference of 20% or more between the base costs claimed by a receiving party and the costs shown in an estimate of costs filed by that party; and

(b) it appears to the court that—

(i) the receiving party has not provided a satisfactory explanation for that difference; or

(ii) the paying party reasonably relied on the estimate of costs,

the court may regard the difference between the costs claimed and the costs shown in the estimate as evidence that the costs claimed are unreasonable or disproportionate.

Directions Relating to Part 44—General Rules About Costs

Section 7 Solicitor's duty to notify client: Rule 44.2

7.1 For the purposes of rule 44.2 'client' includes a party for whom a solicitor is acting and any other person (for example, an insurer, a trade union or the LSC) who has instructed the solicitor to act or who is liable to pay his fees.

7.2 Where a solicitor notifies a client of an order under that rule, he must also explain why the order came to be made.

7.3 Although rule 44.2 does not specify any sanction for breach of the rule the court may, either in the order for costs itself or in a subsequent order, require the solicitor to produce to the court evidence showing that he took reasonable steps to comply with the rule.

Section 8 Court's discretion and circumstances to be taken into account when exercising its discretion as to costs: Rule 44.3

8.1 Attention is drawn to the factors set out in this rule which may lead the court to depart from the general rule stated in rule 44.3(2) and to make a different order about costs.

8.2 In a probate claim where a defendant has in his defence given notice that he requires the will to be proved in solemn form (see paragraph 8.3 of the practice direction supplementing Part 57), the court will not make an order for costs against the defendant unless it appears that there was no reasonable ground for opposing the will. The term 'probate claim' is defined in rule 57.1(2).

8.3 (1) The court may make an order about costs at any stage in a case.

(2) In particular the court may make an order about costs when it deals with any application, makes any order or holds any hearing and that order about costs may relate to the costs of that application, order or hearing.

(3) Rule 44.3A(1) provides that the court will not assess any additional liability until the conclusion of the proceedings or the part of the proceedings to which the funding arrangement relates. (Paragraphs 2.4 and 2.5 above explain when proceedings are concluded. As to the time when detailed assessment may be carried out see paragraphs 28.1, below)

8.4 In deciding what order to make about costs the court is required to have regard to all the circumstances including any payment into court or admissible offer to settle made by a party which is drawn to the court's attention (whether or not it is made in accordance with Part 36). Where a claimant has made a Part 36 offer and fails to obtain a judgment which is more advantageous than that offer, that circumstance alone will not lead to a reduction in the costs awarded to the claimant under this rule.

8.5 There are certain costs orders which the court will commonly make in proceedings before trial. The following table sets out the general effect of these orders. The table is not an exhaustive list of the orders which the court may make.

Term	Effect
• Costs • Costs in any event	The party in whose favour the order is made is entitled to the costs in respect of the part of the proceedings to which the order relates, whatever other costs orders are made in the proceedings.
• Costs in the case • Costs in the application	The party in whose favour the court makes an order for costs at the end of the proceedings is entitled to his costs of the part of the proceedings to which the order relates.
• Costs reserved	The decision about costs is deferred to a later occasion, but if no later order is made the costs will be costs in the case.
• Claimant's/defendant's costs in case/application	If the party in whose favour the costs order is made is awarded costs at the end of the proceedings, that party is entitled to his costs of the part of the proceedings to which the order relates. If any other party is awarded costs at the end of the proceedings, the party in whose favour the final costs order is made is not liable to pay the costs of any other party in respect of the part of the proceedings to which the order relates.

Term	Effect
• Costs thrown away	Where, for example, a judgment or order is set aside, the party in whose favour the costs order is made is entitled to the costs which have been incurred as a consequence. This includes the costs of— (a) preparing for and attending any hearing at which the judgment or order which has been set aside was made; (b) preparing for and attending any hearing to set aside the judgment or order in question; (c) preparing for and attending any hearing at which the court orders the proceedings or the part in question to be adjourned; (d) any steps taken to enforce a judgment or order which has subsequently been set aside.
• Costs of and caused by	Where, for example, the court makes this order on an application to amend a statement of case, the party in whose favour the costs order is made is entitled to the costs of preparing for and attending the application and the costs of any consequential amendment to his own statement of case.
• Costs here and below	The party in whose favour the costs order is made is entitled not only to his costs in respect of the proceedings in which the court makes the order but also to his costs of the proceedings in any lower court. In the case of an appeal from a Divisional Court the party is not entitled to any costs incurred in any court below the Divisional Court.
• No order as to costs • Each party to pay his own costs	Each party is to bear his own costs of the part of the proceedings to which the order relates whatever costs order the court makes at the end of the proceedings.

8.6 Where, under rule 44.3(8), the court orders an amount to be paid before costs are assessed—
(1) the order will state that amount; and
(2) if no other date for payment is specified in the order, rule 44.8 (Time for complying with an order for costs) will apply.

Fees of counsel

8.7 (1) This paragraph applies where the court orders the detailed assessment of the costs of a hearing at which one or more counsel appeared for a party.
(2) Where an order for costs states the opinion of the court as to whether or not the hearing was fit for the attendance of one or more counsel, a costs officer conducting a detailed assessment of costs to which that order relates will have regard to the opinion stated.
(3) The court will generally express an opinion only where:
(a) the paying party asks it to do so;
(b) more than one counsel appeared for a party; or
(c) the court wishes to record its opinion that the case was not fit for the attendance of counsel.

Fees payable to conveyancing counsel appointed by the court to assist it

8.8 (1) Where the court refers any matter to the conveyancing counsel of the court the fees payable to counsel in respect of the work done or to be done will be assessed by the court in accordance with rule 44.3.
(2) An appeal from a decision of the court in respect of the fees of such counsel will be dealt with under the general rules as to appeals set out in Part 52. If the appeal is against the decision of an authorised court officer, it will be dealt with in accordance with rules 47.20 to 47.23.

Section 9 Costs orders relating to funding arrangements: Rule 44.3A

9.1 Under an order for payment of 'costs' the costs payable will include an additional liability incurred under a funding arrangement.

9.2 (1) If before the conclusion of the proceedings the court carries out a summary assessment of the base costs it may identify separately the amount allowed in respect of: solicitors' charges; counsels' fees; other disbursements; and any value added tax (VAT). (Sections 13 and 14 of this Practice Direction deal with summary assessment)
(2) If an order for the base costs of a previous application or hearing did not identify separately the amounts allowed for solicitor's charges, counsel's fees and other disbursements, a court which later makes an assessment of an additional liability may apportion the base costs previously ordered.

Section 10 Limits on recovery under funding arrangements: Rule 44.3B

10.1 In a case to which rule 44.3B(1)(c) or (d) applies the party in default may apply for relief from the sanction. He should do so as quickly as possible after he becomes aware of the default. An application, supported by evidence, should be made under Part 23 to a costs judge or district judge of the court which is dealing with the case. (Attention is drawn to rules 3.8 and 3.9 which deal with sanctions and relief from sanctions)

10.2 Where the amount of any percentage increase recoverable by counsel may be affected by the outcome of the application, the solicitor issuing the application must serve on counsel a copy of the application notice and notice of the hearing as soon as practicable and in any event at least 2 days before the hearing. Counsel may make written submissions or may attend and make oral submissions at the hearing.

(Paragraph 1.4 contains definitions of the terms 'counsel' and 'solicitor')

Section 11 Factors to be taken into account in deciding the amount of costs: Rule 44.5

11.1 In applying the test of proportionality the court will have regard to rule 1.1(2)(c). The relationship between the total of the costs incurred and the financial value of the claim may not be a reliable guide. A fixed percentage cannot be applied in all cases to the value of the claim in order to ascertain whether or not the costs are proportionate.

11.2 In any proceedings there will be costs which will inevitably be incurred and which are necessary for the successful conduct of the case. Solicitors are not required to conduct litigation at rates which are uneconomic. Thus in a modest claim the proportion of costs is likely to be higher than in a large claim, and may even equal or possibly exceed the amount in dispute.

11.3 Where a trial takes place, the time taken by the court in dealing with a particular issue may not be an accurate guide to the amount of time properly spent by the legal or other representatives in preparation for the trial of that issue.

11.4 Where a party has entered into a funding arrangement the costs claimed may, subject to rule 44.3B, include an additional liability.

11.5 In deciding whether the costs claimed are reasonable and (on a standard basis assessment) proportionate, the court will consider the amount of any additional liability separately from the base costs.

11.6 In deciding whether the base costs are reasonable and (if relevant) proportionate the court will consider the factors set out in rule 44.5.

11.7 Subject to paragraph 17.8(2), when the court is considering the factors to be taken into account in assessing an additional liability, it will have regard to the facts and circumstances as they reasonably appeared to the solicitor or counsel when the funding arrangement was entered into and at the time of any variation of the arrangement.

11.8 (1) In deciding whether a percentage increase is reasonable relevant factors to be taken into account may include:

(a) the risk that the circumstances in which the costs, fees or expenses would be payable might or might not occur;

(b) the legal representative's liability for any disbursements;

(c) what other methods of financing the costs were available to the receiving party.

(2) Omitted.

11.9 A percentage increase will not be reduced simply on the ground that, when added to base costs which are reasonable and (where relevant) proportionate, the total appears disproportionate.

11.10 In deciding whether the cost of insurance cover is reasonable, relevant factors to be taken into account include:

(1) where the insurance cover is not purchased in support of a conditional fee agreement with a success fee, how its cost compares with the likely cost of funding the case with a conditional fee agreement with a success fee and supporting insurance cover;

(2) the level and extent of the cover provided;

(3) the availability of any pre-existing insurance cover;

(4) whether any part of the premium would be rebated in the event of early settlement;

(5) the amount of commission payable to the receiving party or his legal representatives or other agents.

11.11 Where the court is considering a provision made by a membership organisation, rule 44.3B(1):

(b) provides that any such provision which exceeds the likely cost to the receiving party of the premium of an insurance policy against the risk of incurring a liability to pay the costs of other parties to the proceedings is not recoverable. In such circumstances the court will, when assessing the additional liability, have regard to the factors set out in paragraph 11.10 above, in addition to the factors set out in rule 44.5.

Section 12 Procedure for assessing costs: Rule 44.7

12.1 Where the court does not order fixed costs (or no fixed costs are provided for) the amount of costs payable will be assessed by the court. This rule allows the court making an order about costs either:

(a) to make a summary assessment of the amount of the costs; or

(b) to order the amount to be decided in accordance with Part 47 (a detailed assessment).

12.2 An order for costs will be treated as an order for the amount of costs to be decided by a detailed assessment unless the order otherwise provides.

12.3 Whenever the court awards costs to be assessed by way of detailed assessment it should consider whether to exercise the power in rule 44.3(8) (Courts Discretion as to Costs) to order the paying party to pay such sum of money as it thinks just on account of those costs.

Section 13 Summary assessment: general provisions

13.1 Whenever a court makes an order about costs which does not provide for fixed costs to be paid the court should consider whether to make a summary assessment of costs.

13.2 The general rule is that the court should make a summary assessment of the costs:

(1) at the conclusion of the trial of a case which has been dealt with on the fast track, in which case the order will deal with the costs of the whole claim; and

(2) at the conclusion of any other hearing, which has lasted not more than one day, in which case the order will deal with the costs of the application or matter to which the hearing related. If this hearing disposes of the claim, the order may deal with the costs of the whole claim;

(3) in hearings in the Court of Appeal to which Paragraph 14 of the Practice Direction supplementing Part 52 (Appeals) applies; unless there is good reason not to do so e.g. where the paying party shows substantial grounds for disputing the sum claimed for costs that cannot be dealt with summarily or there is insufficient time to carry out a summary assessment.

13.3 The general rule in paragraph 13.2 does not apply to a mortgagee's costs incurred in mortgage possession proceedings or other proceedings relating to a mortgage unless the mortgagee asks the court to make an order for his costs to be paid by another party. Paragraphs 50.3 and 50.4 deal in more detail with costs relating to mortgages.

13.4 Where an application has been made and the parties to the application agree an order by consent without any party attending, the parties should agree a figure for costs to be inserted in the consent order or agree that there should be no order for costs. If the parties cannot agree the costs position, attendance on the appointment will be necessary but, unless good reason can be shown for the failure to deal with costs as set out above, no costs will be allowed for that attendance.

13.5 (1) It is the duty of the parties and their legal representatives to assist the judge in making a summary assessment of costs in any case to which paragraph 13.2 above applies, in accordance, with the following paragraphs.

(2) Each party who intends to claim costs must prepare a written statement of the costs he intends to claim showing separately in the form of a schedule:

(a) the number of hours to be claimed;
(b) the hourly rate to be claimed;
(c) the grade of fee earner;
(d) the amount and nature of any disbursement to be claimed, other than counsel's fee for appearing at the hearing;
(e) the amount of solicitor's costs to be claimed for attending or appearing at the hearing;
(f) the fees of counsel to be claimed in respect of the hearing; and
(g) any value added tax (VAT) to be claimed on these amounts.

(3) The statement of costs should follow as closely as possible Form N260 and must be signed by the party or his legal representative. Where a litigant is an assisted person or is a LSC funded client or is represented by a solicitor in the litigant's employment the statement of costs need not include the certificate appended at the end of Form N260.

(4) The statement of costs must be filed at court and copies of it must be served on any party against whom an order for payment of those costs is intended to be sought. The statement of costs should be filed and the copies of it should be served as soon as possible and in any event not less than 24 hours before the date fixed for the hearing.

(5) Where the litigant is or may be entitled to claim an additional liability the statement filed and served need not reveal the amount of that liability.

13.6 The failure by a party, without reasonable excuse, to comply with the foregoing paragraphs will be taken into account by the court in deciding what order to make about the costs of the claim, hearing or application, and about the costs of any further hearing or detailed assessment hearing that may be necessary as a result of that failure.

13.7 If the court makes a summary assessment of costs at the conclusion of proceedings the court will specify separately:

(1) the base costs, and if appropriate, the additional liability allowed as solicitor's charges, counsel's fees, other disbursements and any VAT; and

(2) the amount which is awarded under Part 46 (Fast Track Trial Costs).

13.8 The court awarding costs cannot make an order for a summary assessment of costs by a costs officer. If a summary assessment of costs is appropriate but the court awarding costs is unable to do so on the day, the court must give directions as to a further hearing before the same judge.

13.9 The court will not make a summary assessment of the costs of a receiving party who is an assisted person or LSC funded client.

13.10 A summary assessment of costs payable by an assisted person or LSC funded client is not by itself a determination of that person's liability to pay those costs (as to which see rule 44.17 and paragraphs 21.1 to 23.17 of this Practice Direction).

13.11 (1) The court will not make a summary assessment of the costs of a receiving party who is a child or patient within the meaning of Part 21 unless the solicitor acting for the child or patient has waived the right to further costs (see paragraph 51.1 below).

(2) The court may make a summary assessment of costs payable by a child or patient.

13.12 (1) Attention is drawn to rule 44.3A which prevents the court from making a summary assessment of an additional liability before the conclusion of the proceedings or the part of the proceedings to which the funding arrangement relates. Where this applies, the court should nonetheless make a summary assessment of the base costs of the hearing or application unless there is a good reason not to do so.

(2) Where the court makes a summary assessment of the base costs all statements of costs and costs estimates put before the judge will be retained on the court file.

13.13 The court will not give its approval to disproportionate and unreasonable costs. Accordingly:

(a) When the amount of the costs to be paid has been agreed between the parties the order for costs must state that the order is by consent.

(b) If the judge is to make an order which is not by consent, the judge will, so far as possible, ensure that the final figure is not disproportionate and/or unreasonable having regard to Part 1 of the CPR. The judge will retain this responsibility notwithstanding the absence of challenge to individual items in the make-up of the figure sought. The fact that the paying party is not disputing the amount of costs can however be taken as some indication that the amount is proportionate and reasonable. The judge will therefore intervene only if satisfied that the costs are so disproportionate that it is right to do so.

Section 14 Summary assessment where costs claimed include an additional liability

Orders made before the conclusion of the proceedings

14.1 The existence of a conditional fee agreement or other funding arrangement within the meaning of rule 43.2 is not by itself a sufficient reason for not carrying out a summary assessment.

14.2 Where a legal representative acting for the receiving party has entered into a conditional fee agreement the court may summarily assess all the costs (other than any additional liability).

14.3 Where costs have been summarily assessed an order for payment will not be made unless the court has been satisfied that in respect of the costs claimed, the receiving party is at the time liable to pay to his legal representative an amount equal to or greater than the costs claimed. A statement in the form of the certificate appended at the end of Form N260 may be sufficient proof of liability. The giving of information under rule 44.15 (where that rule applies) is not sufficient.

14.4 The court may direct that any costs, for which the receiving party may not in the event be liable, shall be paid into court to await the outcome of the case, or shall not be enforceable until further order, or it may postpone the receiving party's right to receive payment in some other way.

Orders made at the conclusion of the proceedings

14.5 Where there has been a trial of one or more issues separately from other issues, the court will not normally order detailed assessment of the additional liability until all issues have been tried unless the parties agree.

14.6 Rule 44.3A(2) sets out the ways in which the court may deal with the assessment of the costs where there is a funding arrangement. Where the court makes a summary assessment of the base costs:
(1) The order may state separately the base costs allowed as (a) solicitor's charges, (b) counsel's fees, (c) any other disbursements and (d) any VAT;
(2) the statements of costs upon which the judge based his summary assessment will be retained on the court file.

14.7 Where the court makes a summary assessment of an additional liability at the conclusion of proceedings, that assessment must relate to the whole of the proceedings; this will include any additional liability relating to base costs allowed by the court when making a summary assessment on a previous application or hearing.

14.8 Paragraph 13.13 applies where the parties are agreed about the total amount to be paid by way of costs, or are agreed about the amount of the base costs that will be paid. Where they disagree about the additional liability the court may summarily assess that liability or make an order for a detailed assessment.

14.9 In order to facilitate the court in making a summary assessment of any additional liability at the conclusion of the proceedings the party seeking such costs must prepare and have available for the court a bundle of documents which must include—
(1) a copy of every notice of funding arrangement (Form N251) which has been filed by him;
(2) a copy of every estimate and statement of costs filed by him;
(3) a copy of the risk assessment prepared at the time any relevant funding arrangement was entered into and on the basis of which the amount of the additional liability was fixed.

Section 15 Costs on the small claims track and fast track: Rule 44.9

15.1 (1) Before a claim is allocated to one of those tracks the court is not restricted by any of the special rules that apply to that track.
(2) Where a claim has been allocated to one of those tracks, the special rules which relate to that track will apply to work done before as well as after allocation save to the extent (if any) that an order for costs in respect of that work was made before allocation.
(3) (i) This paragraph applies where a claim, issued for a sum in excess of the normal financial scope of the small claims track, is allocated to that track only because an admission of part of the claim by the defendant reduces the amount in dispute to a sum within the normal scope of that track.
(See also paragraph 7.4 of the practice direction supplementing CPR Part 26)
(ii) On entering judgment for the admitted part before allocation of the balance of the claim the court may allow costs in respect of the proceedings down to that date.

Section 16 Costs following allocation and reallocation: Rule 44.11

16.1 This paragraph applies where the court is about to make an order to re-allocate a claim from the small claims track to another track.

16.2 Before making the order to re-allocate the claim, the court must decide whether any party is to pay costs to any other party down to the date of the order to re-allocate in accordance with the rules about costs contained in Part 27 (The Small Claims Track).

16.3 If it decides to make such an order about costs, the court will make a summary assessment of those costs in accordance with that Part.

Section 17 Costs-only proceedings: Rule 44.12A

17.1 A claim form under this rule should not be issued in the High Court unless the dispute to which the agreement relates was of such a value or type that had proceedings been begun they would have been commenced in the High Court.

17.2 A claim form which is to be issued in the High Court at the Royal Courts of Justice will be issued in the Supreme Court Costs Office.

17.3 Attention is drawn to rule 8.2 (in particular to paragraph (b)(ii)) and to rule 44.12A(3). The claim form must:

(1) identify the claim or dispute to which the agreement to pay costs relates;

(2) state the date and terms of the agreement on which the claimant relies;

(3) set out or have attached to it a draft of the order which the claimant seeks;

(4) state the amount of the costs claimed; and,

(5) state whether the costs are claimed on the standard or indemnity basis. If no basis is specified the costs will be treated as being claimed on the standard basis.

17.4 The evidence to be filed and served with the claim form under Rule 8.5 must include copies of the documents on which the claimant relies to prove the defendant's agreement to pay costs.

17.5 A costs judge or a district judge has jurisdiction to hear and decide any issue which may arise in a claim issued under this rule irrespective of the amount of the costs claimed or of the value of the claim to which the agreement to pay costs relates. A costs officer may make an order by consent under paragraph 17.7, or an order dismissing a claim under paragraph 17.9 below.

17.6 When the time for filing the defendant's acknowledgement of service has expired, the claimant may by letter request the court to make an order in the terms of his claim, unless the defendant has filed an acknowledgement of service stating that he intends to contest the claim or to seek a different order.

17.7 Rule 40.6 applies where an order is to be made by consent. An order may be made by consent in terms which differ from those set out in the claim form.

17.8 (1) An order for costs made under this rule will be treated as an order for the amount of costs to be decided by a detailed assessment to which Part 47 and the practice directions relating to it apply. Rule 44.4(4) (determination of basis of assessment) also applies to the order.

(2) In cases in which an additional liability is claimed, the costs judge or district judge should have regard to the time when and the extent to which the claim has been settled and to the fact that the claim has been settled without the need to commence proceedings.

17.9 (1) For the purposes of rule 44.12A(4)(b)—

(a) a claim will be treated as opposed if the defendant files an acknowledgment of service stating that he intends to contest the making of an order for costs or to seek a different remedy; and

(b) a claim will not be treated as opposed if the defendant files an acknowledgment of service stating that he disputes the amount of the claim for costs.

(2) An order dismissing the claim will be made as soon as an acknowledgment of service opposing the claim is filed. The dismissal of a claim under rule 44.12A(4) does not prevent the claimant from issuing another claim form under Part 7 or Part 8 based on the agreement or alleged agreement to which the proceedings under this rule related.

17.10 (1) Rule 8.9 (which provides that claims issued under Part 8 shall be treated as allocated to the multi-track) shall not apply to claims issued under this rule. A claim issued under this rule may be dealt with without being allocated to a track.

(2) Rule 8.1(3) and Part 24 do not apply to proceedings brought under rule 44.12A.

17.11 Nothing in this rule prevents a person from issuing a claim form under Part 7 or Part 8 to sue on an agreement made in settlement of a dispute where that agreement makes provision for costs, nor from claiming in that case an order for costs or a specified sum in respect of costs.

Section 18 Court's powers in relation to misconduct: Rule 44.14

18.1 Before making an order under rule 44.14 the court must give the party or legal representative in question a reasonable opportunity to attend a hearing to give reasons why it should not make such an order.

18.2 Conduct before or during the proceedings which gave rise to the assessment which is unreasonable or improper includes steps which are calculated to prevent or inhibit the court from furthering the overriding objective.

18.3 Although rule 44.14(3) does not specify any sanction for breach of the obligation imposed by the rule the court may, either in the order under paragraph (2) or in a subsequent order, require the solicitor to produce to the court evidence that he took reasonable steps to comply with the obligation.

Section 19 Providing information about funding arrangements: Rule 44.15

19.1 (1) A party who wishes to claim an additional liability in respect of a funding arrangement must give any other party information about that claim if he is to recover the additional liability. There is no requirement to specify the amount of the additional liability separately nor to state how it is calculated until it falls to be assessed. That principle is reflected in rules 44.3A and 44.15, in the following paragraphs and in Sections 6, 13, 14 and 31 of this Practice Direction. Section 6 deals with estimates of costs, Sections 13 and 14 deal with summary assessment and Section 31 deals with detailed assessment.

(2) In the following paragraphs a party who has entered into a funding arrangement is treated as a person who intends to recover a sum representing an additional liability by way of costs.

(3) Attention is drawn to paragraph 57.9 of this Practice Direction which sets out time limits for the provision of information where a funding arrangement is entered into between 31 March and 2 July 2000 and proceedings relevant to that arrangement are commenced before 3 July 2000.

Method of giving information

19.2 (1) In this paragraph, 'claim form' includes petition and application notice, and the notice of funding to be filed or served is a notice containing the information set out in Form N251.

(2) (a) A claimant who has entered into a funding arrangement before starting the proceedings to which it relates must provide information to the court by filing the notice when he issues the claim form.

(b) He must provide information to every other party by serving the notice. If he serves the claim form himself he must serve the notice with the claim form. If the court is to serve the claim form, the court will also serve the notice if the claimant provides it with sufficient copies for service.

(3) A defendant who has entered into a funding arrangement before filing any document:

(a) must provide information to the court by filing notice with his first document. A 'first document' may be an acknowledgement of service, a defence, or any other document, such as an application to set aside a default judgment;

(b) must provide information to every party by serving notice. If he serves his first document himself he must serve the notice with that document. If the court is to serve his first document the court will also serve the notice if the defendant provides it with sufficient copies for service.

(4) In all other circumstances a party must file and serve notice within 7 days of entering into the funding arrangement concerned.

(5) There is no requirement in this Practice Direction for the provision of information about funding arrangements before the commencement of proceedings. Such provision is however recommended and may be required by a pre-action protocol.

Notice of change of information

19.3 (1) Rule 44.15 imposes a duty on a party to give notice of change if the information he has previously provided is no longer accurate. To comply he must file and serve notice containing the information set out in Form N251. Rule 44.15(3) may impose other duties in relation to new estimates of costs.

(2) Further notification need not be provided where a party has already given notice:

(a) that he has entered into a conditional fee agreement with a legal representative and during the currency of that agreement either of them enters into another such agreement with an additional legal representative; or

(b) of some insurance cover, unless that cover is cancelled or unless new cover is taken out with a different insurer.

(3) Part 6 applies to the service of notices.

(4) The notice must be signed by the party or by his legal representative.

Information which must be provided

19.4 (1) Unless the court otherwise orders, a party who is required to supply information about a funding arrangement must state whether he has—

entered into a conditional fee agreement which provides for a success fee within the meaning of section 58(2) of the Courts and Legal Services Act 1990;

taken out an insurance policy to which section 29 of the Access to Justice Act 1999 applies;

made an arrangement with a body which is prescribed for the purpose of section 30 of that Act or more than one of these.

(2) Where the funding arrangement is a conditional fee agreement, the party must state the date of the agreement and identify the claim or claims to which it relates (including Part 20 claims if any).

(3) Where the funding arrangement is an insurance policy, the party must state the name and address of the insurer, the policy number and the date of the policy, and must identify the claim or claims to which it relates (including Part 20 claims if any).

(4) Where the funding arrangement is by way of an arrangement with a relevant body the party must state the name of the body and set out the date and terms of the undertaking it has given and must identify the claim or claims to which it relates (including Part 20 claims if any).

(5) Where a party has entered into more than one funding arrangement in respect of a claim, for example a conditional fee agreement and an insurance policy, a single notice containing the information set out in Form N251 may contain the required information about both or all of them.

19.5 Where the court makes a Group Litigation Order, the court may give directions as to the extent to which individual parties should provide information in accordance with rule 44.15.

(Part 19 deals with Group Litigation Orders)

Section 20 Procedure where legal representative wishes to recover from his client an agreed percentage increase which has been disallowed or reduced on assessment: Rule 44.16

20.1 (1) Attention is drawn to Regulation 3(2)(b) of the Conditional Fee Agreements Regulations 2000 and to Regulation 5(2)(b) of the Collective Conditional Fee Agreements Regulations 2000, which provide that some or all of a success fee ceases to be payable in certain circumstances.

(2) Rule 44.16 allows the court to adjourn a hearing at which the legal representative acting for the receiving party applies for an order that a disallowed amount should continue to be payable under the agreement.

20.2 In the following paragraphs 'counsel' means counsel who has acted in the case under a conditional fee agreement which provides for a success fee. A reference to counsel includes a reference to any person who appeared as an advocate in the case and who is not a partner or employee of the solicitor or firm which is conducting the claim or defence (as the case may be) on behalf of the receiving party.

Procedure following summary assessment

20.3 (1) If the court disallows any amount of a legal representative's percentage increase, the court will, unless sub-paragraph (2) applies, give directions to enable an application to be made by the legal representative for the disallowed amount to be payable by his client, including, if appropriate, a direction that the application will be determined by a costs judge or district judge of the court dealing with the case.

(2) The court that has made the summary assessment may then and there decide the issue whether the disallowed amount should continue to be payable, if:

(a) the receiving party and all parties to the relevant agreement consent to the court doing so;

(b) the receiving party (or, if corporate, an officer) is present in court; and

(c) the court is satisfied that the issue can be fairly decided then and there.

Procedure following detailed assessment

20.4 (1) Where detailed assessment proceedings have been commenced, and the paying party serves points of dispute (as to which see Section 34 of this Practice Direction), which show that he is seeking a reduction in any percentage increase charged by counsel on his fees, the solicitor acting for the receiving party must within 3 days of service deliver to counsel a copy of the relevant points of dispute and the bill of costs or the relevant parts of the bill.

(2) Counsel must within 10 days thereafter inform the solicitor in writing whether or not he will accept the reduction sought or some other reduction. Counsel may state any points he wishes to have made in a reply to the points of dispute, and the solicitor must serve them on the paying party as or as part of a reply.

(3) Counsel who fails to inform the solicitor within the time limits set out above will be taken to accept the reduction unless the court otherwise orders.

20.5 Where the paying party serves points of dispute seeking a reduction in any percentage increase charged by a legal representative acting for the receiving party, and that legal representative intends, if necessary, to apply for an order that any amount of the percentage disallowed as against the paying party shall continue to be payable by his client, the solicitor acting for the receiving party must, within 14 days of service of the points of dispute, give to his client a clear written explanation of the nature of the relevant point of dispute and the effect it will have if it is upheld in whole or in part by the court, and of the client's right to attend any subsequent hearings at court when the matter is raised.

20.6 Where the solicitor acting for a receiving party files a request for a detailed assessment hearing it must if appropriate, be accompanied by a certificate signed by him stating:

(1) that the amount of the percentage increase in respect of counsel's fees or solicitor's charges is disputed;

(2) whether an application will be made for an order that any amount of that increase which is disallowed should continue to be payable by his client;

(3) that he has given his client an explanation in accordance with paragraph 20.5; and

(4) whether his client wishes to attend court when the amount of any relevant percentage increase may be decided.

20.7 (1) The solicitor acting for the receiving party must within 7 days of receiving from the court notice of the date of the assessment hearing, notify his client, and if appropriate, counsel, in writing of the date, time and place of the hearing.

(2) Counsel may attend or be represented at the detailed assessment hearing and may make oral or written submissions.

20.8 (1) At the detailed assessment hearing, the court will deal with the assessment of the costs payable by one party to another, including the amount of the percentage increase, and give a certificate accordingly.

(2) The court may decide the issue whether the disallowed amount should continue to be payable under the relevant conditional fee agreement without an adjournment if:

(a) the receiving party and all parties to the relevant agreement consent to the court deciding the issue without an adjournment;
(b) the receiving party (or, if corporate, an officer or employee who has authority to consent on behalf of the receiving party) is present in court; and
(c) the court is satisfied that the issue can be fairly decided without an adjournment.

(3) In any other case the court will give directions and fix a date for the hearing of the application.

Section 21 Application of costs rules: Rule 44.17

21.1 Rule 44.17(b) excludes the costs rules to the extent that regulations under the Legal Aid Act 1988 make different provision. The primary examples of such regulations are the regulations providing prescribed rates (with or without enhancement).

21.2 Rule 44.17(a) also excludes the procedure for the detailed assessment of costs in cases to which Section 11 of the Access to Justice Act 1999 applies, whether it applies in whole or in part. In these excluded cases the procedure for determination of costs is set out in Section 22 of this Practice Direction.

21.3 Section 11 of the Access to Justice Act 1999 provides special protection against liability for costs for litigants who receive funding by the LSC (Legal Services Commission) as part of the Community Legal Service. Any costs ordered to be paid by a LSC funded client must not exceed the amount which is reasonable for him to pay having regard to all the circumstances including:
(a) the financial resources of all the parties to the proceedings; and
(b) their conduct in connection with the dispute to which the proceedings relate.

21.4 In this Practice Direction 'cost protection' means the limit on costs awarded against a LSC funded client set out in Section 11(1) of the Access to Justice Act 1999.
'partner' has the meaning given by the Community Legal Service (Costs) Regulations 2000.

21.5 Whether or not cost protection applies depends upon the 'level of service' for which funding was provided by the LSC in accordance with the Funding Code approved under section 9 of the Access to Justice Act 1999. The levels of service referred to are:
(1) Legal Help—advice and assistance about a legal problem, not including representation or advocacy in proceedings.
(2) Help at Court—advocacy at a specific hearing, where the advocate is not formally representing the client in the proceedings.
(3) Family Mediation.
(4) Legal Representation—representation in actual or contemplated proceedings. Legal Representation can take the form of Investigative

Help (limited to investigating the merits of a potential claim) or Full Representation.

(5) Approved Family Help—this can take the form of Help with Mediation (legal advice in support of the family mediation process) or General Family Help (help negotiating a settlement to a family dispute without recourse to adversarial litigation).

(6) Support Funding—partial funding in expensive cases that are primarily being funded privately, under or with a view to a conditional fee agreement. Support Funding can take the form of Investigative Support (equivalent to Investigative Help) or Litigation Support (equivalent to Full Representation).

21.6 Levels of service (4) (5) and (6) are provided under a certificate (similar to a legal aid certificate). The certificate will state which level of service is covered. Where there are proceedings, a copy of the certificate will be lodged with the court.

21.7 Cost protection does not apply where:

(1) the LSC funded client receives Help at Court;

(2) the LSC funded client receives Litigation Support (but see further, paragraph 21.8);

(3) the LSC funded client receives Investigative Support (except where the proceedings for which Investigative Support was given are not pursued after the certificate is discharged). Investigative Support will not normally cover the issue of proceedings (except for disclosure), but cost protection may be relevant if the defendant seeks an assessment of pre-action costs;

(4) the LSC funded client receives Legal Help only i.e. where the solicitor is advising, but not representing a litigant in person. However, where the LSC funded client receives Legal Help e.g. to write a letter before action, but later receives Legal Representation or Approved Family Help in respect of the same dispute, cost protection does apply to all costs incurred by the receiving party in the funded proceedings or prospective proceedings.

21.8 Where cost protection does not apply, the court may award costs in the normal way. In the case of Litigation Support, costs that are not covered by the LSC funded client's insurance are usually payable by the LSC rather than the funded client, and the court should order accordingly (see Regulation 6 of the Community Legal Service (Cost Protection) Regulations 2000).

21.9 Where work is done before the issue of a certificate, cost protection does not apply to those costs, except where:

(1) pre-action Legal Help is given and the LSC funded client subsequently receives Legal Representation or Approved Family Help in the same dispute; or

(2) where urgent work is undertaken immediately before the grant of an emergency certificate when no emergency application could be made as

the LSC's offices were closed, provided that the solicitor seeks an emergency certificate at the first available opportunity and the certificate is granted.

21.10 If a LSC funded client's certificate is revoked, costs protection does not apply to work done before or after revocation.

21.11 If a LSC funded client's certificate is discharged, costs protection only applies to costs incurred before the date on which funded services ceased to be provided under the certificate. This may be a date before the date on which the certificate is formally discharged by the LSC (Burridge v Stafford: Khan v Ali [2000] 1 WLR 927, [1999] 4 All ER 660 C.A.).

Assessing an LSC funded client's resources

21.12 The first £100,000 of the value of the LSC funded client's interest in the main or only home is disregarded when assessing his or her financial resources for the purposes of S.11 and cannot be the subject of any enforcement process by the receiving party. The receiving party cannot apply for an order to sell the LSC funded client's home, but could secure the debt against any value exceeding £100,000 by way of a charging order.

21.13 The court may only take into account the value of the LSC funded client's clothes, household furniture, tools and implements of trade to the extent that it considers that having regard to the quantity or value of the items, the circumstances are exceptional.

21.14 The LSC funded client's resources include the resources of his partner, unless the partner has a contrary interest in the dispute in respect of which funded services are provided.

21.15 (1) Where a LSC funded client is acting in a representative, fiduciary or official capacity, the court shall not take the personal resources of the party into account for the purposes of either a Section 11 order or costs against the Commission, but shall have regard to the value of any property or estate or the amount of any fund out of which the party is entitled to be indemnified, and may also have regard to the resources of any persons who are beneficially interested in the property, estate or fund.

(2) Similarly, where a party is acting as a litigation friend to a client who is a child or a patient, the court shall not take the personal resources of the litigation friend into account in assessing the resources of the client.

(3) The purpose of this provision is to ensure that any liability is determined with reference to the value of the property or fund being used to pay for the litigation, and the financial position of those who may benefit from or rely on it.

Costs against the LSC

21.16 Regulation 5 of the Community Legal Service (Cost Protection) Regulations 2000 governs when costs can be awarded against the LSC. This provision only applies where cost protection applies and the costs ordered to be paid by the LSC funded client do not fully meet the costs that would have been ordered to be paid by him if cost protection did not apply.

21.17 In this Section and the following two Sections of this Practice Direction 'non-funded party' means a party to proceedings who has not received LSC funded services in relation to these proceedings under a legal aid certificate or a certificate issued under the LSC Funding Code other than a certificate which has been revoked.

21.18 The following criteria set out in Regulation 5 must be satisfied before the LSC can be ordered to pay the whole or any part of the costs incurred by a non-funded party:

(1) the proceedings are finally decided in favour of a non-funded party;
(2) unless there is good reason for delay (and the application for funded services was made on or after 3 December 2001) the non-funded party provides written notice of intention to seek an order against the LSC within three months of the making of the section 11(1) costs order;
(3) the court is satisfied that it is just and equitable in the circumstances that provision for the costs should be made out of public funds; and
(4) where costs are incurred in a court of first instance, the following additional criteria must also be met:
    (i) the proceedings were instituted by the LSC funded client;
    (ii) the non-funded party is an individual; and
    (iii) the non-funded party will suffer severe financial hardship unless the order is made.

('Section 11(1) costs order' is defined in paragraph 22.1, below)

21.19 In determining whether conditions (3) and (4) are satisfied, the court shall take into account the resources of the non-funded party and his partner, unless the partner has a contrary interest.

Effect of appeals

21.20 (1) An order for costs can only be made against the LSC when the proceedings (including any appeal) are finally decided. Therefore, where a court of first instance decides in favour of a non-funded party and an appeal lies, any order made against the LSC shall not take effect unless:
    (a) where permission to appeal is required, the time limit for permission to appeal expires, without permission being granted;
    (b) where permission to appeal is granted or is not required, the time limit for appeal expires without an appeal being brought.

(2) Accordingly, if the LSC funded client appeals, any earlier order against the LSC can never take effect. If the appeal is unsuccessful, an application can be made to the appeal court for a fresh order.

Section 22 Orders for costs to which Section 11 of the Access to Justice Act 1999 applies

22.1 In this Practice Direction: 'order for costs to be determined' means an order for costs to which Section 11 of the Access to Justice Act 1999 applies under which the amount of costs payable by the LSC funded client is to be determined by a costs judge or district judge under Section 23 of this Practice Direction.

'order specifying the costs payable' means an order for costs to which Section 11 of the Act applies and which specifies the amount which the LSC funded client is to pay.

'full costs' means, where an order to which Section 11 of the Act applies is made against a LSC funded client, the amount of costs which that person would, had cost protection not applied, have been ordered to pay.

'determination proceedings' means proceedings to which paragraphs 22.1 to 22.10 apply.

'Section 11(1) costs order' means an order for costs to be determined or an order specifying the costs payable other than an order specifying the costs payable which was made in determination proceedings.

'statement of resources' means:

(1) a statement, verified by a statement of truth, made by a party to proceedings setting out:
   (a) his income and capital and financial commitments during the previous year and, if applicable, those of his partner;
   (b) his estimated future financial resources and expectations and, if applicable, those of his partner ('partner' is defined in paragraph 21.4, above);
   (c) a declaration that he and, if applicable, his partner, has not deliberately foregone or deprived himself of any resources or expectations;
   (d) particulars of any application for funding made by him in connection with the proceedings; and,
   (e) any other facts relevant to the determination of his resources; or
(2) a statement, verified by a statement of truth, made by a client receiving funded services, setting out the information provided by the client under Regulation 6 of the Community Legal Service (Financial) Regulations 2000, and stating that there has been no significant change in the client's financial circumstances since the date on which the information was provided or, as the case may be, details of any such change.

'Regional Director' means any Regional Director appointed by the LSC and any member of his staff authorised to act on his behalf.

22.2 Regulations 8 to 13 of the Community Legal Service (Costs) Regulations 2000 as amended set out the procedure for seeking costs against a funded client and the LSC. The effect of these Regulations is set out in this section and the next section of this Practice Direction.

22.3 As from 5 June 2000, Regulations 9 to 13 of the Community Legal Service (Costs) Regulations 2000 as amended also apply to certificates issued under the Legal Aid Act 1988 where costs against the assisted person fall to be assessed under Regulation 124 of the Civil Legal Aid (General) Regulations 1989. In this section and the next section of this Practice Direction the expression 'LSC funded client' includes an assisted person (defined in rule 43.2).

22.4 Regulation 8 of the Community Legal Service (Costs) Regulations 2000 as amended provides that a party intending to seek an order for costs against a LSC funded client may at any time file and serve on the LSC funded client a statement of resources. If that statement is served 7 or more days before a date fixed for a hearing at which an order for costs may be made, the LSC funded client must also make a statement of resources and produce it at the hearing.

22.5 If the court decides to make an order for costs against a LSC funded client to whom cost protection applies it may either:
- (1) make an order for costs to be determined; or
- (2) make an order specifying the costs payable.

22.6 If the court makes an order for costs to be determined it may also:
- (1) state the amount of full costs; or
- (2) make findings of facts, e.g., concerning the conduct of all the parties which are to be taken into account by the court in the subsequent determination proceedings.

22.7 The court will not make an order specifying the costs payable unless:
- (1) it considers that it has sufficient information before it to decide what amount is a reasonable amount for the LSC funded client to pay in accordance with Section 11 of the Act; and
- (2) either:
  - (a) the order also states the amount of full costs; or
  - (b) the court considers that it has sufficient information before it to decide what amount is a reasonable amount for the LSC funded client to pay in accordance with Section 11 of the Act and is satisfied that, if it were to determine the full costs at that time, they would exceed the amounts specified in the order.

22.8 Where an order specifying the costs payable is made and the LSC funded client does not have cost protection in respect of all of the costs awarded in that order, the order must identify the sum payable (if any) in respect of which the LSC funded client has cost protection and the sum payable (if any) in respect of which he does not have cost protection.

22.9 The court cannot make an order under Regulations 8 to 13 of the Community Legal Service (Costs) Regulations 2000 as amended except in proceedings to which the next section of this Practice Direction applies.

Section 23 Determination proceedings and similar proceedings under the Community Legal Service (Costs) Regulations 2000

23.1 This section of this Practice Direction deals with:
- (1) proceedings subsequent to the making of an order for costs to be determined;

(2) variations in the amount stated in an order specifying the amount of costs payable; and

(3) the late determination of costs under an order for costs to be determined;

(4) appeals in respect of determination.

23.2 In this section of this Practice Direction 'appropriate court office' means:

(1) the district registry or county court in which the case was being dealt with when the Section 11(1) order was made, or to which it has subsequently been transferred; or

(2) in all other cases, the Supreme Court Costs Office.

23.2A (1) This paragraph applies where the appropriate office is any of the following county courts:

Barnet, Bow, Brentford, Bromley, Central London, Clerkenwell, Croydon, Edmonton, Ilford, Kingston, Lambeth, Mayors and City of London, Romford, Shoreditch, Uxbridge, Wandsworth, West London, Willesden and Woolwich.

(2) Where this paragraph applies:

(i) a receiving party seeking an order specifying costs payable by an LSC funded client and/or by the Legal Services Commission under this section must file his application in the Supreme Court Costs Office and, for all purposes relating to that application, the Supreme Court Costs Office will be treated as the appropriate office in that case; and

(ii) unless an order is made transferring the application to the Supreme Court Costs Office as part of the High Court, an appeal from any decision made by a costs judge shall lie to the Designated Civil Judge for the London Group of County Courts or such judge as he shall nominate. The appeal notice and any other relevant papers should be lodged at the Central London Civil Justice Centre.

23.3 (1) A receiving party seeking an order specifying costs payable by an LSC funded client and/or by the LSC may within 3 months of an order for costs to be determined, file in the appropriate court office an application in Form N244 accompanied by:

(a) the receiving party's bill of costs (unless the full costs have already been determined);

(b) the receiving party's statement of resources (unless the court is determining an application against a costs order against the LSC and the costs were not incurred in the court of first instance); and

(c) if the receiving party intends to seek costs against the LSC, written notice to that effect.

(2) If the LSC funded client's liability has already been determined and is less than the full costs, the application will be for costs against the LSC only. If the LSC funded client's liability has not yet been determined, the receiving party must indicate if costs will be sought against the LSC if the funded client's liability is determined as less than the full costs. (The LSC

funded client's certificate will contain the addresses of the LSC funded client, his solicitor, and the relevant Regional Office of the LSC.)

23.4 The receiving party must file the above documents in the appropriate court office and (where relevant) serve copies on the LSC funded client and the Regional Director. In respect of applications for funded services made before 3 December 2001 a failure to file a request within the 3 months time limit specified in Regulation 10(2) is an absolute bar to the making of a costs order against the LSC. Where the application for funded services was made on or after 3 December 2001 the court does have power to extend the 3 months time limit, but only if the applicant can show good reason for the delay.

23.5 On being served with the application, the LSC funded client must respond by filing a statement of resources and serving a copy of it on the receiving party (and the Regional Director where relevant) within 21 days. The LSC funded client may also file and serve written points disputing the bill within the same time limit. (Under rule 3.1 the court may extend or shorten this time limit.)

23.6 If the LSC funded client fails to file a statement of resources without good reason, the court will determine his liability (and the amount of full costs if relevant) and need not hold an oral hearing for such determination.

23.7 When the LSC funded client files a statement or the 21 day period for doing so expires, the court will fix a hearing date and give the relevant parties at least 14 days notice. The court may fix a hearing without waiting for the expiry of the 21 day period if the application is made only against the LSC.

23.8 Determination proceedings will be listed for hearing before a costs judge or district judge. The determination of the liability on the LSC funded client will be listed as a private hearing.

23.9 Where the LSC funded client does not have cost protection in respect of all of the costs awarded, the order made by the costs judge or district judge must in addition to specifying the costs payable, identify the full costs in respect of which cost protection applies and the full costs in respect of which cost protection does not apply.

23.10 The Regional Director may appear at any hearing at which a costs order may be made against the LSC. Instead of appearing, he may file a written statement at court and serve a copy on the receiving party. The written statement should be filed and a copy served, not less than 7 days before the hearing.

Variation of an order specifying the costs payable

23.11 (1) This paragraph applies where the amount stated in an order specifying the costs payable plus the amount ordered to be paid by the LSC is less than the full costs to which cost protection applies.

(2) The receiving party may apply to the court for a variation of the amount which the LSC funded client is required to pay on the ground that there has been a significant change in the client's circumstances since the date of the order.

23.12 On an application under paragraph 23.11, where the order specifying the costs payable does not state the full costs:

(1) the receiving party must file with his application the receiving party's statement of resources and bill of costs and copies of these documents should be served with the application;

(2) the LSC funded client must respond to the application by making a statement of resources which must be filed at court and served on the receiving party within 21 days thereafter. The LSC funded client may also file and serve written points disputing the bill within the same time limit;

(3) the court will, when determining the application assess the full costs identifying any part of them to which cost protection does apply and any part of them to which cost protection does not apply.

23.13 On an application under paragraph 23.11 the order specifying the costs payable may be varied as the court thinks fit. That variation must not increase:

(1) the amount of any costs ordered to be paid by the LSC; and

(2) the amount payable by the LSC funded client, to a sum which is greater than the amount of the full costs plus the costs of the application.

23.14 (1) Where an order for costs to be determined has been made but the receiving party has not applied, within the 3-month time limit under paragraph 23.2, the receiving party may apply on any of the following grounds for a determination of the amount which the funded client is required to pay:

(a) there has been a significant change in the funded client's circumstances since the date of the order for costs to be determined; or

(b) material additional information about the funded client's financial resources is available which could not with reasonable diligence have been obtained by the receiving party at the relevant time; or

(c) there were other good reasons for the failure by the receiving party to make an application within the time limit.

(2) An application for costs payable by the LSC cannot be made under this paragraph.

23.15 (1) Where the receiving party has received funded services in relation to the proceedings, the LSC may make an application under paragraphs 23.11 and 23.14 above.

(2) In respect of an application under paragraph 23.11 made by the LSC, the LSC must file and serve copies of the documents described in paragraph 23.12(1).

23.16 An application under paragraph 23.11, 23.14 and 23.15 must be commenced before the expiration of 6 years from the date on which the court made the order specifying the costs payable, or (as the case may be) the order for costs to be determined.

23.17 Applications under paragraphs 23.11, 23.14 and 23.15 should be made in the appropriate court office and should be made in Form N244 to be listed for a hearing before a costs judge or district judge.

Appeals

23.18 (1) Save as mentioned above any determination made under Regulation 9 or 10 of the Costs Regulations is final (Regulation 11(1)). Any party with a financial interest in the assessment of the full costs, other than a funded party, may appeal against that assessment in accordance with CPR Part 52 (Regulation 11(2) and CPR rule 47.20).

(2) The receiving party or the Commission may appeal on a point of law against the making of a costs order against the Commission, against the amount of costs the Commission is required to pay or against the court's refusal to make such an order (Regulation 11(4)).

Directions Relating to Part 45—Fixed Costs

Section 24 Fixed costs in small claims

24.1 Under Rule 27.14 the costs which can be awarded to a claimant in a small claims track case include the fixed costs payable under Part 45 attributable to issuing the claim.

24.2 Those fixed costs shall be the sum of:

(a) the fixed commencement costs calculated in accordance with Table 1 of Rule 45.2; and

(b) the appropriate court fee or fees paid by the claimant.

Section 24A Claims to which Part 45 does not apply

24A In a claim to which Part 45 does not apply, no amount shall be entered on the claim form for the charges of the claimant's solicitor, but the words 'to be assessed' shall be inserted.

Section 25 Fixed costs on the issue of a default costs certificate

25.1 Unless paragraph 24.2 applies or unless the court orders otherwise, the fixed costs to be included in a default costs certificate are £80 plus a sum equal to any appropriate court fee payable on the issue of the certificate.

25.2 The fixed costs included in a certificate must not exceed the maximum sum specified for costs and court fee in the notice of commencement.

Section 25A Road traffic accidents: fixed recoverable costs in costs-only proceedings

Scope

25A.1 Section II of Part 45 ('the Section') provides for certain fixed costs to be recoverable between parties in respect of costs incurred in disputes which are settled prior to proceedings being issued. The Section applies to road traffic accident disputes as defined in rule 45.7(4)(a), where the accident which gave rise to the dispute occurred on or after 6th October 2003.

25A.2 The Section does not apply to disputes where the total agreed value of the damages is within the small claims limit or exceeds £10,000. Rule 26.8(2) sets out how the financial value of a claim is assessed for the purposes of allocation to track.

25A.3 Fixed recoverable costs are to be calculated by reference to the amount of agreed damages which are payable to the receiving party. In calculating the amount of these damages—

(a) account must be taken of both general and special damages and interest;
(b) any interim payments made must be included;
(c) where the parties have agreed an element of contributory negligence, the amount of damages attributed to that negligence must be deducted;
(d) any amount required by statute to be paid by the compensating party directly to a third party (such as sums paid by way of compensation recovery payments and National Health Service expenses) must not be included.

25A.4 The Section applies to cases which fall within the scope of the Uninsured Drivers Agreement dated 13 August 1999. The section does not apply to cases which fall within the scope of the Untraced Drivers Agreement dated 14 February 2003.

Fixed recoverable costs formula

25A.5 The amount of fixed costs recoverable is calculated by totalling the following—

(a) the sum of £800;
(b) 20% of the agreed damages up to £5,000; and
(c) 15% of the agreed damages between £5,000 and £10,000.

For example, agreed damages of £7,523 would result in recoverable costs of £2,178.45 i.e.

$$£800 + (20\% \text{ of } £5,000) + (15\% \text{ of } £2,523).$$

Additional costs for work in specified areas

25A.6 The area referred to in rule 45.9(2) consists of (within London) the county court districts of Barnet, Bow, Brentford, Central London, Clerkenwell, Edmonton, Ilford, Lambeth, Mayors and City of London, Romford, Shoreditch, Wandsworth, West London, Willesden and Woolwich and (outside London) the county court districts of Bromley, Croydon, Dartford, Gravesend and Uxbridge.

Multiple claimants

25A.7 Where there is more than one potential claimant in relation to a dispute and two or more claimants instruct the same solicitor or firm of solicitors, the provisions of the section apply in respect of each claimant.

Information to be included in the claim form

25A.8 Costs-only proceedings are commenced using the procedure set out in rule 44.12A. A claim form should be issued in accordance with Part 8. Where the claimant is claiming an amount of costs which exceed the amount of the fixed recoverable costs he must include on the claim form details of the exceptional circumstances which he considers justifies the additional costs.

25A.9 The claimant must also include on the claim form details of any disbursements or success fee he wishes to claim. The disbursements that may be claimed are set out in rule 45.10(1). If the disbursement falls within 45.10(2)(d) (disbursements that have arisen due to a particular feature of the dispute) the claimant must give details of the particular feature of the dispute and why he considers the disbursement to be necessary.

Disbursements and success fee

25A.10 If the parties agree the amount of the fixed recoverable costs and the only dispute is as to the payment of, or amount of, a disbursement or as to the amount of a success fee, then proceedings should be issued under rule 44.12A in the normal way and not by reference to Section II of Part 45.

Section 25B Fixed recoverable success fees in employer's liability disease claims

25B.1 The following table is a non-exclusive list of the conditions that will fall within Type A and Type B claims for the purposes of Rule 45.23.

Claim type	Description
A	Asbestosis Mesothelioma Bilateral Pleural Thickening Pleural Plaques
B	Repetitive Strain Injury/WRULD Carpal Tunnel Syndrome caused by Repetitive Strain Injury Occupational Stress

Directions Relating to Part 46—Fast Track Trial Costs

Section 26 Scope of Part 46: Rule 46.1

26.1 Part 46 applies to the costs of an advocate for preparing for and appearing at the trial of a claim in the fast track.

26.2 It applies only where, at the date of the trial, the claim is allocated to the fast track. It does not apply in any other case, irrespective of the final value of the claim.

26.3 In particular it does not apply to:

(a) the hearing of a claim which is allocated to the small claims track with the consent of the parties given under rule 26.7(3); or

(b) a disposal hearing at which the amount to be paid under a judgment or order is decided by the court (see paragraph 12.8 of the Practice Direction which supplements Part 26 (Case Management—Preliminary Stage)).

Cases which settle before trial

26.4 Attention is drawn to rule 44.10 (limitation on amount court may award where a claim allocated to the fast track settles before trial).

Section 27 Power to award more or less than the amount of fast track trial costs: Rule 46.3

27.1 Rule 44.15 (providing information about funding arrangements) sets out the requirement to provide information about funding arrangements to the court and other parties. Section 19 of this Practice Direction sets out the information to be provided and when this is to be done.

27.2 Section 11 of this Practice Direction explains how the court will approach the question of what sum to allow in respect of additional liability.

27.3 The court has the power, when considering whether a percentage increase is reasonable, to allow different percentages for different items of costs or for different periods during which costs were incurred.

Directions Relating to Part 48—Costs—Special Cases

Section 50 Amount of costs where costs are payable pursuant to contract: Rule 48.3

50.1 Where the court is assessing costs payable under a contract, it may make an order that all or part of the costs payable under the contract shall be disallowed if it is satisfied by the paying party that costs have been unreasonably incurred or are unreasonable in amount.

50.2 Rule 48.3 only applies if the court is assessing costs payable under a contract. It does not—

(1) require the court to make an assessment of such costs; or

(2) require a mortgagee to apply for an order for those costs that he has a contractual right to recover out of the mortgage funds.

50.3 The following principles apply to costs relating to a mortgage—

(1) An order for the payment of costs of proceedings by one party to another is always a discretionary order: section 51 of the Supreme Court Act 1981.

(2) Where there is a contractual right to the costs the discretion should ordinarily be exercised so as to reflect that contractual right.

(3) The power of the court to disallow a mortgagee's costs sought to be added to the mortgage security is a power that does not derive from section 51, but from the power of the courts of equity to fix the terms on which redemption will be allowed.

(4) A decision by a court to refuse costs in whole or in part to a mortgagee litigant may be—
   (a) a decision in the exercise of the section 51 discretion;
   (b) a decision in the exercise of the power to fix the terms on which redemption will be allowed;
   (c) a decision as to the extent of a mortgagee's contractual right to add his costs to the security; or
   (d) a combination of two or more of these things.

   The statements of case in the proceedings or the submissions made to the court may indicate which of the decisions has been made.

(5) A mortgagee is not to be deprived of a contractual or equitable right to add costs to the security merely by reason of an order for payment of costs made without reference to the mortgagee's contractual or equitable rights, and without any adjudication as to whether or not the mortgagee should be deprived of those costs.

50.4 (1) Where the contract entitles a mortgagee to—
   (a) add the costs of litigation relating to the mortgage to the sum secured by it;
   (b) require a mortgagor to pay those costs; or
   (c) both,

   the mortgagor may make an application for the court to direct that an account of the mortgagee's costs be taken.

(Rule 25.1(1)(n) provides that the court may direct that a party file an account)

(2) The mortgagor may then dispute an amount in the mortgagee's account on the basis that it has been unreasonably incurred or is unreasonable in amount.

(3) Where a mortgagor disputes an amount, the court may make an order that the disputed costs are assessed under rule 48.3.

Section 51 Costs where money is payable by or to a child or patient: Rule 48.5

51.1 The circumstances in which the court need not order the assessment of costs under rule 48.5(3) are as follows:
   (a) where there is no need to do so to protect the interests of the child or patient or his estate;
   (b) where another party has agreed to pay a specified sum in respect of the costs of the child or patient and the solicitor acting for the child or patient has waived the right to claim further costs;
   (c) where the court has decided the costs payable to the child or patient by way of summary assessment and the solicitor acting for the child or patient has waived the right to claim further costs;
   (d) where an insurer or other person is liable to discharge the costs which the child or patient would otherwise be liable to pay to his solicitor and

the court is satisfied that the insurer or other person is financially able to discharge those costs.

Section 52 Litigants in person: Rule 48.6

52.1 In order to qualify as an expert for the purpose of rule 48.6(3)(c) (expert assistance in connection with assessing the claim for costs), the person in question must be a:

(1) barrister;
(2) solicitor;
(3) Fellow of the Institute of Legal Executives;
(4) Fellow of the Association of Law Costs Draftsmen;
(5) law costs draftsman who is a member of the Academy of Experts;
(6) law costs draftsman who is a member of the Expert Witness Institute.

52.2 Where a litigant in person wishes to prove that he has suffered financial loss he should produce to the court any written evidence he relies on to support that claim, and serve a copy of that evidence on any party against whom he seeks costs at least 24 hours before the hearing at which the question may be decided.

52.3 Where a litigant in person commences detailed assessment proceedings under rule 47.6 he should serve copies of that written evidence with the notice of commencement.

52.4 The amount, which may be allowed to a litigant in person under rule 46.3(5)(b) and rule 48.6(4), is £9.25 per hour.

52.5 Attention is drawn to rule 48.6(6)(b). A solicitor who, instead of acting for himself, is represented in the proceedings by his firm or by himself in his firm name, is not, for the purpose of the Civil Procedure Rules, a litigant in person.

Section 53 Personal liability of legal representative for costs—wasted costs orders: Rule 48.7

53.1 Rule 48.7 deals with wasted costs orders against legal representatives. Such orders can be made at any stage in the proceedings up to and including the proceedings relating to the detailed assessment of costs. In general, applications for wasted costs are best left until after the end of the trial.

53.2 The court may make a wasted costs order against a legal representative on its own initiative.

53.3 A party may apply for a wasted costs order—

(1) by filing an application notice in accordance with Part 23; or
(2) by making an application orally in the course of any hearing.

53.4 It is appropriate for the court to make a wasted costs order against a legal representative, only if—

(1) the legal representative has acted improperly, unreasonably or negligently;
(2) his conduct has caused a party to incur unnecessary costs; and

(3) it is just in all the circumstances to order him to compensate that party for the whole or part of those costs.

53.5 The court will give directions about the procedure that will be followed in each case in order to ensure that the issues are dealt with in a way which is fair and as simple and summary as the circumstances permit.

53.6 As a general rule the court will consider whether to make a wasted costs order in two stages—

(1) in the first stage, the court must be satisfied—

(a) that it has before it evidence or other material which, if unanswered, would be likely to lead to a wasted costs order being made; and

(b) the wasted costs proceedings are justified notwithstanding the likely costs involved.

(2) at the second stage (even if the court is satisfied under paragraph (1)) the court will consider, after giving the legal representative an opportunity to give reasons why the court should not make a wasted costs order, whether it is appropriate to make a wasted costs order in accordance with paragraph 53.4 above.

53.7 On an application for a wasted costs order under Part 23 the court may proceed to the second stage described in paragraph 53.6 without first adjourning the hearing if it is satisfied that the legal representative has already had a reasonable opportunity to give reasons why the court should not make a wasted costs order. In other cases the court will adjourn the hearing before proceeding to the second stage.

53.8 On an application for a wasted costs order under Part 23 the application notice and any evidence in support must identify—

(1) what the legal representative is alleged to have done or failed to do; and

(2) the costs that he may be ordered to pay or which are sought against him.

53.9 A wasted costs order is an order—

(1) that the legal representative pay a specified sum in respect of costs to a party; or

(2) for costs relating to a specified sum or items of work to be disallowed.

53.10 Attention is drawn to rule 44.3A(1) and (2) which respectively prevent the court from assessing any additional liability until the conclusion of the proceedings (or the part of the proceedings) to which the funding arrangement relates, and set out the orders the court may make at the conclusion of the proceedings.

APPENDIX F

Guideline Hourly Rates

Guideline Hourly Rates for Solicitors

Band one grade guideline rates for summary assessment—January 2005

Band One Grade*	A**	B	C	D
Guideline Rates	184	163	137	100

Aldershot, Farnham, Bournemouth (including Poole)
Birmingham Inner
Bristol
Cambridge City, Harlow
Canterbury, Maidstone, Medway & Tunbridge Wells
Cardiff (Inner)
Chelmsford South, Essex & East Suffolk
Fareham, Winchester
Hampshire, Dorset, Wiltshire, Isle of Wight
Kingston, Guildford, Reigate, Epsom
Leeds Inner (within 2 kilometres radius of the City Art Gallery)
Lewes
Liverpool, Birkenhead
Manchester Central
Newcastle—City Centre (within a 2 mile radius of St Nicholas Cathedral)
Norwich City
Nottingham City
Oxford, Thames Valley
Southampton, Portsmouth
Swindon, Basingstoke
Watford

Band two grade guideline rates for summary assessment—January 2005

Band Two Grade*	A**	B	C	D
Guideline Rates	173	152	126	95

Bath, Cheltenham and Gloucester, Taunton, Yeovil
Bury
Chelmsford North, Cambridge County, Peterborough, Bury St E, Norfolk, Lowestoft
Chester & North Wales
Coventry, Rugby, Nuneaton, Stratford and Warwick
Exeter, Plymouth
Hull (City)
Leeds Outer, Wakefield & Pontefract
Leigh
Lincoln
Luton, Bedford, St Albans, Hitchin, Hertford
Manchester Outer, Oldham, Bolton, Tameside
Newcastle (other than City Centre)
Nottingham & Derbyshire
Sheffield, Doncaster and South Yorkshire
Southport
St Helens
Stockport, Altrincham, Salford
Swansea, Newport, Cardiff (Outer)
Wigan
Wolverhampton, Walsall, Dudley & Stourbridge
York, Harrogate

Band three grade guideline rates for summary assessment —January 2005

Band Three Grade*	A**	B	C	D
Guideline Rates	158	142	121	90

Birmingham Outer
Bradford (Dewsbury, Halifax, Huddersfield, Keighley & Skipton)
Cumbria
Devon, Cornwall
Grimsby, Skegness
Hull Outer
Kidderminster

Northampton & Leicester
Preston, Lancaster, Blackpool, Chorley, Accrington, Burnley, Blackburn, Rawenstall & Nelson
Scarborough & Ripon
Stafford, Stoke, Tamworth
Teesside
Worcester, Hereford, Evesham and Redditch
Shrewsbury, Telford, Ludlow, Oswestry
South & West Wales

London band grades guideline rates for summary assessment —January 2005

Grade*	A**	B	C	D
City of London: EC1, EC2, EC3, EC4	359	259	198	122
Central London: W1, WC1, WC2, SW1	276	210	171	110
Outer London: (All other London post codes: W, NW, N, E, SE, SW and Bromley, Croydon, Dartford, Gravesend and Uxbridge)	198–232	149–198	144	105

*There are four grades of fee earner:

A. Solicitors with over 8 years' post-qualification experience including at least 8 years' litigation experience.
B. Solicitors and legal executives with over 4 years' post-qualification experience including at least 4 years' litigation experience.
C. Other solicitors and legal executives and fee earners of equivalent experience.
D. Trainee solicitors, para-legals and fee earners of equivalent experience.

Note: 'legal executive' means a Fellow of the Institute of Legal Executives.

**An hourly rate in excess of the guideline figures may be appropriate for Grade A fee earners in substantial and complex litigation where other factors, including the value of the litigation, the level of complexity, the urgency or importance of the matter as well as any international element would justify a significantly higher rate to reflect higher average costs.

Guidelines for Counsel's Fees

The following table sets out figures based on Supreme Court Costs Office statistics dealing with run of the mill proceedings in the Queens Bench and Chancery Division and in the Administrative Court. The table gives figures for cases lasting up to an hour and up to half a day, in respect of counsel up to five years call, up to 10 years call and over 10 years call. It is emphasized that these figures are not recommended rates but it is hoped that they may provide a helpful starting point for judges when assessing counsel's fees. The appropriate fee in any particular case may be more or less than the figures appearing in the table, depending upon the circumstances.

Table of Counsel's Fees

	1 hour hearing	1
Queens Bench		
Junior up to 5 years call	£245	£425
Junior 5–10 years call	£365	£725
Junior 10+ years call	£550	£1,100
Chancery Division		
Junior up to 5 years call	£275	£525
Junior 5–10 years call	£470	£880
Junior 10+ years call	£715	£1,320
Administrative Court		
Junior up to 5 years call	£360	£550
Junior 5–10 years call	£660	£1,100
Junior 10+ years call	£935	£1,650

The Ready Reckoner[1]

Prospects of Success %	Success Fee %
100	0
90	11
80	25
75	33.3
70	43
65	54
60	67
50	100

[1] The Ready Reckoner was first published in Bawdon, Napier and Wignall *Conditional Fees: A Survival Guide* (1995) and is reproduced here by permission of the Law Society © The Law Society 1995

INDEX

The manufacturer's authorised representative in the EU for product safety is Oxford University Press España S.A. of el Parque Empresarial San Fernando de Henares, Avenida de Castilla, 2 – 28830 Madrid (www.oup.es/en or product.safety@oup.com). OUP España S.A. also acts as importer into Spain of products made by the manufacturer.

www.ingramcontent.com/pod-product-compliance
Ingram Content Group UK Ltd.
Pitfield, Milton Keynes, MK11 3LW, UK
UKHW012145150926
475595UK00011B/215
* 9 7 8 0 1 9 9 2 9 8 2 1 1 *